# Camino Portugués

## Lisbon – Porto – Santiago

maps - mapas - mappe - karten

Camino da Costa

Camino Central

Senda Litoral

Variante Espiritual

John Brierley

ISBN: 978-1-912216-31-4



British Library Cataloguing-in-Publication Data.
A catalogue record for this book is available from the British Library.



Printed and bound in Czechia

Published by

CAMINO GUIDES
An imprint of Kaminn Media Ltd
272 Bath Street,
Glasgow, G2 4JR

Tel: +44 (0)141 354 1758
Fax: +44 (0)141 354 1759

Email: info@caminoguides.com
www.caminoguides.com

•Portugal GMT +0 ✆+351 ---------->

•España GMT +1 ✆ +34 ---------->

01 – 13

14 – 18

19 – 24

15a – 21a

22v – 24v

## MAP LEGEND: Symbols & Abbreviations

| | |
|---|---|
| Total km | Total distance for stage |
| *equiv.* | Adjusted for cumulative climb (each 100m vertical +10 mins) |
| 850m Alto | Contours / High point of each stage |
| < A H > | Intermediate accommodation (*often less busy / quieter*) |
| 3.5 | Precise distance between points (3.5 km = ± 1 hour) |
| 50m > / ^ / < | Interim distances 50m right> / s/o=straight on^ / <left |
| | Natural path / forest track / gravel *senda* |
| | Quiet country lane (asphalt) |
| | Secondary road (*grey*: asphalt) / Roundabout *rotonda* |
| N-11 | Main road [N-] *Nacional* (*red*: additional traffic and hazard) |
| A-1 | Motorway *autopista* (*blue*: conventional motorway colour) |
| | Railway *ferrocarril* / Station *estación* |
| | Main Waymarked route (*yellow*: ± 80% of pilgrims) |
| | Alternative Scenic route (*green*: more remote / less pilgrims) |
| | Alternative road route (*grey*: more asphalt & traffic) |
| | Optional detour *desvío* (*turquoise:* to point of interest) |
| | Primary Path of pilgrimage (***purple***: inner path of Soul) |
| | Crossing *cruce* / Option *opción* / Extra care *¡cuidado!* |
| | Windmill *molino* / Viewpoint *punto de vista* / Radio mast |
| | National boundary / Provincial boundary *límite provincial* |
| | River *río* / Riverlet Stream *arroyo / rego* |
| | Sea or lake *Mar o lago* / Woodland *bosques* |
| | Church *iglesia* / Chapel *capilla* / Wayside cross *cruceiro* |
| | Drinking font *fuente* [ ] / Café-Bar / Shop (*mini*)*mercado* |
| *menú V.* | Restaurant / *menú peregrino* / *V. Vegetariano(a)* |
| | Tourist office *turismo* / Manor house *pazo* / Rest area *picnic* |
| | Pharmacy *farmacia* / Hospital / Post office *correos* |
| | Airport / Bus station *estación de autobús / gasolinera* |
| *XIIc.* | Ancient monument / 12th century |
| H P C | Hotels •*H-H** €30-90 / Pension •*P** €20-35 / •*CR (B&B)* €35-75 |
| *x12* €35-45 | Number of private rooms *x12* €35(single)-45 (double) *approx* |
| H A A | *Off* route lodging / reported closed – check for updates |
| A 1 2 J | Pilgrim hostel(s) *Albergue* ●*Alb.* + Youth hostel ●*Juventude* |
| [32 ] | Number of bed spaces (usually bunk beds *literas*) €5-€17 |
| [ ÷4] +12 | ÷ number of dormitories / *+12* number of private rooms €30+ |
| Par. | Parish hostel *Parroquial* donation *donativo* / €5 |
| Conv. | Convent or monastery hostel *donativo* / €5 |
| Mun/ Xunta | Municipal hostel €5+ / Galician government *Xunta* €8 |
| Asoc. | Association hostel €8+ |
| Priv. (*) | Private hostel (network*) €10-17 |
| | *[all prices average (low season) for comparison purposes only]* |
| p.55 | Town plan *plan de la ciudad* with page number |
| (Pop.– Alt. m) | Town population – altitude in metres |
| | City suburbs / outskirts *afueras* (*grey*) |
| | Historical centre *centro histórico / barrio antiguo* (*brown*) |

**Introduction:** We have too much paraphernalia in our lives. This slim ***maps only*** edition seeks to lighten the load. This has been made possible by the selfless work of pilgrim associations that have waymarked all routes. It is difficult to get lost if we remain present to each moment and attentive for the yellow arrows that point the way to Santiago – mindfulness is the key. However, this *maps only* version cannot substitute for the more detailed information contained in the full guide. If you are travelling with a smart phone or other digital device, we recommend you download the eBook version with full details of •*alternative routes* •*lodging* •*historical notes and* •*intimations of the mystical path*. Take time to familiarise yourself with the map symbols & abbreviations opposite. Note these maps direct you *to* Santiago; if you intend to walk 'in reverse' *from* Santiago to Lisbon or Porto – source alternative maps. Check for updates at *www.caminoguides.com*

This edition includes the main ***Camino Central*** ● ● ● from Lisbon to Santiago and the coastal routes from Porto ***Camino da Costa*** ● ● ● plus the seashore ***Senda Litoral*** ● ● ●. This latter route is exposed to windblown sand from Atlantic winds but recent and ongoing improvements has widened its appeal. The ***Variante Espiritual:*** ● ● ● via Ría Arousa is also included.

These multilingual maps recognise the international fellowship of the camino, helping foster a sense of camaraderie and communion; a shared spiritual intention that lies at the heart of pilgrimage. It is this transcendent focus that distinguishes pilgrimage from long distance walking. We recommend you source a guidebook with notes on how best to prepare for an extended trip of this nature such as the companion book ***A Pilgrim's Guide to the Camino Portugués*** *A Practical & Mystical Manual for the Modern-day Pilgrim* with detailed information.

All of us travel two paths simultaneously; the outer path along which we haul our body and the inner pathway of soul. We need to be mindful of both and take time to prepare ourselves accordingly. The traditional way of the pilgrim is to travel alone, by foot, carrying all the material possessions we might need for the journey ahead. This provides the first lesson for the pilgrim – to leave behind all that is superfluous and to travel with only the barest necessities. Preparation for the inner path is similar – we start by letting go of psychic waste accumulated over the years; resentments, prejudices and outmoded belief systems. With an open mind and open heart we will more readily assimilate the lessons to be found along this ancient Path of Enquiry.

We have been asleep a long time. Despite the chaotic world around us, or perhaps because of it, something is stirring us to awaken from our collective amnesia. A sign of this awakening is the number of people drawn to walk the caminos. The hectic pace of modern life, experienced not only in our work but also our family and social lives, spins us ever outwards away from our centre. We have allowed ourselves to be thrown onto the surface of our lives – mistaking busy-ness for aliveness, but this superficial existence is inherently purposeless.

Pilgrimage offers us an opportunity to slow down and allow some spaciousness into our lives. In this quieter space we can reflect on the deeper significance of our lives and the reasons why we came here. The camino encourages us to ask the perennial question – who am I? And, crucially, it provides time for answers to be understood and integrated. Don't rush the camino – take the time it takes because it may well prove a pivotal turning point in your life. Whichever route we take, our ultimate Destination is assured. The only real choice we have is how long it takes us to arrive...

*Bom caminho – John Brierley*

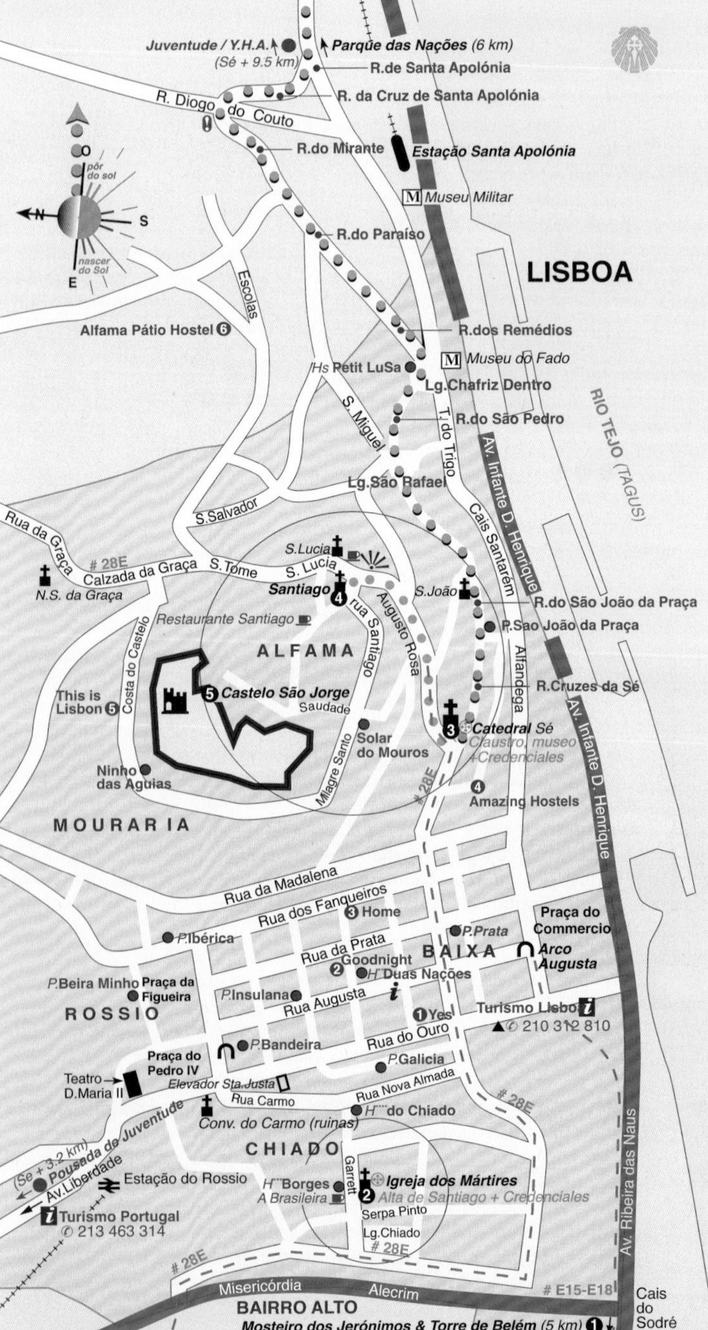

LISBOA
Juventude / Y.H.A.
(Sé + 9.5 km)
Parque das Nações (6 km)
R.de Santa Apolónia
R. da Cruz de Santa Apolónia
R. Diogo do Couto
R.do Mirante
Estação Santa Apolónia
Museu Militar
R.do Paraíso
O
pôr do sol
N
S
nascer do Sol
E
Escolas
Alfama Pátio Hostel 6
R.dos Remédios
Hs Petit LuSa
Museu do Fado
Lg.Chafriz Dentro
R.do São Pedro
RIO TEJO (TAGUS)
S. Miguel
T. do Trigo
Av. Infante D. Henrique
Lg.São Rafael
S.Salvador
Cais Santarém
Rua da Graça
# 28E
Calzada da Graça
S.Tome
S. Lucia
S.Lucia
N.S. da Graça
Santiago 4
Augusto Rosa
S.João
R.do São João da Praça
P.Sao João da Praça
Restaurante Santiago
rua Santiago
ALFAMA
Costa do Castelo
Alfandega
R.Cruzes da Sé
5 Castelo São Jorge
Saudade
This is Lisbon 5
3 Catedral Sé
Claustro, museo +Credenciales
Solar do Mouros
Milagre Santo
Ninho das Aguias
4 Amazing Hostels
MOURARIA
Rua da Madalena
Rua dos Fanqueiros
3 Home
Praça do Commercio
P.Ibérica
P.Prata
Rua da Prata
BAIXA
Arco Augusta
2 Goodnight
H Duas Nações
P.Beira Minho
Praça da Figueira
P.Insulana
Rua Augusta
Turismo Lisboa
ROSSIO
1 Yes
© 210 312 810
Rua do Ouro
Praça do Pedro IV
P.Bandeira
P.Galicia
Teatro D.Maria II
Elevador Sta.Justa
Rua Carmo
Rua Nova Almada
H do Chiado
Pousada de Juventude
(Se + 3.2 km)
Conv. do Carmo (ruinas)
CHIADO
Garrett
Av.Liberdade
Estação do Rossio
H Borges
A Brasileira
Igreja dos Mártires
2 Alta de Santiago + Credenciales
Serpa Pinto
Lg.Chiado
Turismo Portugal
© 213 463 314
Av. Ribeira das Naus
Misericórdia
Alecrim
# E15-E18
Cais do Sodré
BAIRRO ALTO
Mosteiro dos Jerónimos & Torre de Belém (5 km) 1

**Portugal** – GMT + 0 / ✆ +351. Telefone fixo: 2. Número de telemóvel / m: 9 **LISBOA: ❶ Turismo** Aeroporto ✆ 218 450 660 (07:00-24:00). **Lisboa Centro** ❶ Turismo Lisboa / Welcome Center Praça do Comércio ✆ 210 312 810 (09.00-18.00). ❶Turismo (ask me) Rossio Paça D. Pedro IV ✆ 213 259 131 (10.00-13.00 / 14.00-18.00). Santa Apolonia Estação da CP - Terminal Int. ✆ 218 821 606 (08.00-13.00). ● **Associação de Peregrinos**: ✣ *credenciales*: ***Via Lusitana*** ✆ 915 595 213. ✣ ***APAAS*** ✆ 966 426 851. ✣ ***Basílica dos Mártires*** Rua Serpa Pinto ✆ 213 462 465 (10:00-17:00). ✣ ***Catedral*** *Sé* (09:30-18:30).

▌**Hostels** www.hostelworld.com (€12-20): ❶ **Yes** ✆ 213 427 171 r/S. Julião,148. ❷ **Goodnight** ✆ 215 989 153 r/Correiros, 113. ❸ **Home Lisbon** ✆ 218 885 312 r/S. Nicolau, 13. ❹ **Amazing Hostels** *Sé / Alfama* ✆ 964 453 972 Beco Arco Escuro, 6. ❺ **This is Lisbon** ✆ 218 014 549 r/Costa do Castelo, 63. ❻ **Alfama Pátio** ✆ 218 883 127 r/Escolas Gerais, 3. •*P* **São João de Praça** €25-45 incl. ✆ 218 862 591 r/São João de Praça, 97. •*H**** **Borges** *40x* €38+ ✆ 213 461 951 r/ Garrett 108 opp. *Basilica dos Mártires (credencial)* adj. café *A Brasileira*. ▌(€12-18) ●**Pousadas de Juventude *Hi Lisboa*** ✆ 925 665 072 r/ Andrade Corvo, 46 *(Sé + 3.1 km)*. ●***Moscavide YHA*** ✆ 218 920 890 Rua de Moscavide Lt 47-101 *(Sé + 9.5 km)*.

● **Monumentos históricos** ❶ ***Mosteiro dos Jerónimos*** *XV* e *Torre de Belém XVI* Praça do Império (10:00-17:30) ❷ ***Basílica dos Mártires*** *XVIII* Rua Garrett (10:00-17:00) ❸ ***Catedral*** *Sé XII* (# 28E) (09:30-18:30) ❹ ***Igreja de Santiago*** rua Santiago. ❺ ***Castelo São Jorge*** *XI* Rua de Santa Cruz do Castelo (9:00-21:00).

❸ Catedral *Catedral Claustro*

❹ Catedral *Igreja de Santiago*

❸ Catedral Ca*Catedral Entrada*

❺ Catedral Ca*Castelo São Jorge*

## 01 LISBOA – ALVERCA (Verdelha)

| | | |
|---|---|---|
| | 17.7 | 51% |
| | 4.2 | 14% |
| | 10.3 | 35% |
| Total km | **32.2** km *(20.0 ml)* | |

Total ascent **550**m ±*1.0 hr*
Alto Alpriarte 60m *(197 ft)*
<A H> Moscavide **9.4** km Alpriate **22.5**
Rail *estação: •Santa Ápolónia •Oriente •Sacavém •Santa Iria •Póvoa*

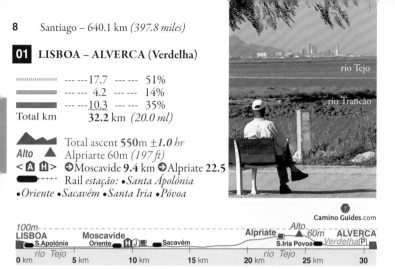

Camino Guides.com

100m LISBOA S.Apolónia Moscavide Oriente Sacavém Alpriate Alto 60m S.Iria Povoa ALVERCA Verdelha río Tejo 0 km 5 km 10 km 15 km 20 km 25 km 30

**Parque das Nações *Moscavide*** (+0.8 km): •*H*** **IBIS** *110x* €60 ✆ 210 730 470 *www.ibis.com r/do Mar Vermelho* and on *Av. Dom João II* •*H**** **TRYP Lisboa Oriente** *206x* €92-105 ✆ 218 930 000 *www.melia.com* and •*H**** **Tivoli Oriente** *280x* €96+ ✆ 218 915 100 *www.minorhotels.com* ***Moscavide: [+0.8km]:*** ●**Pousada de Juventude** *Asoc.[92÷6]* €14 *+20x* €30 ✆ 218 920 890 *www.pousadasjuventude.pt/en* r/Moscavide Lt 47-101. **Alpriate** *Alb.* **Alpriate** *Asoc. closed.* *Grillus (Zézinhas).* **Santa Iria** (+2.0 km N-10 - Galp): •*H**** **VIP Santa Iria** *124x* €63+ ✆ 210 032 300 *www.viphotels.com* adj. •*Hs* **Miratejo** *36x* €40 ✆ 219 591 216. **Verdelha de Baixo** (+1.3 km): ***Estrada de Alfarrobeira*** @**Nº1** / *Hs* ❶ *P* **Faia** *8x* €20-30 ✆ 219 596 197 m: 931 612 110. @**Nº10** ❷*P* **Alfa10** *15x* €15-30 ✆ 219 580 475 *www.alfa10.pt* @**Nº17** ❸*P* **A Lanterna** *6x* €15-30 ✆ 219 576 488. @**Nº23** + 550m ❹*P* **Silvina Ferreira** *20x* €20-30 ✆ 219 583 911. **Sol Rio** *x5* €55 ✆ 939 250 251 N-10.

Parque das Nações *Ponte Vasco Gama Gama*
Queen of England *Catarina de Bragança*

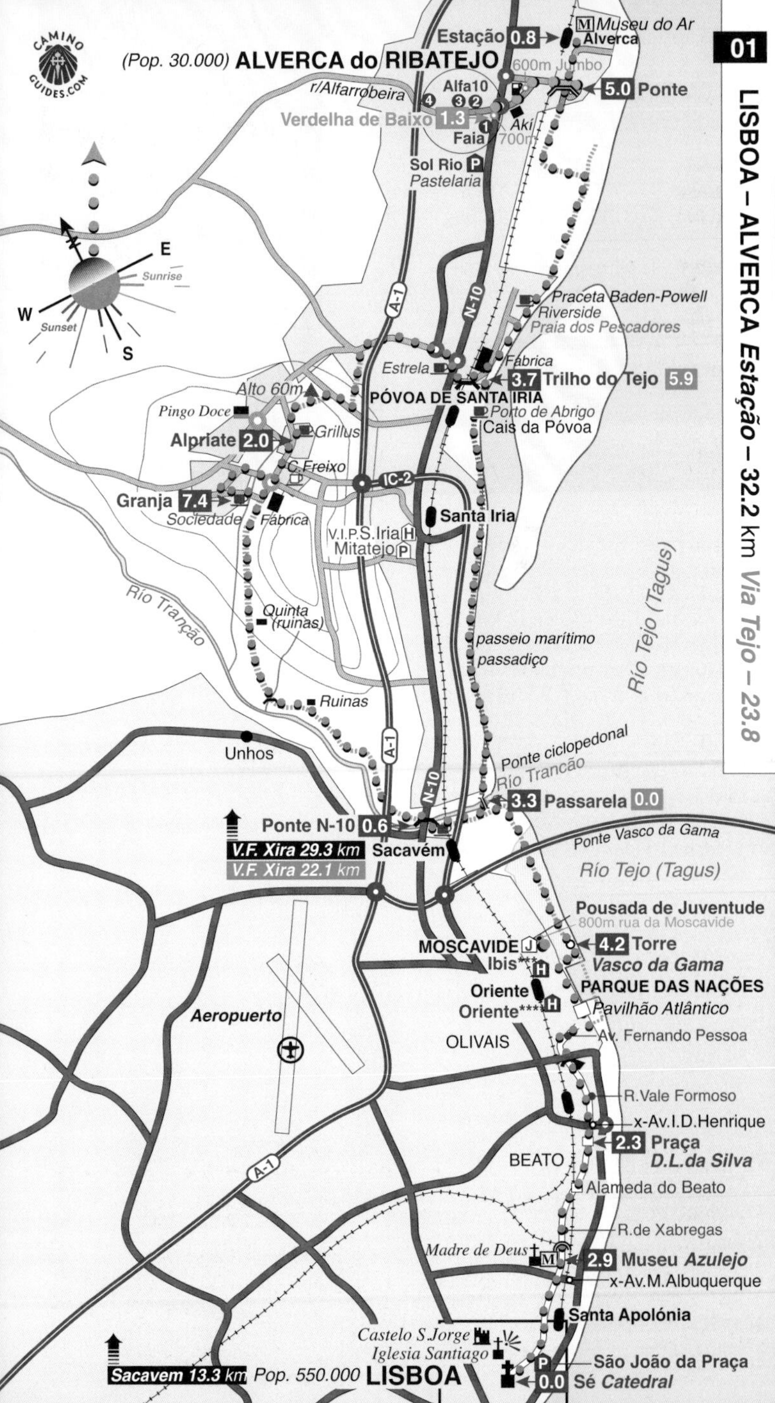
01
LISBOA – ALVERCA Estação – 32.2 km Via Tejo – 23.8
(Pop. 30.000) ALVERCA do RIBATEJO
Estação 0.8
Museu do Ar
Alverca
600m Jumbo
5.0 Ponte
r/Alfarrobeira
Alfa10
Verdelha de Baixo 1.3
Akí
Faia
700m
Sol Rio
Pastelaria
E
Sunrise
W
Sunset
S
A-1
N-10
Praceta Baden-Powell
Riverside
Praia dos Pescadores
Fábrica
Estrela
3.7 Trilho do Tejo 5.9
Alto 60m
PÓVOA DE SANTA IRIA
Pingo Doce
Porto de Abrigo
Cais da Póvoa
Grillus
Alpriate 2.0
C.Freixo
IC-2
Granja 7.4
Sociedade
Fábrica
Santa Iria
V.I.P.S.Iria
Mitatejo
Río Tejo (Tagus)
Río Trancão
Quinta (ruinas)
passeio marítimo
passadiço
Ruinas
Unhos
Ponte ciclopedonal
Río Trancão
3.3 Passarela 0.0
Ponte N-10 0.6
V.F. Xira 29.3 km
V.F. Xira 22.1 km
Sacavém
Ponte Vasco da Gama
Río Tejo (Tagus)
Pousada de Juventude
800m rua da Moscavide
MOSCAVIDE
4.2 Torre
Vasco da Gama
Ibis***
PARQUE DAS NAÇÕES
Oriente
Oriente***
Pavilhão Atlântico
Aeropuerto
OLIVAIS
Av. Fernando Pessoa
R.Vale Formoso
x-Av.I.D.Henrique
2.3 Praça
D.L.da Silva
BEATO
A-1
Alameda do Beato
R.de Xabregas
Madre de Deus
2.9 Museu Azulejo
x-Av.M.Albuquerque
Santa Apolónia
Castelo S.Jorge
Iglesia Santiago
São João da Praça
Sacavem 13.3 km
Pop. 550.000 LISBOA
0.0 Sé Catedral

## 02 ALVERCA *estação* – AZAMBUJA

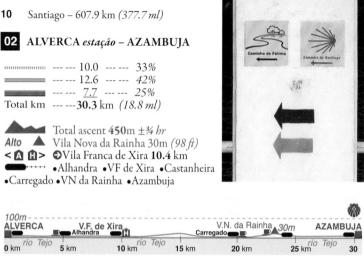

--- --- 10.0 --- --- 33%
--- --- 12.6 --- --- *42%*
--- --- 7.7 --- --- *25%*
Total km --- ---**30.3** km *(18.8 ml)*

Total ascent **450**m ±¾ *hr*
Alto Vila Nova da Rainha 30m *(98 ft)*
< A H > Vila Franca de Xira **10.4** km
•Alhandra •VF de Xira •Castanheira •Carregado •VN da Rainha •Azambuja

100m
ALVERCA | Alhandra | V.F. de Xira | Carregado | V.N. da Rainha 30m | AZAMBUJA
río Tejo | río Tejo | río Tejo
0 km | 5 km | 10 km | 15 km | 20 km | 25 km | 30

■ **Alverca do Ribatejo:** —. ■ **Vila Franca de Xira: Posto de Turismo** *Câmara Municipal* © 263 285 605 Praça Afonso de Albuquerque. •*P* **Ribatejana** Vilatejo *10x* €15-25 © 263 272 991 m: 925 912 679 (Mariano) r/da Praia, 2a. ●*Hs* **DP** *Priv.[16÷4]* €14 *+12x* €32-40 © 263 288 012 m: 926 070 650 *www.hosteldp.com* (Fernando e Carolina) r/António Palha 2. •*Estalagem* **Leziria** €8-25 © 964 774 863 r/da Barroca De Baixo 17 •*Hs* **Maioral** €28-€38 © 263 274 370 trv.do Terreirinho 2. ***N-1*** (**+ 2** km) •*H* **Lezíria Parque** *102x* €60-70 © 263 276 670 *www.continentalhotels.eu* . ■ **Azambuja:** •*H*** **Ouro** *20x* €35-45 © 263 406 530 N-3. ●*Alb.* **Azambuja** *Asoc.[16÷1]* €10 © 914 103 807 *Via Lusitana* 69 rua Vitor Cordon. •*Hs* **Flor da Primavera** *20x* €25-45 © 263 402 545 *www.flordaprimavera.pt* rua Conselheiro Francisco Arouca, 19. •*P* **Jacinto** *4x* €20 © 965 535 677 [m] 263 402 504 Rua dos Campinos, 3C. •*P* **Casa da Rainha** *6x* €35-40 © 969 512 143 *www.casadarainha.pt* Travessa da Rainha, 6.

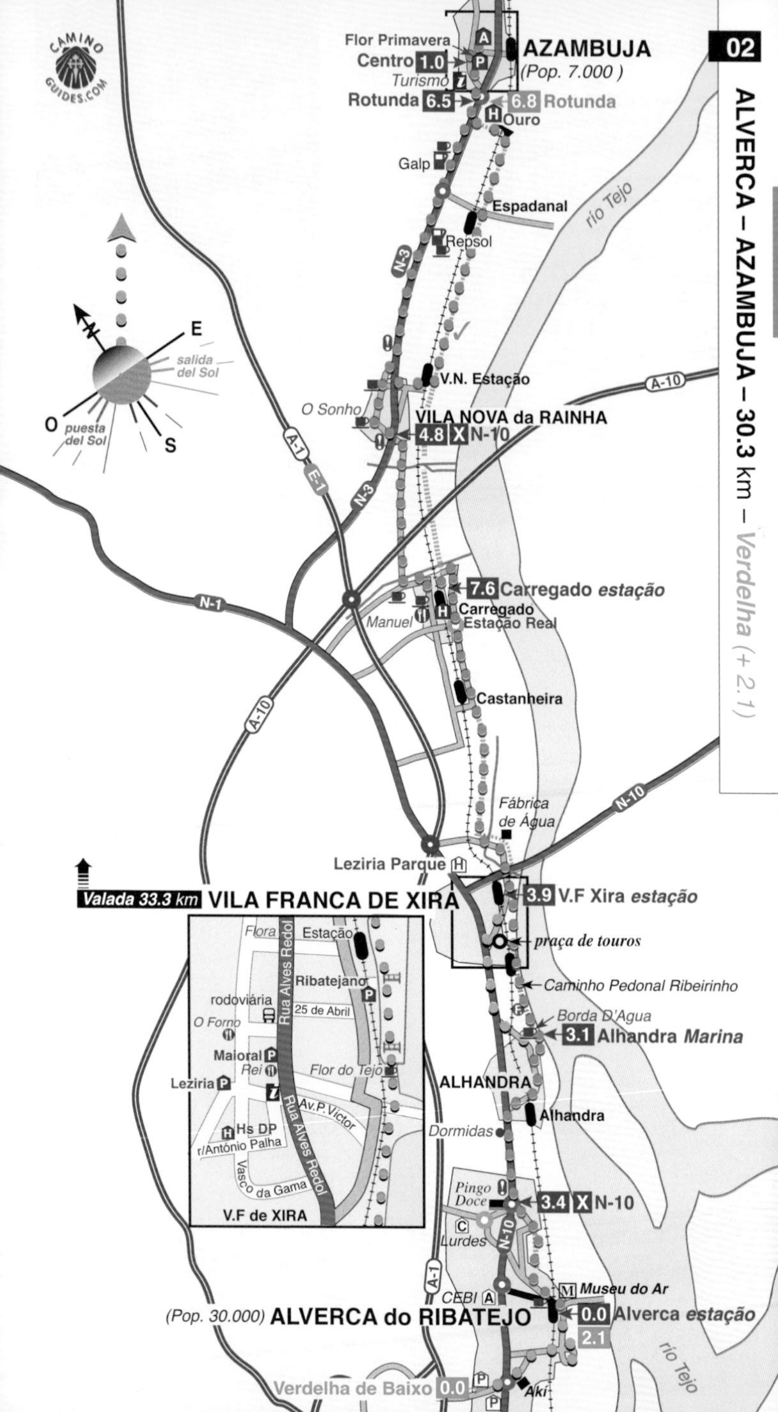
02
ALVERCA – AZAMBUJA – 30.3 km – Verdelha (+ 2.1)
CAMINO GUIDES.COM
AZAMBUJA
(Pop. 7.000 )
Flor Primavera
Centro 1.0
Turismo
Rotunda 6.5
6.8 Rotunda
Ouro
Galp
Espadanal
Repsol
río Tejo
N-3
E
salida del Sol
O
puesta del Sol
S
N
V.N. Estação
O Sonho
VILA NOVA da RAINHA
4.8 X N-10
A-10
A-1
E-1
N-1
7.6 Carregado estação
Carregado
Estação Real
Manuel
Castanheira
Fábrica de Água
N-10
Leziria Parque
Valada 33.3 km
VILA FRANCA DE XIRA
3.9 V.F Xira estação
praça de touros
Caminho Pedonal Ribeirinho
Borda D'Agua
3.1 Alhandra Marina
ALHANDRA
Alhandra
Dormidas
Pingo Doce
3.4 X N-10
Lurdes
CEBI
Museu do Ar
(Pop. 30.000) ALVERCA do RIBATEJO
0.0 Alverca estação
2.1
Verdelha de Baixo 0.0
Aki
Flora
Estação
Rua Alves Redol
Ribatejano
rodoviária
25 de Abril
O Forno
Maioral
Rei
Flor do Tejo
Leziria
Av.P. Victor
Hs DP
r/António Palha
Vasco da Gama
V.F de XIRA

## 03 AZAMBUJA – SANTARÉM

| | | | | |
|---|---|---|---|---|
| | --- --- | 19.2 | --- --- | *58%* |
| | --- --- | 14.0 | --- --- | *42%* |
| | --- --- | 0.0 | --- --- | *0%* |
| Total km | --- --- | **33.2** km | | *(20.6 ml)* |

Total ascent **300**m ±½ *hr*

*Alto* Santarém 135m *(443 ft)*

<A H> Valada **13.4** km Porto Muge **17.0**

•Reguengo •Cataxo •Vale de Santarém •Santarém

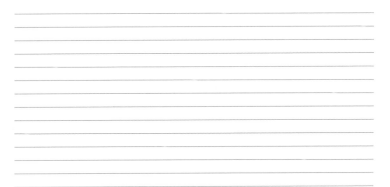

100m
AZAMBUJA
río Tejo
Valada
Port de Muge
Cardaso
Quinta da Burra
río Tejo
*Alto* 135m
SANTARÉM
0 5 km 10 km 15 km 20 km 25 km 30 km

**Valada**: ●*Alb.* **Dois Caminhos** *Priv.[6÷3]* €15 Enrico © 915 657 651 r/D. Diniz, 4. •**Salão Paroquial** Largo da Igreja – floor *suelo.* •*CR* **Casal das Areias** (Morada +300m) €10+ €28-42 Nuno © 932 384 524 www.casaldasareias.com

**Porto de Muge *Morgado:*** •*CR* **Quinta da Marchanta** €30–€40 © 913 553 187. *[+400m •Quinta das* **Palmeiras** *x7 €85-95 © 243 749 272].* ●**Quinta da Burra** [**0.5** km] *currently closed.*

❶ ***Igreja do Hospital de Jesus Cristo*** *XV.* ❷ ***Praça Sá da Bandeira / Igreja N.Sra. da Conceição / Seminário*** *XVII* ***/ Igreja N.Sra da Piedade.*** ❸ ***Igreja de Marvila*** *XVII.* ❹ ***Igreja da Graça*** *XV.* ❺ ***Portas do Sol.*** ❻ ***Porta de Santiago.***

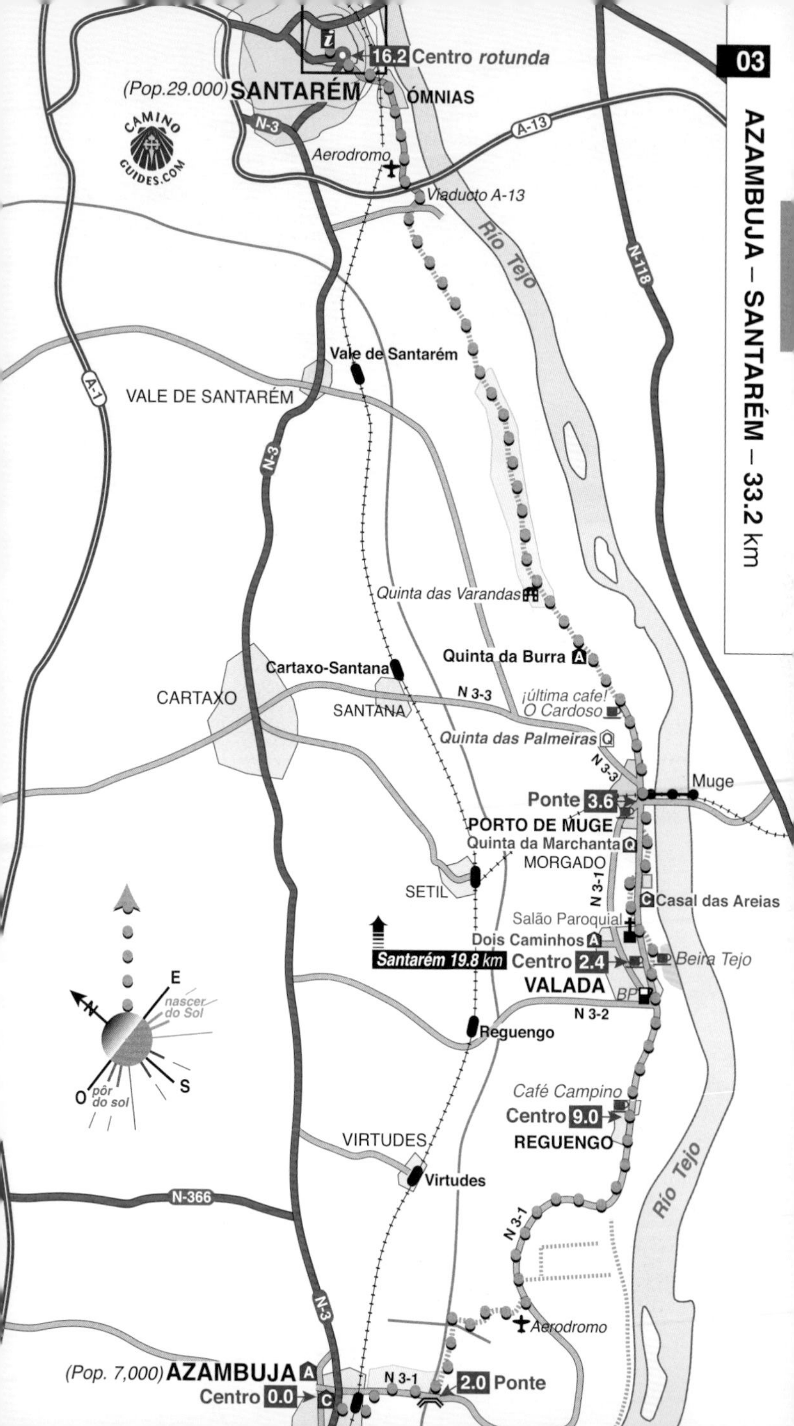

16.2 Centro rotunda
(Pop.29.000) SANTARÉM
ÓMNIAS
CAMINO GUIDES.COM
N-3
A-13
Aerodromo
Viaducto A-13
Río Tejo
N-118
Vale de Santarém
A-1
VALE DE SANTARÉM
N-3
Quinta das Varandas
Quinta da Burra
Cartaxo-Santana
CARTAXO
N 3-3
¡última cafe! O Cardoso
SANTANA
Quinta das Palmeiras
N 3-3
Muge
Ponte 3.6
PORTO DE MUGE
Quinta da Marchanta
MORGADO
N 3-1
SETIL
Casal das Areias
Salão Paroquial
Dois Caminhos
Santarém 19.8 km
Centro 2.4
Beira Tejo
VALADA
BP
E
nascer do Sol
N
N 3-2
Reguengo
S
O
pôr do sol
Café Campino
Centro 9.0
REGUENGO
VIRTUDES
Río Tejo
Virtudes
N-366
N 3-1
N-3
Aerodromo
(Pop. 7,000) AZAMBUJA
N 3-1
2.0 Ponte
Centro 0.0

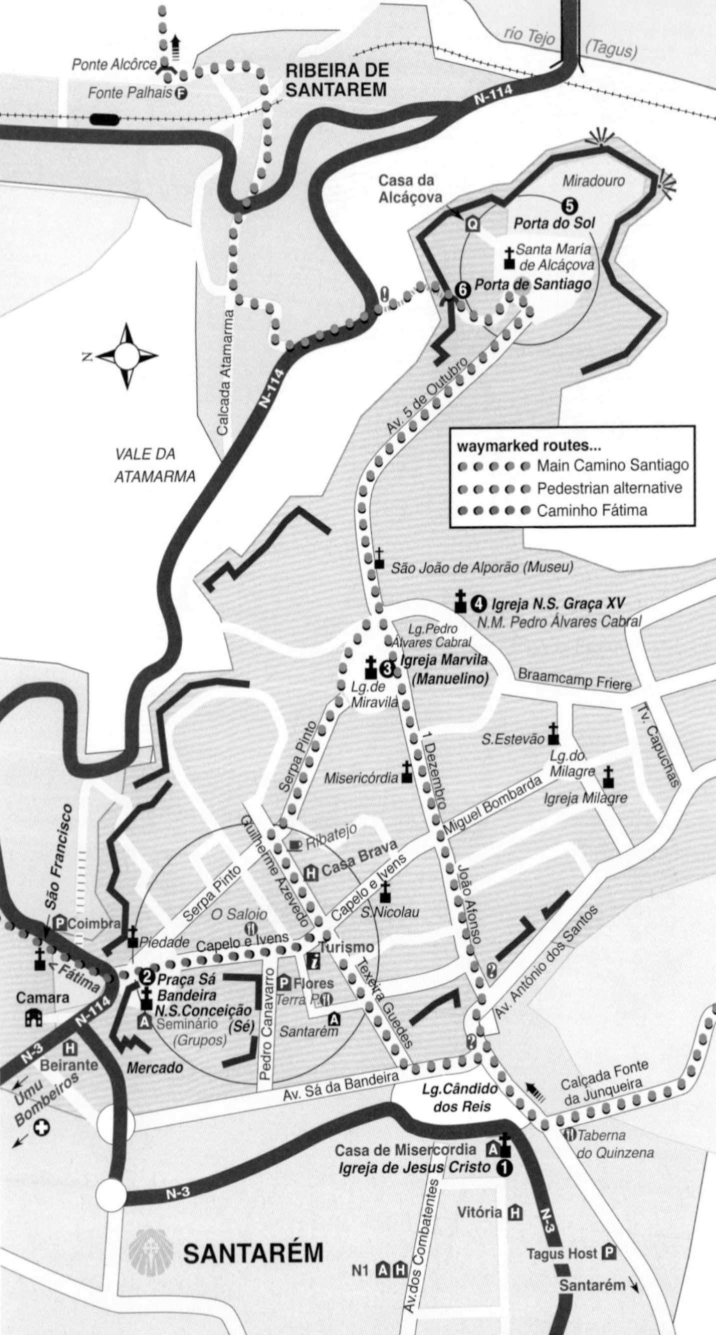

Ponte Alcôrce
Fonte Palhais
RIBEIRA DE SANTAREM
rio Tejo
(Tagus)
N-114
Casa da Alcáçova
Miradouro
5
Porta do Sol
Santa María de Alcáçova
6
Porta de Santiago
Calcada Atamarma
N
N-114
Av. 5 de Outubro
VALE DA ATAMARMA
waymarked routes...
Main Camino Santiago
Pedestrian alternative
Caminho Fátima
São João de Alporão (Museu)
4
Igreja N.S. Graça XV
N.M. Pedro Álvares Cabral
Lg.Pedro Álvares Cabral
3
Igreja Marvila (Manuelino)
Lg.de Miravila
Braamcamp Friere
Serpa Pinto
1 Dezembro
S.Estevão
Lg.do Milagre
Tv. Capuchas
Misericórdia
Miguel Bombarda
Igreja Milagre
São Francisco
Guilherme Azevedo
Ribatejo
Casa Brava
Capelo e Ivens
Serpa Pinto
João Afonso
S.Nicolau
O Saloio
Av. António dos Santos
Coimbra
Piedade
Capelo e Ivens
Turismo
Fátima
2
Praça Sá Bandeira
N.S.Conceição (Sé)
Flores
Terra P.
Texeira Guedes
Camara
N-114
Seminário (Grupos)
Pedro Canavarro
Santarém
N-3
Beirante
Mercado
Umu
Bombeiros
Av. Sá da Bandeira
Lg.Cândido dos Reis
Calçada Fonte da Junqueira
Taberna do Quinzena
Casa de Misercordia
Igreja de Jesus Cristo
1
N-3
Av.dos Combatentes
Vitória
N-3
SANTARÉM
Tagus Host
N1
Santarém

🛈 **Turismo** ✆ 243 304 437 rua Capelo e Ivens, 63.

***Centro:*** *Alb.***Santa Casa da Misericórdia** *Conv.[24÷12!]* €5 ✆ 243 305 260 Largo Cândido dos Reis. *Alb.***Seminário** *Conv.[96÷24] (grupos 10+)* €10+ ✆ *913 023 728 (Sra. Aida)* Praça Sá da Bandeira *(museo €4). Alb.*•**N1 Hostel Apartments** *Priv.[30÷4]*+ €12–€40/60 ✆ 243 350 140 *ww.n1hostelapartments.com* Av. dos Combatentes, 80. *[Alb.Santarém now closed].* •*CH* **Casa Flores** Rua Pedro Canavarro, 9 ✆ 965 612 001 x4 €50+). •*P* **Coimbra** *x4* €15 pp ✆ 243 322 816 Rua 31 de Janeiro, 42. •*Hr* **A Casa Brava** *x16* €75-95 ✆ 912 852 261 R. Guilherme Azevedo 31. •*Hr* **Beirante** *x40* €35+ ✆ 243 322 547 rua Alexandre Herculano (near Mercado). •*H*** **Vitória** *x60* €35-55 ✆ 243 309 130 Rua Visconde de Santarém, 21. •*Hs* **Tagus Host** *12x* €30-37 ✆ 913 476 949 *www.tagushost.pt* Av. Dom Afonso Henriques, 79A. + ***1.3*** *km* •*H***** **Santarém** *x105* €60-70 ✆ 243 330 800 Av Madre Andaluz. + ***1.5*** *km adj. Hospital.* •*H**** **Umu** *x67* €47-57 ✆ 243 377 240 *www.enfis.pt/umu* Av. Bernardo Santareno 38. + **BV** *Mun.[4÷1]* €10 ✆ 243 377 900 Rua Brigadeiro Lino Dias Valente. •**Casa da Alcáçova** *x7* €100+ ✆ 243 304 030 Largo do Alcáçova, 3.

***Praça Sá da Bandeira***

***Mercado** & Azulejo*

río Tejo
*de Santarém*

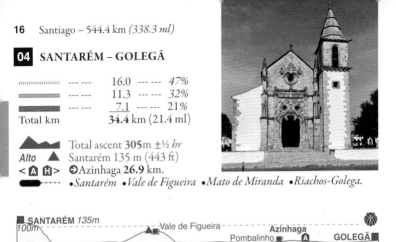

## 04 SANTARÉM – GOLEGÃ

| | | | |
|---|---|---|---|
| | --- --- | 16.0 | --- --- *47%* |
| | --- --- | 11.3 | --- --- *32%* |
| | --- --- | 7.1 | --- --- 21% |
| Total km | | **34.4** km (21.4 ml) | |

Total ascent **305**m ±½ *hr*

*Alto* ▲ Santarém 135 m (443 ft)

<A H> ➲Azinhaga **26.9** km.

•*Santarém* •*Vale de Figueira* •*Mato de Miranda* •*Riachos-Golega.*

SANTARÉM 135m
100m
Vale de Figueira
Azinhaga
Pombalinho
GOLEGÃ
río Tejo
Alviela
Almonda
0 km 5 km 10 km 15 km 20 km 25 km 30 km

■ **Pombalinho:** *[+ **900**m* •*CR.* **Portas** *Alb.[8÷1]* €20 *4x* €58+ ✆ 243 459 044 *www.casadasportas.pt N-365].*

■ **Azinhaga:** ***Rua da Misericordia*** •**Casa da Azinhaga** €70+ ✆ 249 957 146. •**Solar do Espirito Santo** ✆ 249 957 252 €65. **+*1.3*** km ***Rua dos Altos Montijos*** N°68 •*CR* **Casa de Azzancha** *x4* €30pp-€65 incl. ✆ 249 957 253 m: 919 187 773 Helena Santos. *[+4.5 km Mato Miranda* •***Quinta de Miranda*** *€55 ✆ 249 957 115].*

■ **Golegã:** ❶***Posto de Turismo*** ✆ 249 979 002 ***Centro:*** adj. Igreja •**Casa do Adro** €65+ ✆ 966 798 330 (Filipe) Largo da Imaculada Conceição, 58. ***Rua D. João IV*** •**Bombeiros Voluntários** ✆ 249 979 070 floor *suelo.* •**Cavalo Branco** ✆ 249 979 003 €40+ (x3) adj. •**Parque Campismo** ✆ 249 979 003. **N°136** •**Quartos do Lagar** *x5* €25 ✆ 917 591 833 (Josefino). **N°141** •**Pátio da Avó Faustina** €65 ✆ 935 640 545. r/da Cunha Franco Bloco 17 *Alb.*❶ **Inn Golegã** *x12* €15-€35 Elsa ✆ 933 493 397. •**Quinta S. João** €25 incl. ✆ 961 015 131 (adj. Equuspolis). •**Lusitanus** *x6* €40-50 Largo Marquês de Pombal ✆ 249 976 933. ***Rua José Relvas*:** **N°84** ★*Alb.*❷ **Solo Duro** *Priv.[14÷2]* €10 ✆ 249 976 802 *www.casadatiaguida.com* adj. •*CR* **Casa da Tia Guida** €45-60. **N°119** •🍴/*Hs.*O Té €15-35 ✆ 249 976 404. •*H* **Casa do Largo** *x10* €55+ ✆ 249 104 850 Largo 5 de Outubro. Rua Frederico Bonacho dos Anjos 35 *Alb.*❸ **Das Ademas** *Priv.[12÷2]* €10-15 *+2x* €35 ✆ 918 310 195. •*H***** **Lusitano** *x24* €75+ ✆ 249 979 170 *www.hotellusitano.com* Rua Gil Vicente.

Camino a Azinhaga

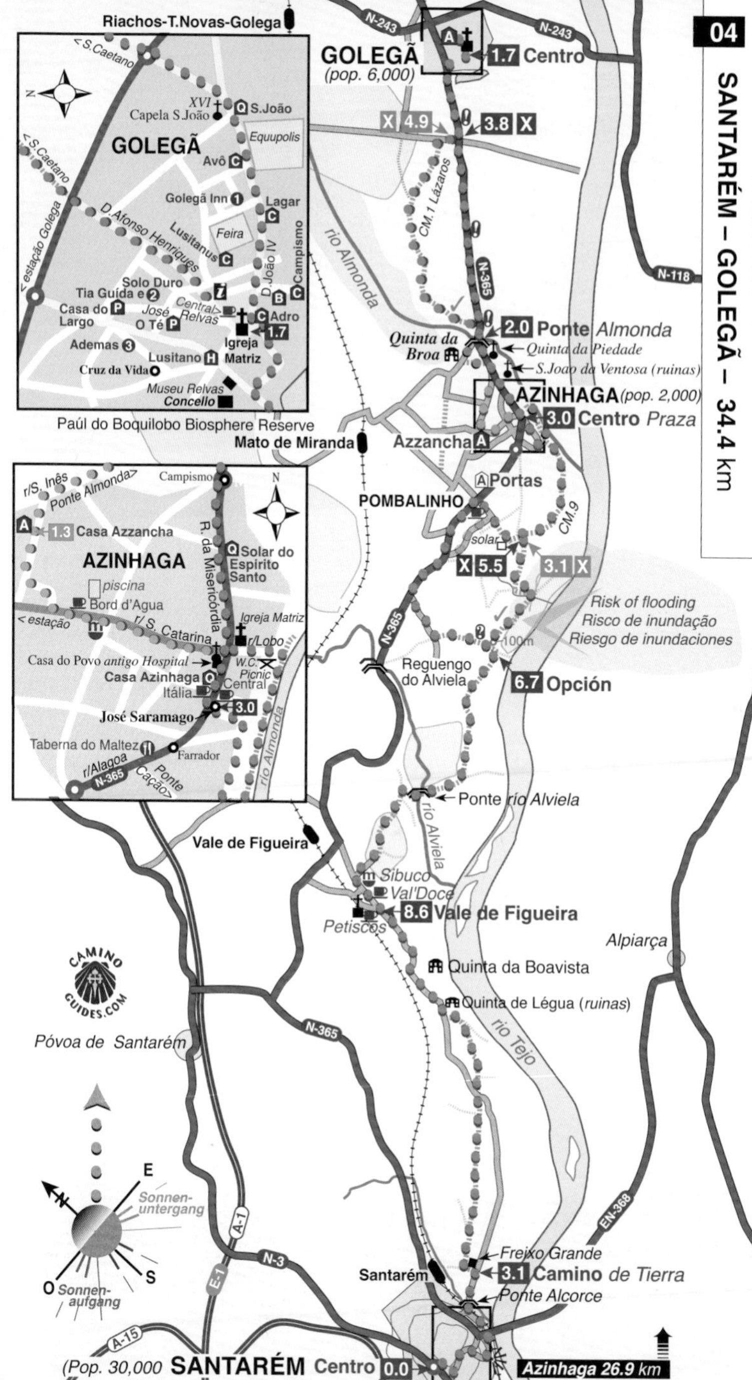
Riachos-T.Novas-Golega
GOLEGÃ
(pop. 6,000)
1.7 Centro
N-243
X 4.9
3.8 X
CM.1 Lázaros
rio Almonda
N-365
N-118
2.0 Ponte Almonda
Quinta da Broa
Quinta da Piedade
S.João da Ventosa (ruinas)
AZINHAGA (pop. 2,000)
3.0 Centro Praza
Paúl do Boquilobo Biosphere Reserve
Mato de Miranda
Azzancha
Portas
POMBALINHO
solar
CM.9
X 5.5
3.1 X
Risk of flooding
Risco de inundação
Riesgo de inundaciones
100m
Reguengo do Alviela
6.7 Opción
Ponte río Alviela
río Alviela
Vale de Figueira
Sibuco
Val'Doce
8.6 Vale de Figueira
Petiscos
Alpiarça
Quinta da Boavista
Quinta de Légua (ruinas)
rio Tejo
N-365
Póvoa de Santarém
CAMINO GUIDES.COM
E
Sonnen-untergang
S
O
Sonnen-aufgang
A-1
N-3
E-1
EN-368
Freixo Grande
Santarém
3.1 Camino de Tierra
Ponte Alcorce
A-15
(Pop. 30,000 SANTARÉM Centro 0.0
Azinhaga 26.9 km
GOLEGÃ
S.Caetano
Capela S.João
XVI
S.João
Equupolis
Avô
Golegã Inn
Lagar
Feira
D.Afonso Henriques
Lusitanus
estação Golega
D.João IV
Campismo
Solo Duro
Tia Guida e
Casa do Largo
José O Té
Central Relvas
Adro
Igreja Matriz
1.7
Ademas
Lusitano
Cruz da Vida
Museu Relvas
Concello
AZINHAGA
r/S. Inês
Ponte Almonda
Campismo
1.3 Casa Azzancha
R. da Misericórdia
Solar do Espirito Santo
piscina
Bord d'Agua
estação
r/ S. Catarina
Igreja Matriz
r/Lobo
Casa do Povo antigo Hospital
W.C. Picnic
Casa Azinhaga
Central
Itália
3.0
José Saramago
Taberna do Maltez
Farrador
r/Alagoa
N-365
Ponte Cação
rio Almonda

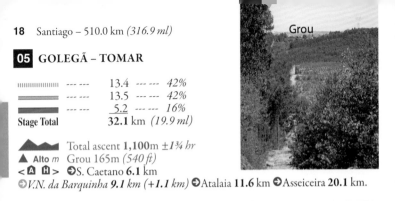

## 05 GOLEGÃ – TOMAR

| | | | |
|---|---|---|---|
| ---- | --- --- | 13.4 | --- --- *42%* |
| ---- | --- --- | 13.5 | --- --- *42%* |
| ---- | --- --- | 5.2 | --- --- *16%* |
| **Stage Total** | | **32.1** km *(19.9 ml)* | |

Total ascent **1,100**m ±*1¾ hr*

▲ Alto *m* Grou 165m *(540 ft)*

<🅐 🅗> ➲S. Caetano **6.1** km ➲*V.N. da Barquinha* ***9.1 km (+1.1 km)*** ➲Atalaia **11.6** km ➲Asseiceira **20.1** km.

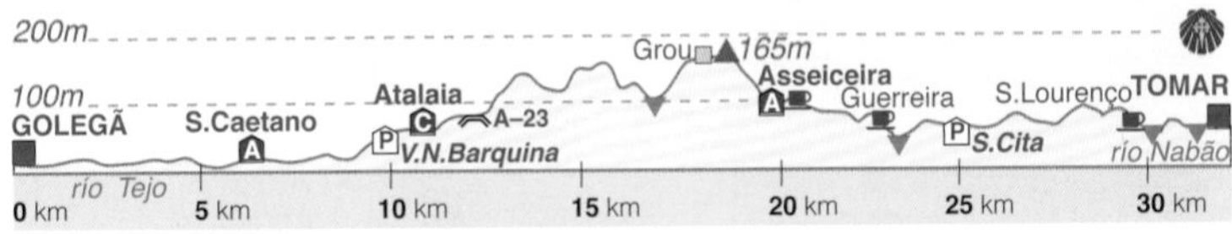


**▌São Caetano:** ●*Alb.* **Casa São Caetano** *Priv.[10÷5]* €15+ incl. ✆ 914 951 076 *(Ana Rita Sanches)* / 917 063 823 *(Alexandre Hachmeister)*. **▌Vila Nova da Barquinha:** *(+ 0.5km)* •*H* **River House** *Art Inn x15* €40-60 ✆ 918 735 242 www.riverhouse.pt Largo 1º Dezembro, 9 & •**Nature House.** •*CR* **Sonetos Do Tejo** *x6* €60-75 ✆ 919 280 663 www.sonetosdotejo.com r/Tejo, 18. **▌*Entroncamento + 3.0 km*** *varios hoteles* **▌Atalaia:** •*CR* **Casa do Patriarca** *x6* €40-60 *Dª Luisa Oliveira* ✆ 249 710 581 www.casadopatriarca.com rua Patriarca Dom José 134. **▌Asseiceira:** ●*Alb.* **D.Dinis** *Mun.[5÷1]* €10 Junta ✆ 249 381 426 **▌Guerreira / *Santa Cita*** *(+ 0.9 km)*: •*P*˙˙ ***Residencial Santa Cita*** ✆ 249 382 533 m: 964 682 805 Largo da Igreja. **▌Glorieta N-110 / *Quinta do Falcão*** *(+ 1.1 km)*: •*P*˙˙ ***Ninho do Falcão*** €35+ ✆ 249 380 070 Estrada do Castelo Bode, 24.

**Ponte A-23** *(woodland paths beyond Atalaia)*

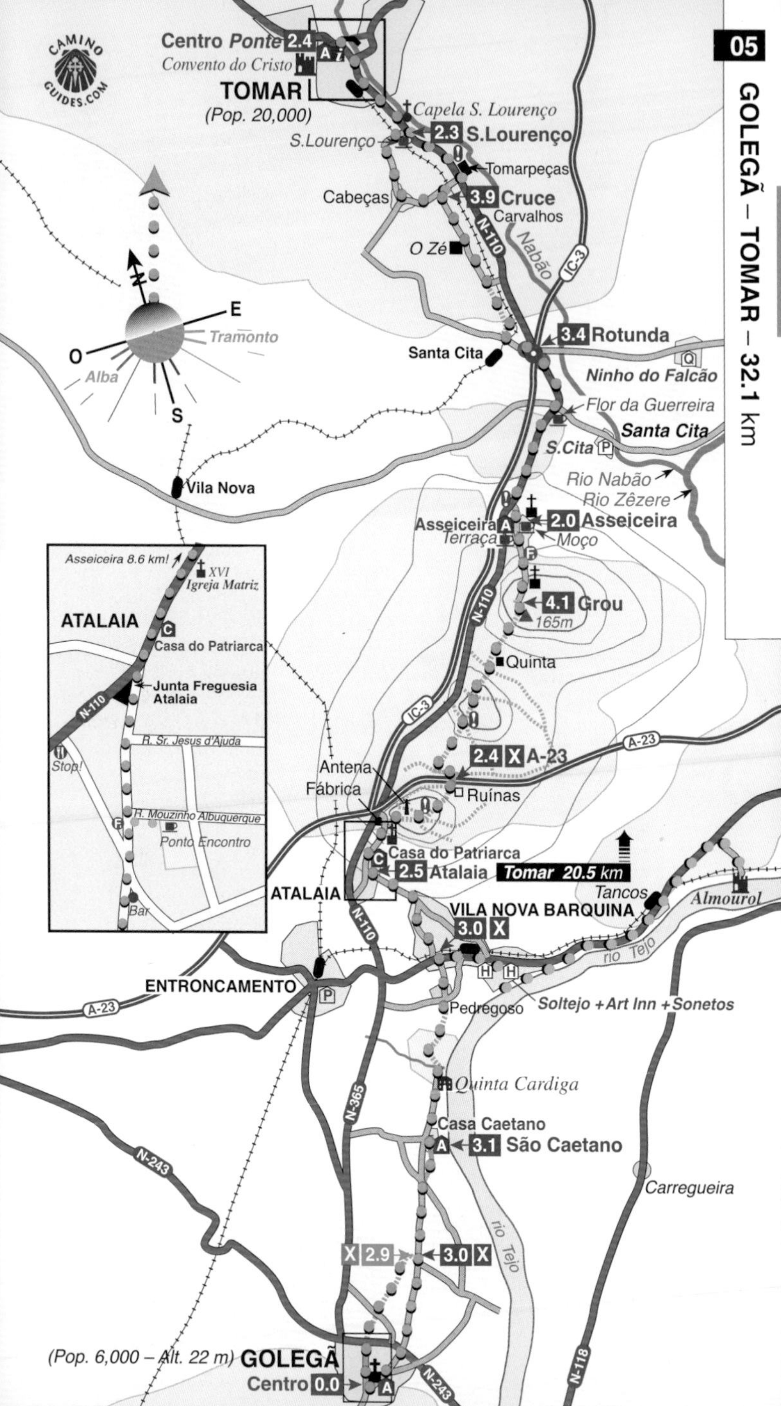
CAMINO GUIDES.COM
Centro Ponte 2.4
Convento do Cristo
TOMAR
(Pop. 20,000)
Capela S. Lourenço
S.Lourenço
2.3 S.Lourenço
Tomarpeças
Cabeças
3.9 Cruce
Carvalhos
O Zé
N-110
Nabão
IC-3
E
Tramonto
O
Alba
S
Santa Cita
3.4 Rotunda
Ninho do Falcão
Flor da Guerreira
Santa Cita
S.Cita
Rio Nabão
Rio Zêzere
Vila Nova
Asseiceira
Terraça
2.0 Asseiceira
Moço
4.1 Grou
165m
Quinta
Asseiceira 8.6 km!
XVI
Igreja Matriz
ATALAIA
Casa do Patriarca
Junta Freguesia Atalaia
R. Sr. Jesus d'Ajuda
Stop!
R. Mouzinho Albuquerque
Ponto Encontro
Bar
A-23
2.4 X A-23
Antena
Fábrica
Ruínas
Casa do Patriarca
2.5 Atalaia
Tomar 20.5 km
ATALAIA
Tancos
Almourol
VILA NOVA BARQUINA
3.0 X
rio Tejo
ENTRONCAMENTO
Soltejo + Art Inn + Sonetos
Pedregoso
Quinta Cardiga
N-365
Casa Caetano
3.1 São Caetano
N-243
Carregueira
X 2.9
3.0 X
rio Tejo
(Pop. 6,000 – Alt. 22 m) GOLEGÃ
Centro 0.0
N-118

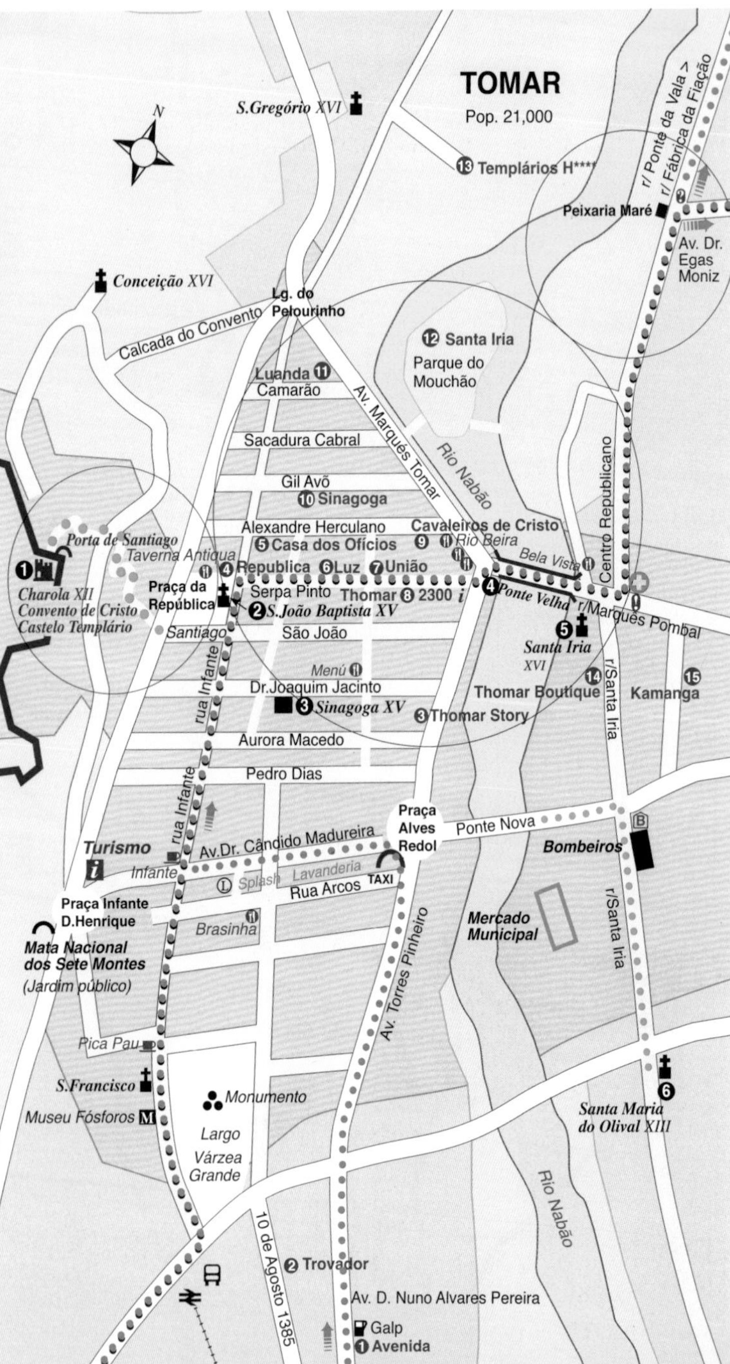

TOMAR
Pop. 21,000
N
S.Gregório XVI
13 Templários H****
r/ Ponte da Vala >
r/ Fábrica da Fiação
Peixaria Maré
Av. Dr. Egas Moniz
Conceição XVI
Lg. do Pelourinho
Calcada do Convento
12 Santa Iria
Parque do Mouchão
11 Luanda
Camarão
Av. Marquês Tomar
Sacadura Cabral
Rio Nabão
Centro Republicano
Gil Avõ
10 Sinagoga
Alexandre Herculano
Cavaleiros de Cristo
5 Casa dos Ofícios
9
Rio Beira
Porta de Santiago
Taverna Antiqua
Bela Vista
1
4 Republica
6 Luz
7 União
Charola XII
Convento de Cristo
Castelo Templário
Praça da República
Serpa Pinto
Thomar 8 2300
4 Ponte Velha
r/Marquês Pombal
2 S.João Baptista XV
Santiago
São João
5
Santa Iria XVI
Menú
rua Infante
Dr.Joaquim Jacinto
14 Thomar Boutique
15 Kamanga
r/Santa Iria
3 Sinagoga XV
3 Thomar Story
Aurora Macedo
Pedro Dias
rua Infante
Praça Alves Redol
Ponte Nova
Turismo
Av.Dr. Cândido Madureira
Bombeiros
Infante
Splash
Lavanderia
TAXI
Rua Arcos
Praça Infante D.Henrique
Brasinha
Av. Torres Pinheiro
Mercado Municipal
r/Santa Iria
Mata Nacional dos Sete Montes
(Jardim público)
Pica Pau
S.Francisco
Monumento
6
Santa Maria do Olival XIII
Museu Fósforos
Largo Várzea Grande
Rio Nabão
10 de Agosto 1385
2 Trovador
Av. D. Nuno Alvares Pereira
Galp
1 Avenida

● **Monumentos históricos: ❶ Convento de Cristo** *XII* / **Castelo** / **Aqueduto dos Pegões** *XVI*. **❷ Igreja de São João Baptista** *XV* / Praza Republica. **❸ Sinagoga e Museo Luso-Hebraico Abraham Zacuto** *XV* Rua Joaquim Jacinto, 73. **❹Ponte Velha** Río Nabão **❺ Capela de Santa Iria. ❻ Igreja de Santa Maria do Olival.**

**❶*Turismo Regional*** 09:30-18:00 ✆ 249 329 800 Av. Dr. Cândido Madureira 531

● ***Lodging:*** **❶** *Hs* **Avenida** *x7* €15-€35 ✆ 960 077 991 Av. Dom Nuno Álvares Pereira, 41 (adj. Galp). **❷** *H*** **Trovador** *x30* €35-40 ✆ 249 322 567 r/10 de Agosto, 22 (adj. bus station). **❸** *P* **Thomar Story** *x12* €45-55 ✆ 925 936 273 r/João Carlos Everard 53 (by river). ***Central:*** **❹** *H***** **Republica** *x19* €125+ ✆ 249 193 400 www.hotelrepublica.pt Praça da República 41. **❺** *H**** **Casa dos Ofícios** *x16* €80+ ✆124 9247 360 www.casadosoficioshotel.pt r/Silva Magalhães N.º 71. ***Rua Serpa Pinto @Nº144*** **❻** *P** **Luz** *x10* €18-25 ✆ 249 312 317 www.residencialluz.com ***@Nº94*** **❼** *P** **União** *x26* €30-40 ✆ 249 323 161.***@Nº43*** albergue run by Sónia Pais ★**❽***Alb.***Thomar 2300** *Priv.[32÷5]* €15 incl. *+4* €25-€35 ✆ 249 324 256 www.hostel2300thomar.com ***@Nº144*** **❾** *H*** **Cavaleiros de Cristo** *x16* €25-40 ✆ 249 321 067 rua Alexandre Herculano,7. **❿** *Hs* **Sinagoga** €30 ✆ 249 323 083 rua Gil Avo,31. **⓫** *P* **Luanda** *x14* €30-40 ✆ 249 323 200 www.residencialuanda.com Av. Marques de Tomar, 15, above *Rst.* on river. – opp. ***far side of rio Nabão:*** the old fashioned **⓬ Estalagem de Santa Iria** *x14* €35-40 ✆ 249 313 326 Parque do Mouchão (rio Nabão). Also on the river (further out of town) **⓭** *H**** **dos Templarios** *x177* €103+ ✆ 249 310 100 www.hoteldostemplarios.com Largo Cândido dos Reis. **Over river:** **⓮** *H**** **Thomar Boutique** €55-65 ✆ 249 323 210 www.thomarboutiquehotel.com r/Santa Iria 14. **⓯** *H*** **Kamanga** *x15* €35-€45 ✆ 249 311 555 www.hotelkamanga.com r/Major Ferreira Amaral, 16 near **Bombeiros Municipais** ✆ 249 329 140 rua de Santa Iria. ● ***Restaurantes:*** Popular 🍴 Taverna Antiqua adj. Praça da República and 🍴 Beira Rio adj. río Nabão. 🍴 Brasinha r/dos Arcos 5.

●**Fátima** *Rodoviaria* €9: Tomar 09:55–Fátima 10:55 / Fátima 18:40–Tomar 19:40.

**Igreja de São João Baptista XV**

**Convento de Cristo XII**

# 06 TOMAR – ALVAIÁZERE

| | | |
|---|---|---|
| | 15.8 | *48%* |
| | 17.4 | *52%* |
| | 0.0 | *0%* |
| **Stage Total** | **33.2** km | *(20.6 ml)* |

Total ascent **1,340**m ±*2¼ hr*

▲ Alto *m* Alvaiázere 330 m (1,080 ft)

< A H > ➲Vila Verde **19.6** km ➲Tojal **23.1** km ➲Cortiça **26.4** km.

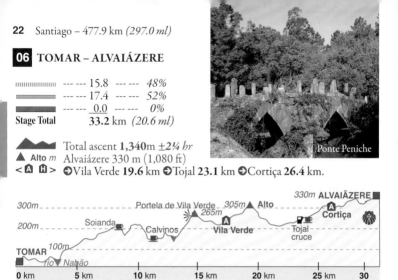

Ponte Peniche

330m ALVAIÃZERE
300m
Portela de Vila Verde 265m
305m Alto
200m
Soianda
Calvinos
Vila Verde
Tojal cruce
Cortiça
TOMAR
100m
rio Nabão
0 km 5 km 10 km 15 km 20 km 25 km 30

**▌Calvinos** ●*Alb.* **Calvinos** *Asoc.[10÷2]* €6 ✆ 927 627 647 r/Capela. **▌Vila Verde *Areias*:** ●*Alb.* **Heart Way** Liede ✆ 938 744 535 rua N.S da luz, 342 Areias check if open. Possible alt.: ●*Alb.* **Casa Paradise** Estrada das Galegas 305. **▌Tojal *Cruce*:** 🍴•*P.* **Tojal Douro** +200m €30 ✆ 925 374 578. **▌*[Ramalhal +1.6 km*** *N-110 [!]* 🍴•*CR.* ***Encontro*** €20-35 Batista ✆ *913 234 298 €20-35].* **▌Cortiça:** ●*Alb.* **Quinta Cortiça** *Priv.[14÷2]* €20 incl. ✆ María 926 923 994 *www.quintadacortica.pt* **▌*Carrasqueiras 2.6 km*** ●*Alb.* **Amigos** *Priv.[12÷1] €10 tipi ✆ 236 656 374 (Paul) Estrada do Nabao N-356].* **▌Outeirinho *+0.6 km*** •*CR* **Ti' Ladeira** *x3* €25 incl. ✆ 927 493 141 *www.tiladeira.com Rua da Ladeira].* **■ Alvaiázere:** •*P* **O Brás** *x12* €15-30 ✆ 236 655 405 [m] 966 495 337 *www.restauranteobras.pt menú* €10. ★●*Alb.* **Pinheiro** *Priv.[20÷2]* €12 ✆ 236 098 343 Carlos [m] 915 440 196 free pick-up *ecogida gratuita.* ***+0.5** km* •**Bombeiros Voluntários** ✆ 236 650 510 Rua dos Bombeiros Voluntários. ☕ *Quintinha (Tita)* rua D. Sancho.

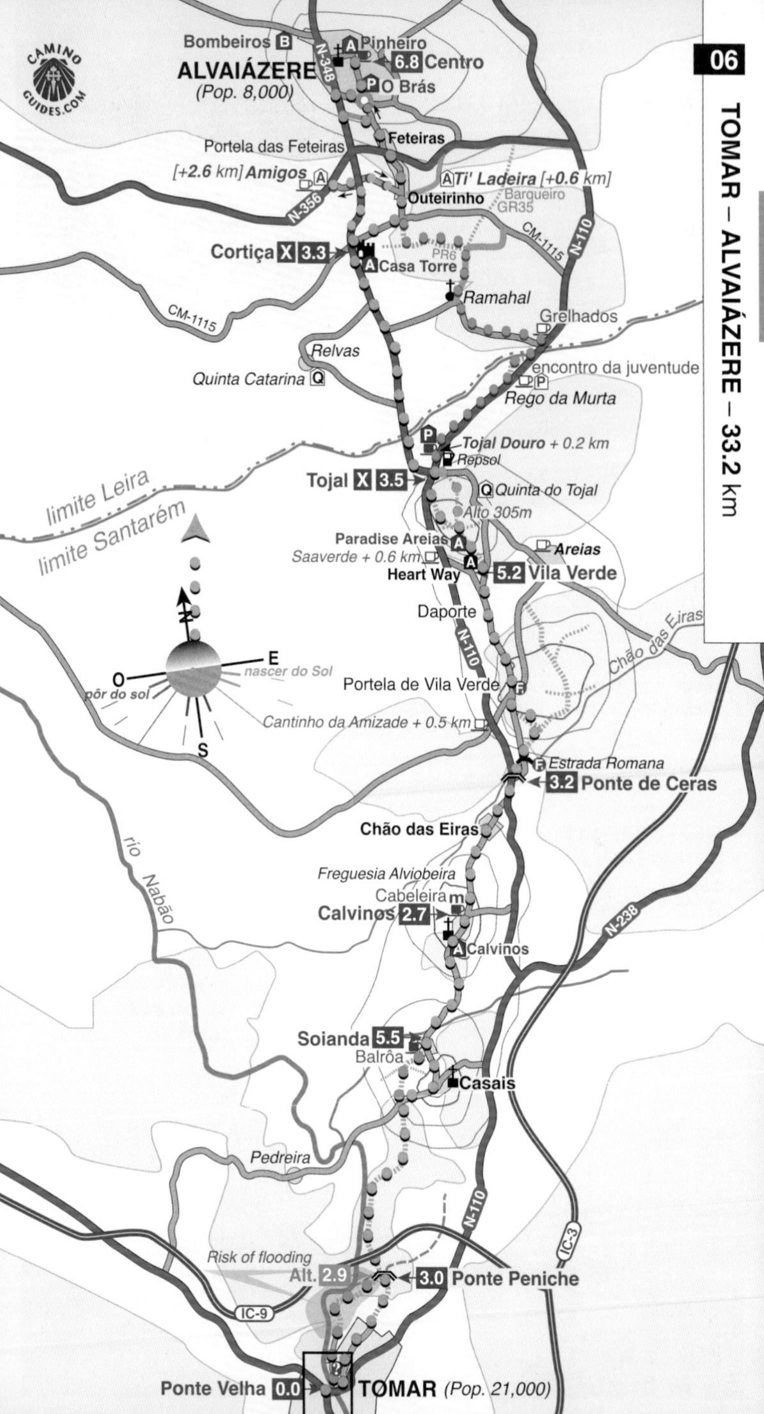
CAMINO GUIDES.COM
Bombeiros
ALVAIÁZERE
(Pop. 8,000)
Pinheiro
6.8 Centro
O Brás
N-348
Feteiras
Portela das Feteiras
[+2.6 km] Amigos
Ti' Ladeira [+0.6 km]
Outeirinho
Barqueiro
GR35
N-356
CM-1115
N-110
Cortiça 3.3
Casa Torre
PR6
Ramahal
CM-1115
Grelhados
Relvas
Quinta Catarina
encontro da juventude
Rego da Murta
Tojal Douro + 0.2 km
Repsol
Tojal 3.5
Quinta do Tojal
Alto 305m
limite Leira
limite Santarém
Paradise Areias
Areias
Saaverde + 0.6 km
Heart Way
5.2 Vila Verde
Daporte
N-110
Chão das Eiras
E
nascer do Sol
O
pôr do sol
S
Portela de Vila Verde
Cantinho da Amizade + 0.5 km
Estrada Romana
3.2 Ponte de Ceras
Chão das Eiras
rio Nabão
Freguesia Alviobeira
Cabeleira
Calvinos 2.7
Calvinos
N-238
Soianda 5.5
Balrôa
Casais
Pedreira
N-110
IC-3
Risk of flooding
Alt. 2.9
3.0 Ponte Peniche
IC-9
Ponte Velha 0.0
TOMAR (Pop. 21,000)

# 07 ALVAIÁZERE – RABAÇAL

| | | |
|---|---|---|
| | 15.7 | *48%* |
| | 17.1 | *52%* |
| | 0.0 | *0%* |
| **Stage Total** | **32.8** km *(20.4 ml)* | |

Total ascent **1,050**m ±*1¾ hr*

▲ Alto *m* Vendas 485 m *(1,590 ft)*

< A H > ➲Ansião **13.2** km ➲Alvorge **23.5** km

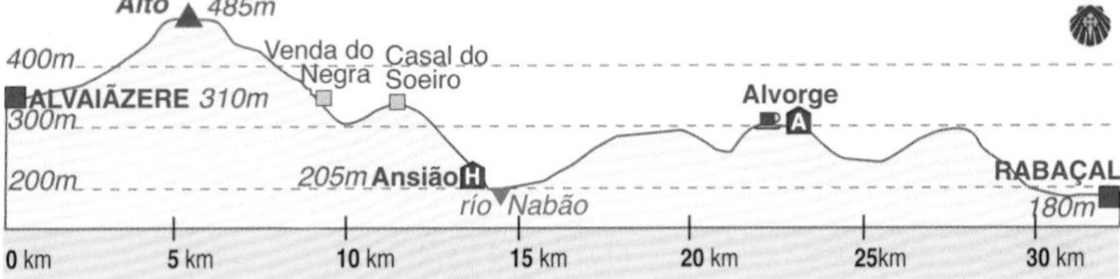

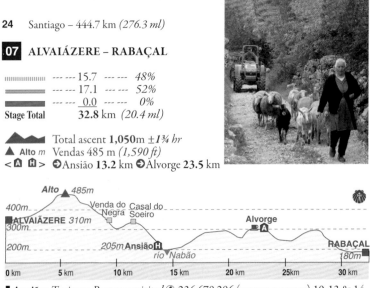

**Ansião**: *Turismo: Praça municipal* © 236 670 206 (summer *verano*) 10-13 & 14-18. •*H*** *spa* **Ansiturismo** *x10* €40-55 © 236 673 337 rua Jerónimo Soares Barbosa 34 adj. *biblioteca*. •*P* **Adega Típica** *x8* €25-40 © 236 677 364 Carlos & João *www.adegatipicadeansiao.com* r/dos Combatentes da Grande Guerra opp. Concello. •**Hostal** adj. tapas bar *Tarouca (Pedro)* ***Av. Dr. Vítor Faveiro*** & •*H* **A Nova Estrela** *Sol* €20-30 © 236 677 415 [m] 918 838 605. •**Bombeiros Voluntários** © 236 670 600. 🍴/•*P.* **Solar da Rainha** €25-35 © 236 676 204 r/Alto dos Pinheiras 339. *[+**1.9** km •Cr **Quinta dos Church** €20 menú €10 © Olga (Church) 914 420 587 opp. Capela de São Brás – free pick-up ecogida gratuita].*

**Alvorge**: ❶*Alb.***O Lagareiro** *Priv.[**10÷2**]* €12-17 *+1* €25-45 Vítor © 913 132 477 r/Boiças, 52 + ❷*Alb.***Alvorge** *Par.[**10÷1**]* €5 Vítor © 913 132 477 *Cruceiro* keys *llaves*. *[+ **1.5** km •CR **Vale Florido** €30+ © 236 981 716 Rua Santo Antonio].* Rua de São Pedro *CR.***Moinho do Cubo** *x1* €50-60 © 969 831 678.

**Rabaçal:** /●*Alb.* **O Bonito** *priv.[**16÷2**]* €10 *x2* €25 Claudia © 916 890 599. •**Pousada do Rabaçal** *x10* €15+ © 918 752 990 Rua da Igreja adj. ***museo romano*** © 239 561 856 €1.50 (10:00-13-00 & 14:00-18:00). *[● **Penela +8** km • Hs Sicó In & Out €15 Zona Industrial. H*** Duecitânia €50+ © 239 700 740].*

Camino de Alvorge

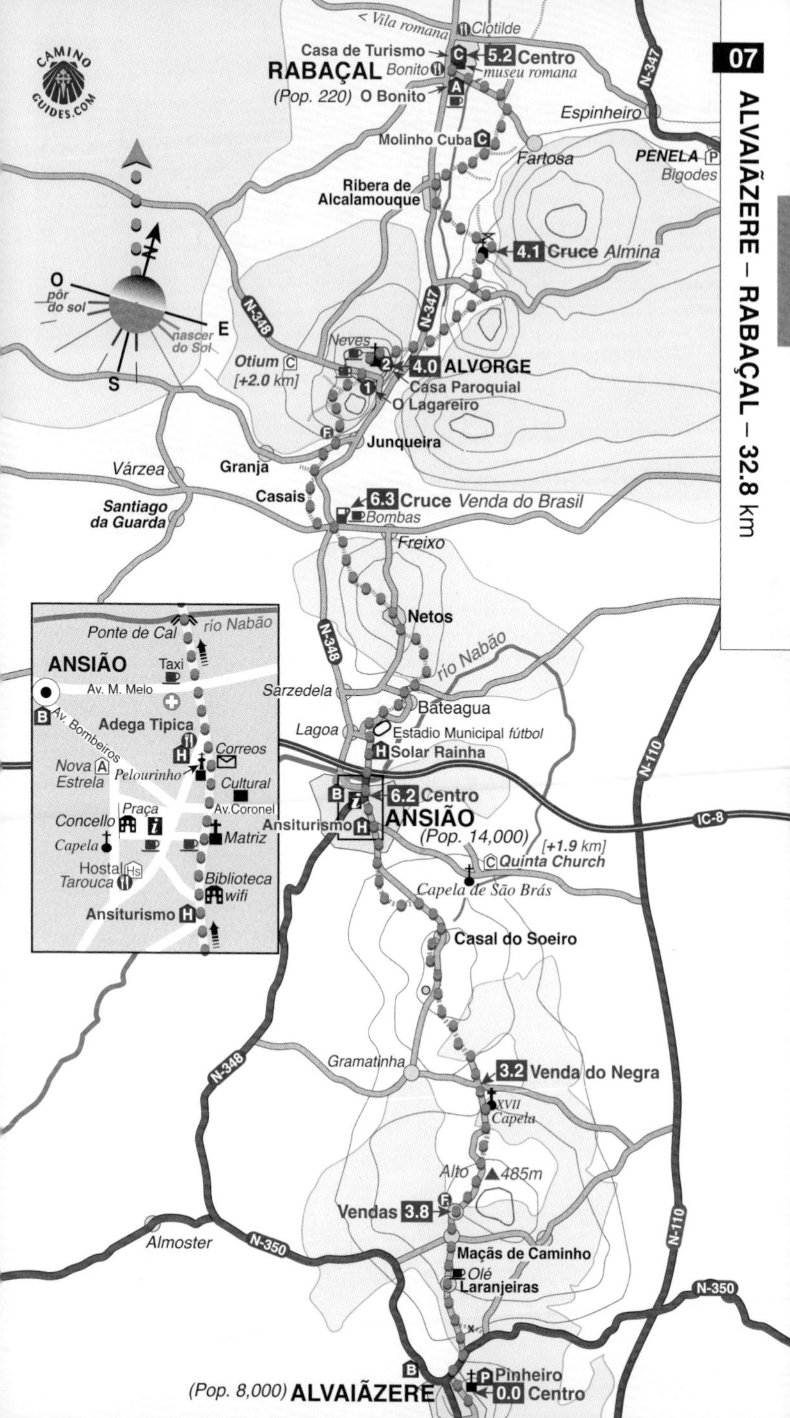
07
ALVAIÃZERE – RABAÇAL – 32.8 km
CAMINO GUIDES.COM
< Vila romana
Clotilde
Casa de Turismo
5.2 Centro
museu romana
RABAÇAL
Bonito
(Pop. 220) O Bonito
Espinheiro
N-347
Molinho Cuba
Fartosa
PENELA
Bigodes
Ribera de Alcalamouque
4.1 Cruce Almina
O
pôr do sol
E
nascer do Sol
S
N-348
N-347
Neves
Otium
[+2.0 km]
4.0 ALVORGE
Casa Paroquial
O Lagareiro
Junqueira
Várzea
Granja
Casais
Santiago da Guarda
6.3 Cruce Venda do Brasil
Bombas
Freixo
Netos
N-348
rio Nabão
Sarzedela
Bateagua
Lagoa
Estadio Municipal fútbol
Solar Rainha
6.2 Centro
ANSIÃO
(Pop. 14,000)
Ansiturismo
[+1.9 km]
Quinta Church
Capela de São Brás
Casal do Soeiro
N-110
IC-8
Ponte de Cal
rio Nabão
ANSIÃO
Taxi
Av. M. Melo
Av. Bombeiros
Adega Tipica
Correos
Nova Estrela
Pelourinho
Cultural
Av.Coronel
Praça
Concello
Matriz
Capela
Hostal Tarouca
Biblioteca wifi
Ansiturismo
N-348
Gramatinha
3.2 Venda do Negra
XVII Capela
Alto
485m
Vendas 3.8
Almoster
N-350
N-110
Maçãs de Caminho
Olé
Laranjeiras
N-350
Pinheiro
(Pop. 8,000) ALVAIÃZERE
0.0 Centro

# 08 RABAÇAL – COIMBRA

| | | |
|---|---|---|
| | --- --- 10.2 --- --- | *35%* |
| | --- --- 15.4 --- --- | *53%* |
| | --- --- 3.6 --- --- | *12%* |
| **Stage Total** | **29.2** km *(18.1 ml)* | |

Total ascent **920**m ±*1½ hr*
▲ Alto *m* Alto Santo Clara 215m *(705 ft)*
<A H> ➲Conímbriga **12.3** km.
➲*Condeixa a Nova* ***12.3*** *+1.0 km]*
➲Cernache **17.6** km . ➲*Palheira* ***22.3*** *+ 0.5 km]* ➲S.Clara **28.2** km.

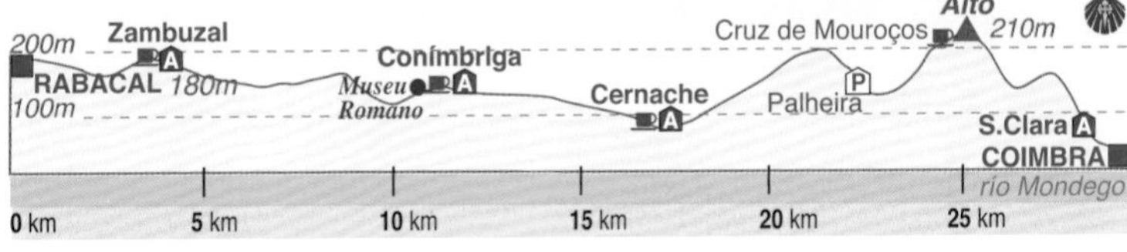


▌**Zambujal:** ●*Alb.* **Casa das Raposas** *priv.[18÷2]* €15-20 ✆ 965 006 277 *(Sérgio Elias)*. ▌**Fonte Coberta** •*Refugio Peregrino Nicolau* tent by donation *cámping*. ▌**Conímbriga:** ●*Alb.* **de Conímbriga** *priv.[8÷1]*. €12 ✆ 962 870 633 Rua da Lagoa, 15. ▌**Condeixa-A-Nova:** *[+ 1 km* •*H***** **do Paço** *x43* €65-79 ✆ 239 944 025 *www.conimbrigahoteldopaco.pt*. •*P* **Borges** €25 ✆ 932 824 949 Rua Dona Maria Elsa Franco Sotto Mayor Nº 65 + @ Nº 53 •**Casa de Hóspedes Ruínas** ✆ 239 941 772. ▌**Cernache:** ●*Alb.***Cernache** *priv.[14÷3]* €8 ✆ 917 619 080 (Pedro) / 968 034 708 Rua Álvaro Anes, 37. ▌**Palheira:** *[****+0.5*** *km* •*CR* ***Jantesta*** *x15 €25+ ✆ 239 437 587 www.bemestar-coimbra.com Rua Da Jantesta, 35]*

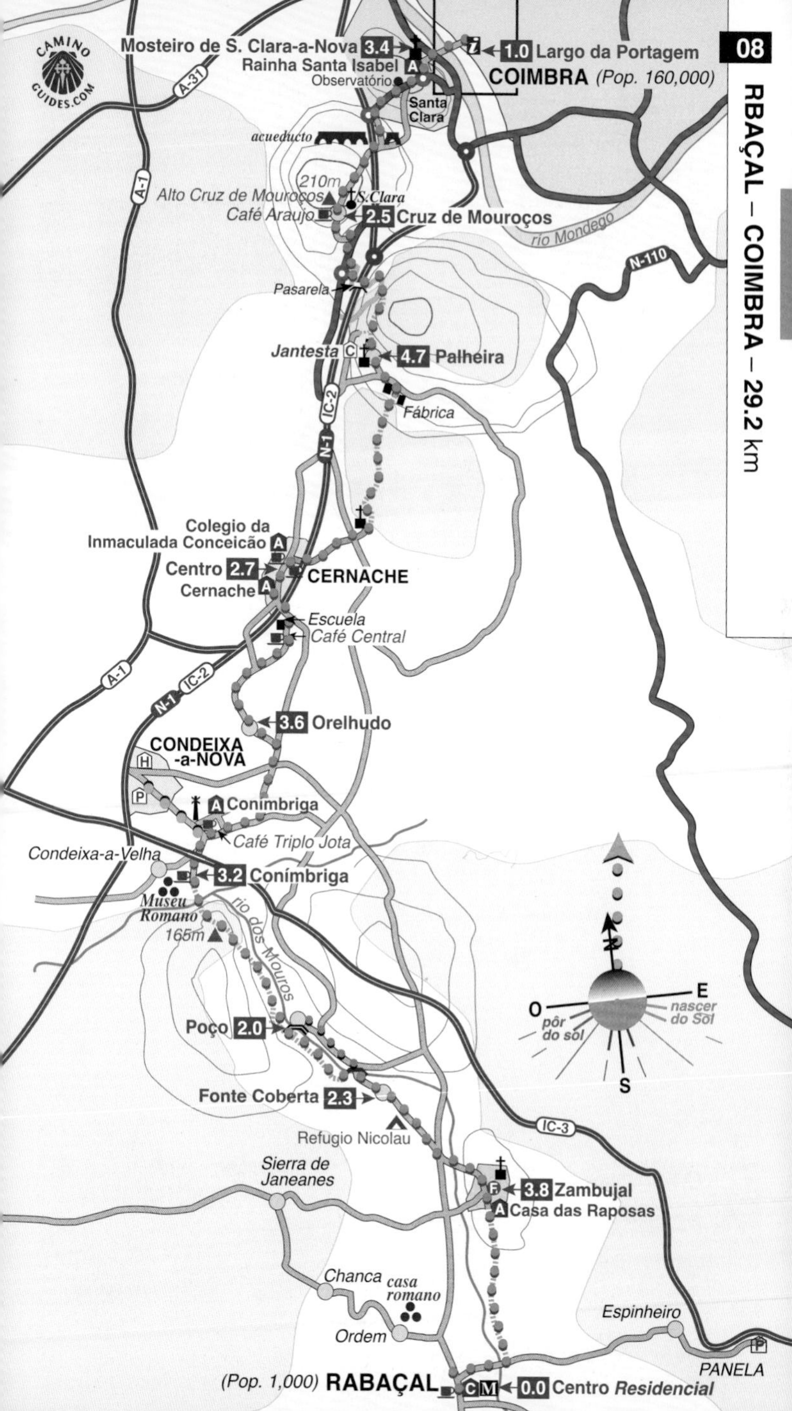
RABAÇAL – COIMBRA – 29.2 km
CAMINO GUIDES.COM
Mosteiro de S. Clara-a-Nova 3.4
Rainha Santa Isabel
Observatório
1.0 Largo da Portagem
COIMBRA (Pop. 160,000)
Santa Clara
acueducto
A-31
A-1
210m
Alto Cruz de Mouroços
S.Clara
Café Araujo
2.5 Cruz de Mouroços
rio Mondego
N-110
Pasarela
Jantesta
4.7 Palheira
Fábrica
IC-2
N-1
Colegio da Inmaculada Conceicão
Centro 2.7
CERNACHE
Cernache
Escuela
Café Central
3.6 Orelhudo
CONDEIXA -a-NOVA
Conimbriga
Café Triplo Jota
Condeixa-a-Velha
3.2 Conímbriga
Museu Romano
rio dos Mouros
165m
E
O
nascer do Sol
pôr do sol
N
S
Poço 2.0
Fonte Coberta 2.3
Refugio Nicolau
IC-3
Sierra de Janeanes
3.8 Zambujal
Casa das Raposas
Chanca
casa romano
Ordem
Espinheiro
PANELA
(Pop. 1,000) RABAÇAL
0.0 Centro Residencial

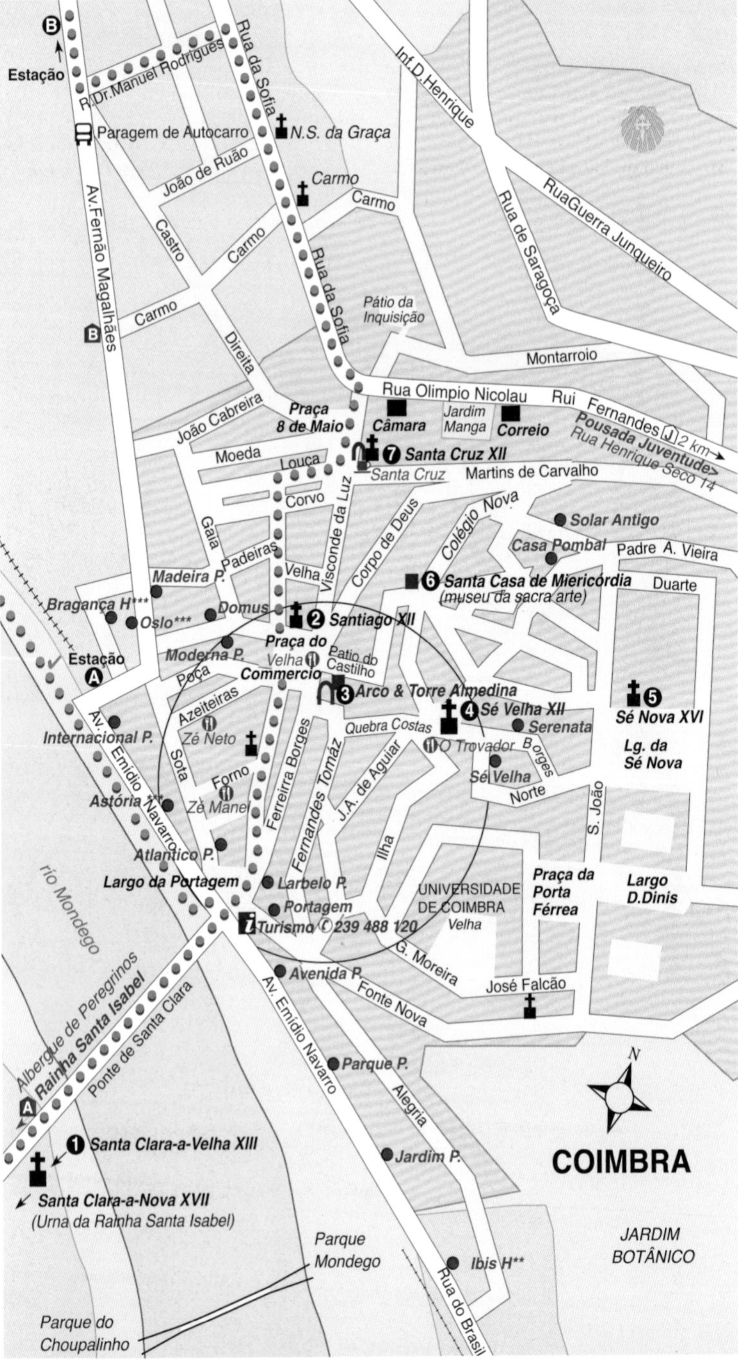
Estação
R.Dr.Manuel Rodrigues
Rua da Sofia
Paragem de Autocarro
N.S. da Graça
João de Ruão
Carmo
Av.Fernão Magalhães
Castro
Carmo
Inf.D.Henrique
Rua de Saragoça
RuaGuerra Junqueiro
Pátio da Inquisição
Montarroio
Direita
Rua Olimpio Nicolau
Rui Fernandes
2 km
Pousada Juventude
Rua Henrique Seco 14
Praça 8 de Maio
Câmara
Jardim Manga
Correio
João Cabreira
Moeda
Louça
Santa Cruz XII
Santa Cruz
Martins de Carvalho
Corvo
Corpo de Deus
Colégio Nova
Solar Antigo
Casa Pombal
Padre A. Vieira
Gaia
Padeiras
Visconde da Luz
Velha
Madeira P.
Santa Casa de Miericórdia
(museu da sacra arte)
Duarte
Bragança H***
Oslo***
Domus
Santiago XII
Praça do Commercio
Patio do Castilho
Velha
Estação
Moderna P.
Poça
Arco & Torre Almedina
Sé Velha XII
Sé Nova XVI
Lg. da Sé Nova
Azeiteiras
Zé Neto
Quebra Costas
Serenata
Internacional P.
Av. Emídio Navarro
Sota
Ferreira Borges
Fernandes Tomáz
J.A. de Aguiar
O Trovador
Borges
Sé Velha
Norte
Forno
Zé Manel
Astória ***
S. João
Ilha
Atlantico P.
rio Mondego
Largo da Portagem
Larbelo P.
UNIVERSIDADE DE COIMBRA
Velha
Praça da Porta Férrea
Largo D.Dinis
Portagem
Turismo © 239 488 120
G. Moreira
Avenida P.
Fonte Nova
José Falcão
Albergue de Peregrinos
Rainha Santa Isabel
Ponte de Santa Clara
Av. Emídio Navarro
Parque P.
Alegria
N
Santa Clara-a-Velha XIII
Jardim P.
COIMBRA
Santa Clara-a-Nova XVII
(Urna da Rainha Santa Isabel)
JARDIM BOTÂNICO
Parque Mondego
Ibis H**
Rua do Brasil
Parque do Choupalinho

● **Monumentos históricos:** ❶ **Convento Santa Clara-a-Velha** *XIII Albergue de Peregrinos (e Túmulo da Rainha Santa).* ❷ **Igreja de Santiago** *XII* rua Visconde da Luz. ❸ **Porta e torre de Almedina** *XII* ❹ **Sé Velha e Claustro** *XII.* ❺ **Sé Nova** *XVI* ❻ **Santa Casa da Misericórdia** XV *(museo da Sacra Arte).* ❼ **Igreja do Mosteiro de Santa Cruz** *XII* Praça 8 de Maio *(Túmulo da Rei Afonso Henriques).*

❶ ***Turismo: Largo da Portagem*** *www.centerofportugal.com/destination/coimbra* Turismo ✆ 239 488 120. ▮ **Hoteles** *(€12pp-€60)* •*Hs* **Portagem** *x8* €15pp ✆ 917 569 143 r/Couraça Estrela 11. •*P.* **Larbelo** ✆ 239 829 092 adj. •*P.* **Atlantico** ✆ 239 826 496. •*H**** **Astória** ✆ 239 853 020. •*P.* **Internacional** ✆ 239 825 503. adj. •*P.* **Avenida** ✆ 239 822 156. adj. *Sé* •*Hs* **Serenata** Largo Sé Velha ✆ 239 853 130 & •*Hs* **Sé Velha** ✆ 239 151 647 r/Norte, 11. •**Casa Pombal** ✆ 239 835 175 r/ Flores 18. •*P.* **Moderna** ✆ 239 825 413, r/Adelino Veiga @N°49 & •*P.* **Dómus** ✆ 239 828 584 @N°62. ●**Juventud** *x70* €12 ✆ 239 829 228 r/ Dr. Henriques Seco bus N° 46. **Bombeiros Voluntários** Av. Fernão Magalhães.

❹ Sé Velha *entrada*

❹ Sé Velha *claustro*

❷ Igreja de Santiago

❼ Igreja do Mosteiro de **Santa Cruz**

## 09 COIMBRA – MEALHADA

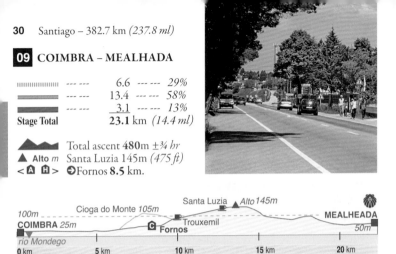

| | | | | |
|---|---|---|---|---|
| | --- --- | 6.6 | --- --- | *29%* |
| | --- --- | 13.4 | --- --- | *58%* |
| | --- --- | 3.1 | --- --- | *13%* |
| **Stage Total** | | **23.1** km | | *(14.4 ml)* |

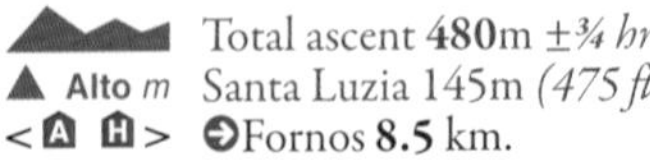

Total ascent **480**m ±¾ *hr*

▲ Alto *m* Santa Luzia 145m *(475 ft)*

<🅐 🅗> ➲Fornos **8.5** km.

100m
Cioga do Monte *105m*
Santa Luzia ▲ *Alto 145m*
MEALHEADA
COIMBRA *25m*
Trouxemil
Fornos
*50m*
*rio Mondego*
0 km
5 km
10 km
15 km
20 km

▌**Fornos:** •*CR* **Casa Morais** *x10* €50-60 ✆ 967 636 029 Rua Da Capela. ▌**Mealhada:** •*P.* **Castela** *x5* €30 ✆ ✆ 231 202 275 r/Doutor Paulo Falcão, 10 adj. Iglesia. •*P.* **Oasis** *x16* €25-40 ✆ 231 202 081 N-1. ▌**Sernadelo:** +***0.6*** km •*H*** ***Quinta dos Três Pinheiros*** *x53 €40-52* ✆ 231 202 391 *www.trespinheiros.com* ●*Alb.***Hilário** *Priv.[***20***÷1] +15* €15-30 ✆ 231 202 117 [m] 916 191 721 (Isabela) Av. da Restauração, 30.

Esplanada da Mealhada

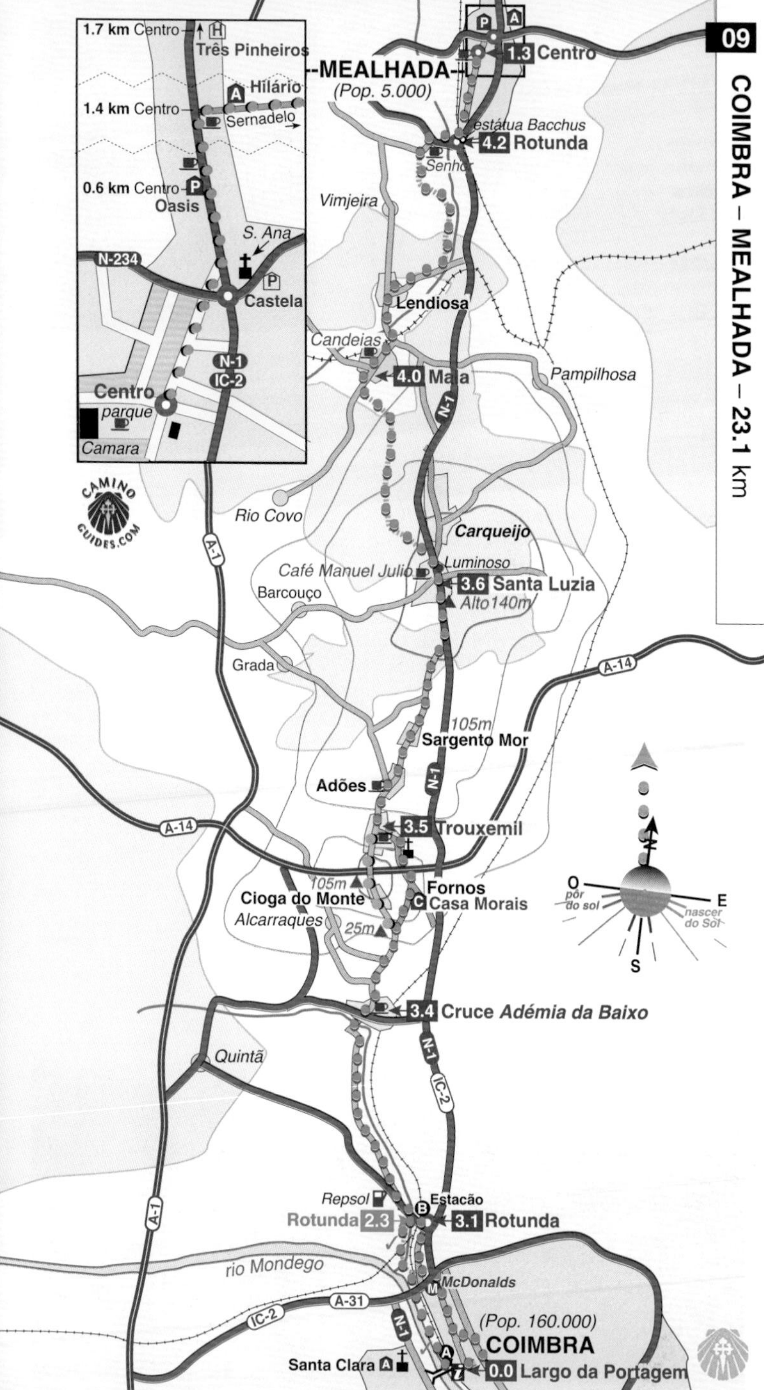

1.7 km Centro
Três Pinheiros
MEALHADA
(Pop. 5.000)
Hilário
1.4 km Centro
Sernadelo
0.6 km Centro
Oasis
S. Ana
N-234
Castela
N-1
IC-2
Centro
parque
Camara
1.3 Centro
estátua Bacchus
4.2 Rotunda
Senhor
Vimjeira
Lendiosa
Candeias
4.0 Mala
Pampilhosa
Rio Covo
Carqueijo
Luminoso
Café Manuel Julio
3.6 Santa Luzia
Alto 140m
Barcouço
Grada
A-14
105m
Sargento Mor
Adões
A-14
3.5 Trouxemil
105m
Fornos
Cioga do Monte
Casa Morais
Alcarraques
25m
O
pôr do sol
E
nascer do Sol
S
3.4 Cruce Adémia da Baixo
Quintã
IC-2
A-1
Repsol
Estacão
Rotunda 2.3
3.1 Rotunda
rio Mondego
McDonalds
A-31
(Pop. 160.000)
COIMBRA
Santa Clara
0.0 Largo da Portagem
CAMINO GUIDES.COM

# 10 MEALHADA – ÁGUEDA

| | | |
|---|---|---|
| | 3.1 | 12% |
| | 20.9 | 82% |
| | 1.4 | 6% |
| **Stage Total** | **25.4** km | *(15.8 ml)* |

Total ascent **160**m ±¼ *hr*

▲ Alto *m* Anadia 85m *(279 ft)*

<A H> ➲Sernadelo **1.5** km. ➲Anadia 7.7
➲*Famalicão **9.1** km + **1.1***

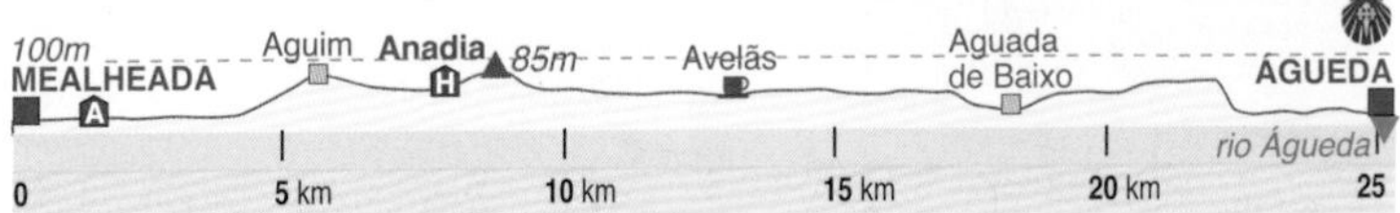


**▌Anadia:** •*H**** **Cabecinho** *x52* €50 ✆ 231 510 940 *www.hotel-cabecinho.com* *[**Famalicão** ●**1.1** km to ●Alb. **Colegio N.S. da Assunção de Cluny** Conv. [**50**÷2] suelo €-donativo ✆ 231 504 167].*

**▌Águeda**: ❶***Turismo*** ✆ 234 601 412. **Lower Town *Baja:*** ❶ *P.* **XPT** *x9* €35-44 ✆ 969 523 545 *www.xpt.pt* r/Vasco da Gama, 37 &@ N°88. 🍴/❷ *P.* **O Ribeirinho** *x7* €35 ✆ 234 623 825. ❸★*P.* **Friends** *Priv.[12÷2]* €18 incl. *x5* €40+ ✆ 234 136 620 r/José Maria Veloso, 8. Praça Conde de Águeda ❹ *H**** **Conde** *x30* €60-90 ✆ 236 610 390 *www.hotelcondedagueda.com* +900m r/Manuel de Sousa Carneiro ❺*H**** **In Gold** *x60* €75+✆ 234 690 170 *www.ingoldhotel.pt* ***Bombeiros Voluntários*** de Águeda Av. 25 de Abril ✆ 234 610 100. **Upper Town *Alta + 1.0 km*** **Lidl** ❻ *P.* **Celeste** *x12* €40+ ✆ 234 602 871 Rua da Misericórdia, 713 (N-1) adj. ★❼ *Alb.***Sto. António** *Priv.[19÷4]* €12 (€17 incl.)

Alb. S.António
Águeda

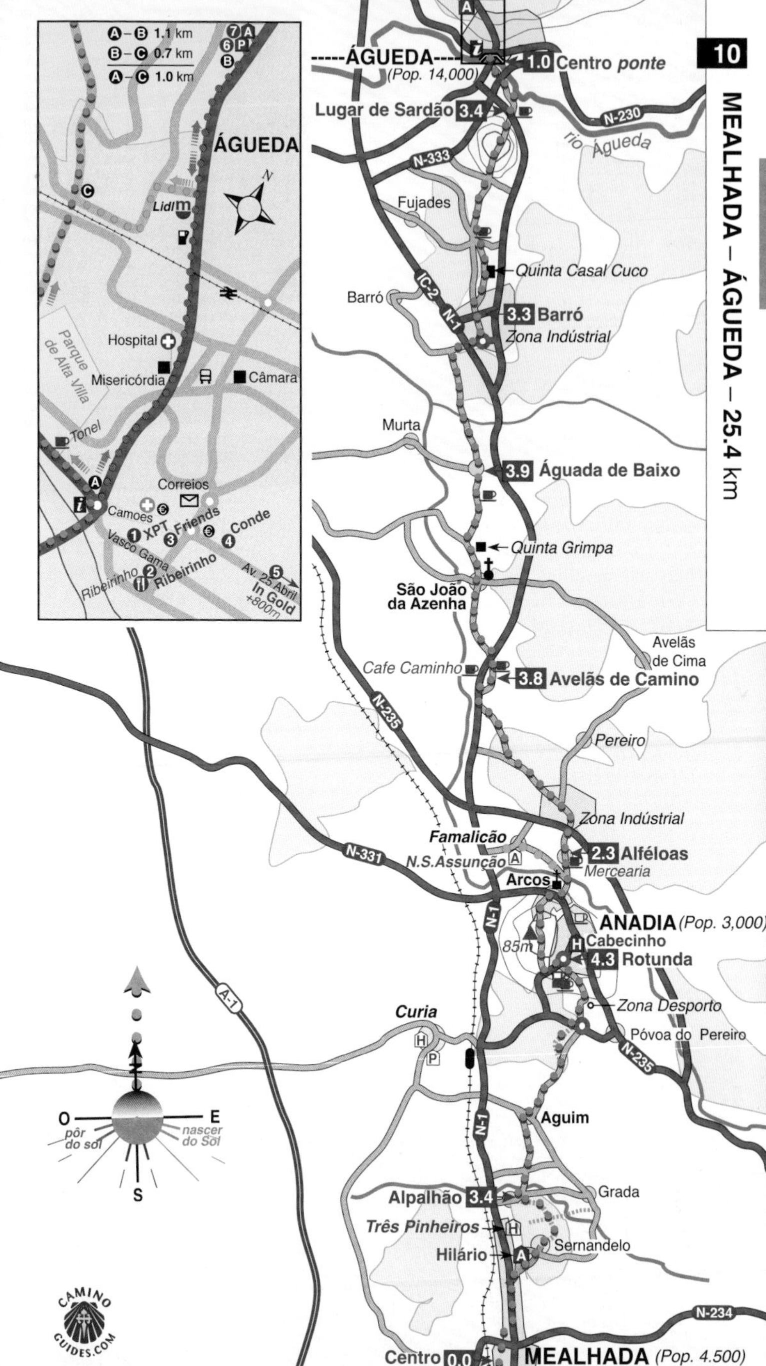

10
MEALHADA – ÁGUEDA – 25.4 km
A – B 1.1 km
B – C 0.7 km
A – C 1.0 km
ÁGUEDA
Lidl
Hospital
Parque de Alta Villa
Misericórdia
Câmara
Tonel
Correios
Camoes
1 XPT
3 Friends
4 Conde
Vasco Gama
2 Ribeirinho
Ribeirinho
Av. 25 Abril
5 In Gold
+800m
ÁGUEDA
(Pop. 14,000)
1.0 Centro ponte
Lugar de Sardão 3.4
N-230
rio Águeda
N-333
Fujades
Quinta Casal Cuco
Barró
IC-2
N-1
3.3 Barró
Zona Indústrial
Murta
3.9 Águada de Baixo
Quinta Grimpa
São João da Azenha
Avelãs de Cima
Cafe Caminho
3.8 Avelãs de Camino
N-235
Pereiro
Zona Indústrial
Famalicão
2.3 Alféloas
N-331
N.S.Assunção
Mercearia
Arcos
ANADIA (Pop. 3,000)
Cabecinho
85m
4.3 Rotunda
Zona Desporto
Curia
Póvoa do Pereiro
N-235
A-1
N-1
O
E
pôr do sol
nascer do Sol
S
Aguim
Alpalhão 3.4
Grada
Três Pinheiros
Sernandelo
Hilário
CAMINO GUIDES.COM
N-234
Centro 0.0
MEALHADA (Pop. 4.500)

## 11 ÁGUEDA – ALBERGARIA *A-VELHA*

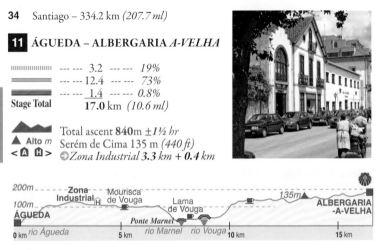

| | | |
|---|---|---|
| | 3.2 | *19%* |
| | 12.4 | *73%* |
| | 1.4 | *0.8%* |
| **Stage Total** | **17.0** km *(10.6 ml)* | |

Total ascent **840**m ±*1½ hr*

▲ Alto *m* Serém de Cima 135 m *(440 ft)*

<A H> *Zona Industrial* ***3.3 km*** + ***0.4 km***

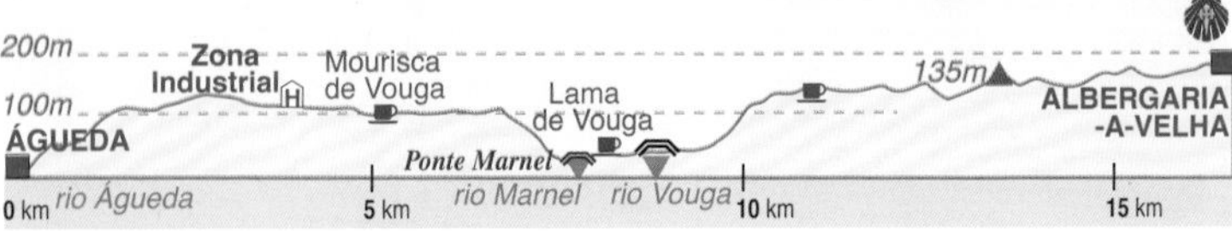


■ **Águeda:** *[zona industrial* ***+0.4*** *km adj. McDonalds. •P.* ***O Trindade*** *x16 €25-40 © 234 645 830 adj. •CR.* ***Castro*** *x22 €20-30* © 234 644 356*]*.

■ **Albergaria-a-velha:** ❶*Alb.* **Rainha D. Teresa** *Asoc.[21÷3]* €8 © 234 529 754 (Via Lusitana) Bernardino Máximo de Albuquerque 14.❷*Estalagem* **dos Padres** €45-€55 incl. Marta Duarte © 930 610 380 www.estalagemdospadres.pt r/ Santo António, 34. ❸*P.* **Parente** €15 © 234 521 271 r/Doutor Brito Guimarães, 11.■ **Outskirts** ***Afueras*****:** ***+0.5*** km ❹*H* **Ribeirotel** *x30* €30+ © 234 524 246 www.ribeirotel.com Areiros, Zona industrial. ***+1.9*** km ●*Motel* **Alameda** *x20* €25-35 © 234 523 402 www.alameda-hotel.com N-1 adj. *gasolinera* Total. 🍴 *Casa Turco* tapas bar (*menú peregrino*) rua 1° Dezembro.

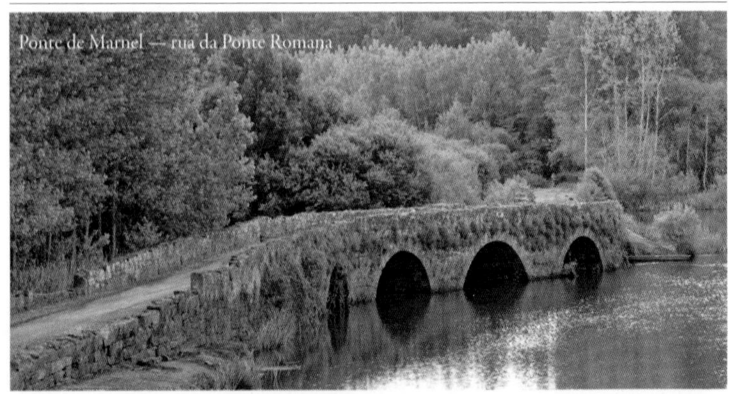

Ponte de Marnel — rua da Ponte Romana

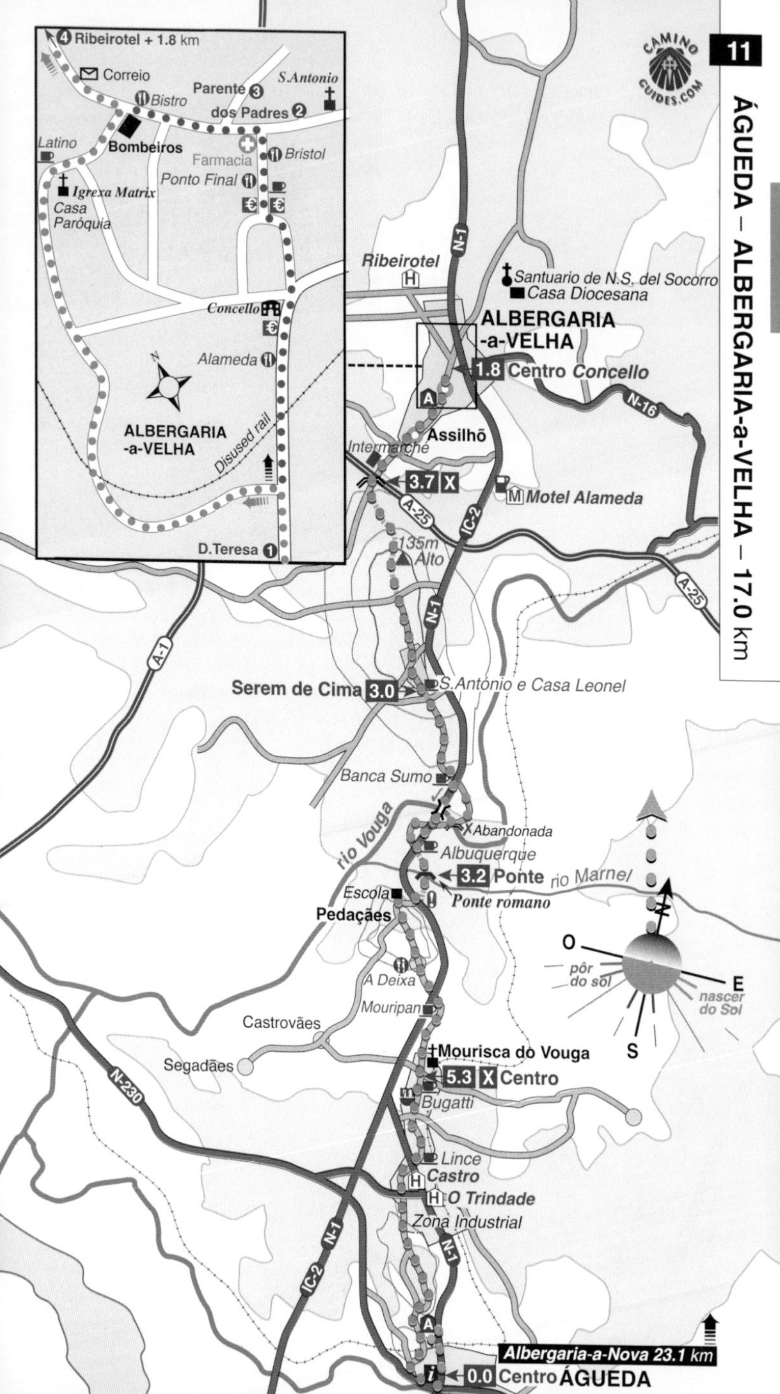
4 Ribeirotel + 1.8 km
Correio
Parente 3
S.Antonio
Bistro
dos Padres 2
Latino
Bombeiros
Farmacia
Bristol
Igrexa Matrix
Ponto Final
Casa Paróquia
Concello
Alameda
ALBERGARIA -a-VELHA
Disused rail
D.Teresa 1
Ribeirotel
Santuario de N.S. del Socorro
Casa Diocesana
ALBERGARIA -a-VELHA
1.8 Centro Concello
N-16
N-1
Assilhõ
Intermarché
3.7 X
Motel Alameda
A-25
IC-2
135m Alto
A-1
Serem de Cima 3.0
S.António e Casa Leonel
Banca Sumo
rio Vouga
Abandonada
Albuquerque
3.2 Ponte
rio Marnel
Ponte romano
Escola
Pedaçães
A Deixa
Mouripan
Castrovães
Segadães
O
pôr do sol
E
nascer do Sol
S
Mourisca do Vouga
5.3 X Centro
Bugatti
N-230
Lince
Castro
O Trindade
Zona Industrial
Albergaria-a-Nova 23.1 km
0.0 Centro ÁGUEDA

## 12 ALBERGARIA-*A-VELHA* – SÃO JOÃO *DE MADEIRA*

Oliveira de Azeméis Câmara

| | | | | |
|---|---|---|---|---|
| | --- --- | 5.7 | --- --- | *19%* |
| | --- --- | 20.9 | --- --- | *69%* |
| | --- --- | 3.6 | --- --- | *12%* |
| **Stage Total** | | **30.2** km | | *(18.7 ml)* |

Total ascent **460**m ±¾ *hr*
▲ Alto *m* São João da Madeira 240m
< A H > ➲Albergaria-a-Nova **6.1** km ➲Outeirinho **9.4** km ➲Bemposta **12.6** ➲Oliveira de Azeméis **20.2** km.

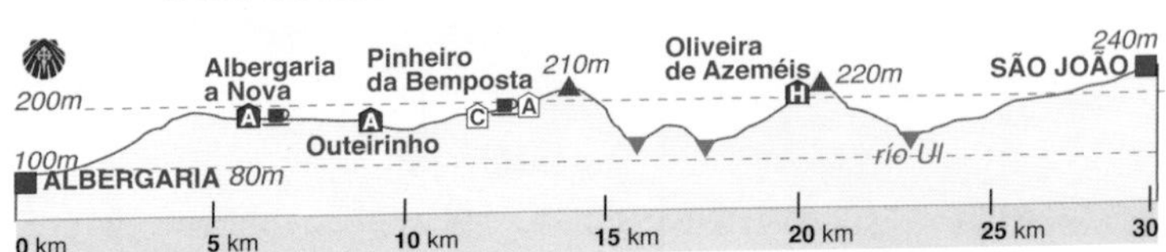


**▌Albergaria-a-Nova:** ●*Alb.* **Albergaria** *Priv.[12÷2]* €10 *+6* €30 ✆ 234 547 068 [m] 919 006 001 *www.albergaria.eu* *Isabel Valente (Belinha)* N-1. **▌Outeirinho** ●*Alb.***Casa Católica** *Priv.[18÷4]* €-donativo ✆ 916 571 106 (Paulo) r/ Silveiras. **▌Pinheiro da Bemposta:** ***+0.3** km* •***Centro Social Paroquial*** Floor *Suelo.* ***+1.6** km* •***Moinho Garcia*** *Priv.[10÷2]* €15 *+5* €25-35 ✆ *935 500 595* *es.alberguemoinhogarcia.com r/Garcia 322.* **■ Oliveira de Azeméis:** ***Turismo*** ✆ 256 674 463 Praca José da Costa. •*H**** **Dighton** *x90* €55-65 ✆ 256 682 191 r/Dr. Albino dos Reis (opp. *Câmara*). •*P* **Anacleto** ±30 ✆ 256 682 541 Av. D. António José de Almeida, 310 (adj. taxis). •**Bombeiros Voluntários** ✆ 256 682 122 *r/dos Bombeiros Voluntários /Av. Dona Maria I (**+1.3** km).* **■ São João da Madeira:** ***Turismo*** ✆ 256 200 285 ***Praça Luís Ribeiro*** **@Nº165** •*P* **Solar São João** *x8* €25-30 ✆ 256 202 540 *www.solarsaojoao.pai.pt* **& @Nº7** •*H*** **A.S. São João** *x36* €35+ ✆ 256 836 100. •*S* **Central Suites 1** €35+ ✆ 936 206 777 *www.centralsuites.pt* r/ António José de Oliveira Júnior 54 +**Suites 2** r/5 de Outubro, 394 +**Suites 3** Av. Dr. Renato Araújo, 105. ●**Santa Casa da Misericórdia** *Priv.[12÷1] suelo* €-Donativo ✆ 256 837 240 r/Manuel Luis Leite Júnior 777. •*H***** **Golden Tulip** *x120* €60-64 ✆ 256 106 700 Av. Adelino Amaro da Costa 573. *[*•**Bombeiros Voluntários** ✆ 256 837 120 r/ Oliveira Figueiredo, Z. Ind. **+2.2** km*]*.

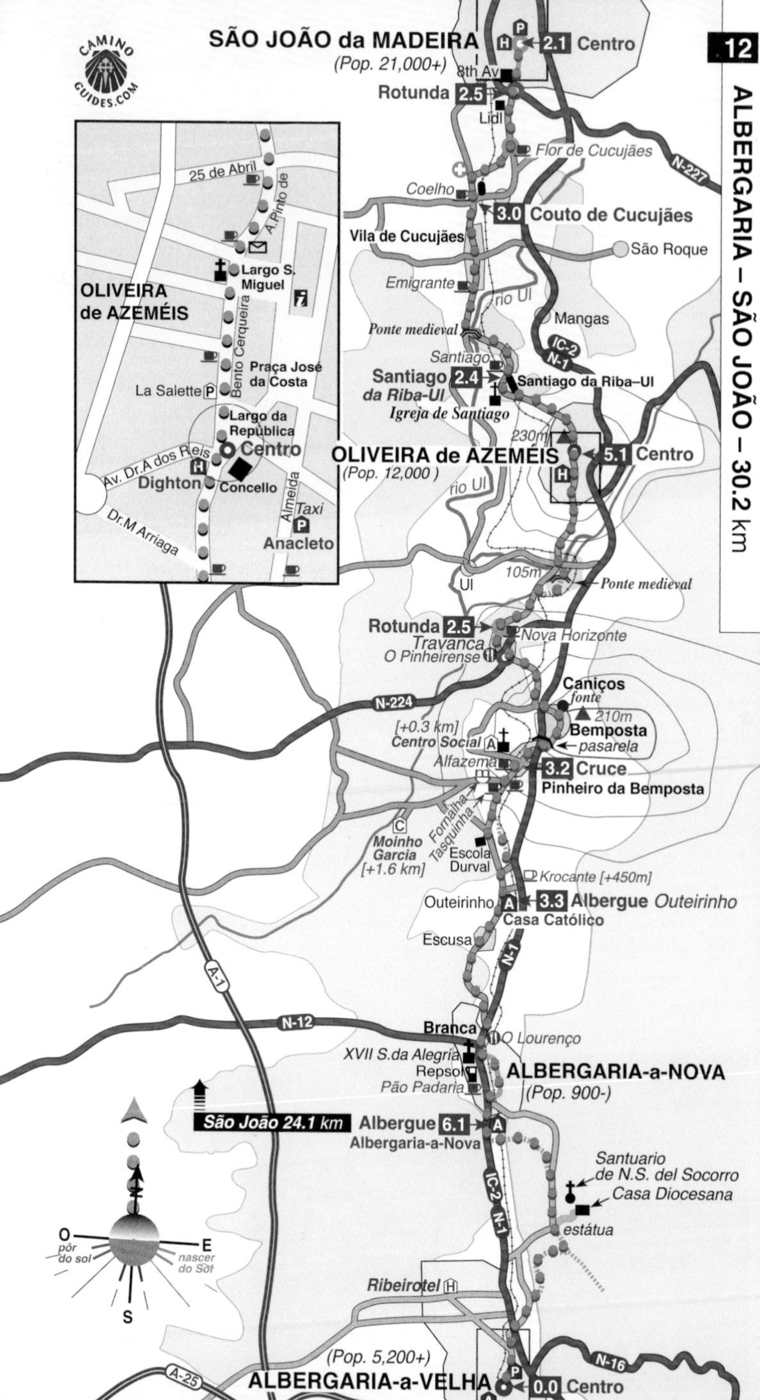
CAMINO GUIDES.COM
SÃO JOÃO da MADEIRA
(Pop. 21,000+)
2.1 Centro
8th Av
Rotunda 2.5
Lidl
Flor de Cucujães
N-227
Coelho
3.0 Couto de Cucujães
Vila de Cucujães
São Roque
Emigrante
rio Ul
Mangas
Ponte medieval
IC-2
N-1
Santiago
Santiago 2.4
da Riba-Ul
Santiago da Riba–Ul
Igreja de Santiago
230m
OLIVEIRA de AZEMÉIS
(Pop. 12,000 )
5.1 Centro
rio Ul
105m
Ul
Ponte medieval
Rotunda 2.5
Travanca
Nova Horizonte
O Pinheirense
Caniços
fonte
210m
Bemposta
pasarela
N-224
[+0.3 km]
Centro Social
Alfazema
3.2 Cruce
Pinheiro da Bemposta
Fornalha
Tasquinha
Moinho
Garcia
[+1.6 km]
Escola
Durval
Krocante [+450m]
Outeirinho
3.3 Albergue Outeirinho
Casa Católico
Escusa
A-1
N-12
Branca
O Lourenço
XVII S.da Alegría
Repsol
Pão Padaria
ALBERGARIA-a-NOVA
(Pop. 900-)
São João 24.1 km
Albergue 6.1
Albergaria-a-Nova
Santuario
de N.S. del Socorro
Casa Diocesana
estátua
O
pôr
do sol
E
nascer
do Sol
N
S
Ribeirotel
(Pop. 5,200+)
A-25
N-16
ALBERGARIA-a-VELHA
0.0 Centro
25 de Abril
A.Pinto de
Largo S.
Miguel
OLIVEIRA
de AZEMÉIS
Bento Cerqueira
Praça José
da Costa
La Salette
Largo da
República
Centro
Av. Dr.A dos Reis
Dighton
Concello
Almeida
Taxi
Anacleto
Dr.M Arriaga

## 13 SÃO JOÃO da MADEIRA – PORTO

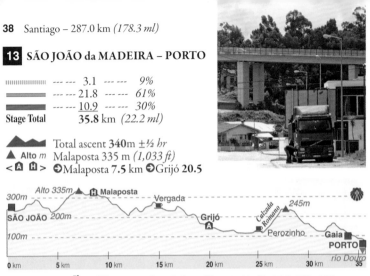

| | | |
|---|---|---|
| | 3.1 | *9%* |
| | 21.8 | *61%* |
| | 10.9 | *30%* |
| **Stage Total** | **35.8** km | *(22.2 ml)* |

Total ascent **340**m ±½ *hr*
Alto *m* Malaposta 335 m *(1,033 ft)*
<A H> Malaposta **7.5** km Grijó **20.5**

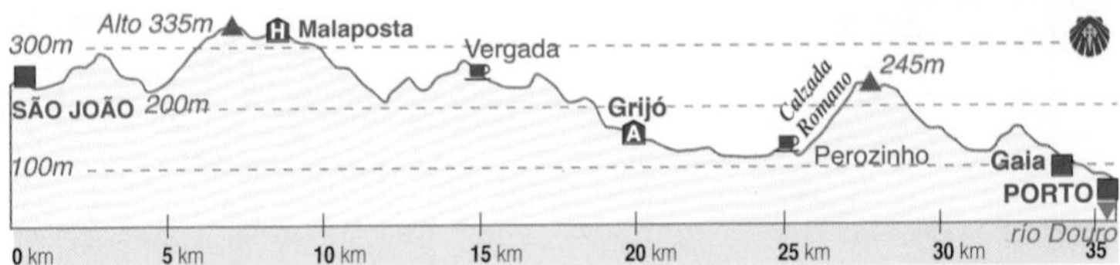


**▌Malaposta:** •*H**** **Feira Pedra Bela** *x60* €35-50 ✆ 256 910 350 www.hotelpedrabela.com r/Malaposta N-1. *[**Detour São Jorge + 2.2 km N-223** hoteles* €20 -50 incl. •*P* ***São Jorge*** *x12 €28-33 ✆ 256 911 303].* **▌Lourosa:** •**B.V.** ✆ 227 443 189 Av. Principal 4030. **▌Grijó:** ●*Alb.* **S. Salvador** *Par.[14÷2]* €7 António Pires ✆ 968 702 769 rua Cardoso Pinto, 274 (adj. Mosteiro). *[+**1.6** km •P **Sobreiro Grosso** ✆ 227 472 130 rua Américo de Oliveira, 807. +**2.1** km •P **Residencial Catavento** ✆ 227 457 583 Largo das Vendas, 88 / N-1].* **▌Vila Nova de Gaia:** •*H*** **Clip** *x89* €49 ✆ 223 745 910 www.cliphotel.pt Av. República, 1559 (opp bp). •*Hs* **Cruz Vermelha** *x9* €20-25 ✆ 913 800 888 r/General Torres, 572 +300m. •*Hs* **Gaia** *x14* €18pp r/Cândido dos Reis, 374 +400m. •*H**** **Sandeman** *Priv.[14÷1]*+ €24 +€120 ✆ 213 461 381 thehouseofsandeman.pt Largo Miguel Bombarda, 3

Serra de Negrelos *calzada romana*

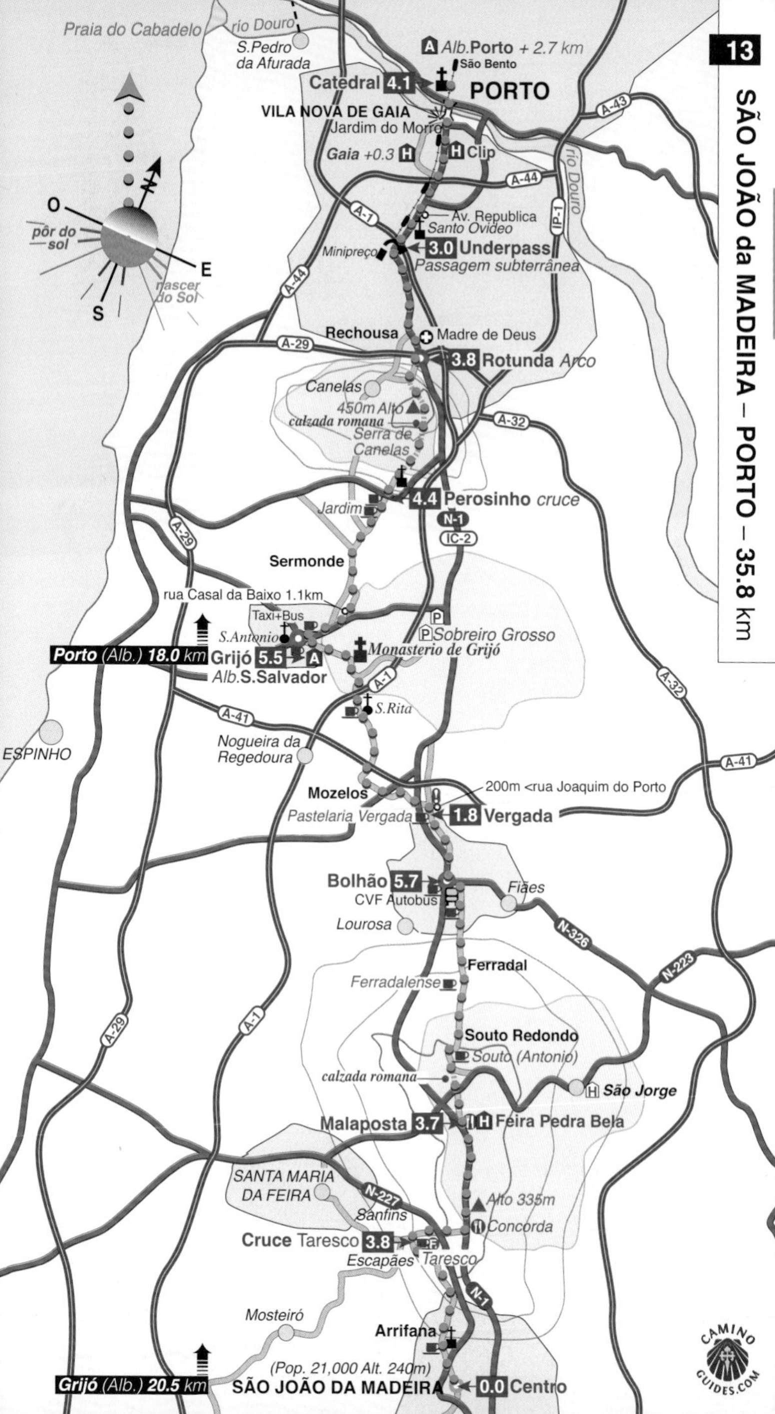

13
SÃO JOÃO da MADEIRA – PORTO – 35.8 km
Praia do Cabadelo
río Douro
S.Pedro da Afurada
Alb.Porto + 2.7 km
São Bento
Catedral 4.1
PORTO
VILA NOVA DE GAIA
Jardim do Morro
Gaia +0.3
Clip
A-43
A-44
río Douro
IP-1
A-1
Av. Republica
Santo Ovideo
Minipreço
3.0 Underpass
Passagem subterrânea
O
pôr do sol
E
nascer do Sol
S
A-44
Rechousa
Madre de Deus
A-29
3.8 Rotunda Arco
Canelas
450m Alto
calzada romana
Serra de Canelas
A-32
Jardim
4.4 Perosinho cruce
N-1
IC-2
A-29
Sermonde
rua Casal da Baixo 1.1km
Taxi+Bus
S.Antonio
Sobreiro Grosso
Monasterio de Grijó
Porto (Alb.) 18.0 km
Grijó 5.5
Alb.S.Salvador
A-1
S.Rita
A-32
A-41
ESPINHO
Nogueira da Regedoura
A-41
200m <rua Joaquim do Porto
Mozelos
Pastelaria Vergada
1.8 Vergada
Bolhão 5.7
CVF Autobus
Fiães
Lourosa
N-326
N-223
Ferradal
Ferradalense
A-1
A-29
Souto Redondo
Souto (Antonio)
calzada romana
São Jorge
Malaposta 3.7
Feira Pedra Bela
SANTA MARIA DA FEIRA
N-227
Sanfins
Alto 335m
Concorda
Cruce Taresco 3.8
Escapães
Taresco
N-1
Mosteiró
Arrifana
(Pop. 21,000 Alt. 240m)
Grijó (Alb.) 20.5 km
SÃO JOÃO DA MADEIRA
0.0 Centro
CAMINO GUIDES.COM

PORTO
Hostels €12+ 1 – 10
A Porto [+500m / 2.6 km from Cathedral]
Vilarinho
Vila do Conde
Igreja Romanica Cedofeita
Boavista
Braga
Rex
Praça República
Rua de Álvares Cabra
N
Largo da Maternidade Julio Dinis
Santiago
rua do Breiner
Rua de Cedofeita
Estoril
Casa Carolina
Gallery 9
Rua Miguel Bombarda
A [+ 1.1 km] Casa Diocesana
Inca
Portuguesa
Malaposta
10 Invictus
S.Marino
Lounge
Praça Carlos Alberto
Trinadade
Ginjal
Lameiras
Bonjardim
Turismo
Paços do Concelho
Praça General Humberto Delgado
Rua do Alamada
Av. Dos Aliados
Rua de Sá da Bandeira
Bolhão
CATARINA
B.V. (Bombeiros)
Campanhã
S.Catarina
Aeroporto
Sagres
Aliados
Paulista
Duas Nações
Downtown 8
rua do Fábrica
Guarany
Intl.
Praça João I
Grande
Carmo
França
Nasoni
Cristal
Paris
Universal
Passos Manuel
Majestic
Brasileira
Praça Liberdade
7 Livraria Lello & Irmão
Douro
Wine 7
Chic Dream
Praça Lisboa
Linha Aeroporto
Linha 500
S.Ildefonso
rua 31 de Janeiro
Caminho por Braga
Jardim Cordoaria
CORDOARIA
6 Torre dos Clérigos
5 Yes
Bragança
8 Estação São Bento
Academia Fotografia
dos Caldeireiros
Poets Inn 6
Triunfo
Rua das Taipas
Best G
4
Caminho por Braga
Rua Chã
Tattva Design
Misericórdia Museu 5
rua das Flores
rua Mouzinho da Silveira
Caminho da Costa
Virtudes
S. Miguel
VITORIA
Oriente
Taipas
Ig.Vitoria
As 7 Maravilhas
r/Belmonte
Caminho Central
WC
Bathala
1 Catedral Sé
Being Porto 3
Bolsa
S.Lourenço
Museu Guerra Junqueiro
< Matasinhos
Comercio
r/Bolsa
Paço Episcopal
Av. V. Peres
rua Nova da Alfândega
Bolsa 4
rua Infante D. Henriques
2 Bluesock
Túnel
Pousada Juventude
A [+ 4.4 km
Francisco 3
2 Casa do Infante
S.Nicolau
Senda Litoral
Funicular
Praça Ribeira
Ribeira
Bebobos
Bars / Cafés
Pestana
Cais de Ribeira
Barca
RIBEIRA
Rio Douro
House of Sandeman 1
Jardim do Morro
Mosteiro da Serra do Pilar
Caves do Vinho do Porto
VILA NOVA DE GAIA

**Portugal**: ✆ **+351**. ❶ ***Turismo Central***: *(09:00–18:00)* Av. dos Aliados *rua Clube dos Fenianos 25* (adj. *câmara)*. ✆ 223 393 472. *www.visitporto.travel* ▮ ***Ribeira***: 63 r/Infante D. Henrique ✆ 222 060 412. ▮ ***Cathedral*** Terreiro da Se ✆ 223 325174 (10:00 – 18:00). ❶ Turismo Portugal: ✆ 927 411 817 Praca D. João I, 43.

**PORTO:** ■ ***Albergues:*** ●★*Alb.* **Peregrinos do Porto** *Priv.[26÷4]* €12+*4* €22-44 ✆ 912 591 321 [m] Óscar Miguel 220 140 515 *www.albergueperegrinosporto.pt* r/Barão de Forester, 954 [+**2.6** km]. ●**N.S. do Rosário de Vilar** *Asoc.[12÷2] €7 +8* €22-38 ✆ 226 056 000 Casa Diocesana, r/Arcediago Vanzeller, 50 [+**2.0** km]. ●**ViaPortuscale** *Asoc.[20÷2]* ✆ 960 227 134 r/Vasco Santana, 264, Senhora da Hora [+**6.9** km]. ●**Pousada de Juventude** *[124÷4]* €13-15 ✆ 226 177 257 r/ Paulo da Gama, 551 [+**4.7** km]. **Bombeiros** *BV. [2÷1]* ✆ 222 055 845 r/Rodrigues Sampaio, 145 [+**0.9** km].

■ ***Hostales Centro:*** *www.hostelworld.com / www.booking.com (€12-20 + privado).* ❶ **House of Sandeman** (V.N. Gaia p.38). ❷ **Bluesock** *[80÷7]* €20 +*8* €60+ ✆ ✆ 227 664 171 *www.bluesockhostels.com/hostel-porto* r/S. João 40 (Ribeira). ❸ **Being Porto** *[12÷1]* €15 +*30* €50-60 ✆ 222 011 977 r/Belomonte, 13. ❹ **Best Guest** *[16÷3]* €18 +*8* €46 ✆ 967 116 157 r/Mouzinho da Silveira, 257. ❺ **Yes Porto!** ✆ 222 082 391 *www.yeshostels.com* r/Arquitecto Nicolau Nazoni 31. ❻ **Poets Inn** €20 +*12* €50 ✆ 223 324 209 r/Caldeireiros, 261. ❼ **Porto Wine** *[40÷7]* €17 +*10* €60+ ✆ 222 013 167 *www.winehostel.pt* Campo dos Martires da Patria 52 (popular). ❽ **Downtown** *[28÷4]* €12 ✆ 223 234 729 Praça Guilherme Gomes Fernandes 66. ❾ **Gallery** *[24÷5]* €27 +*2* €120 ✆ 224 964 313 r/Miguel Bombarda 222. ❿ **Invictus** *[20÷3]* €12 +€44 ✆ 222 024 371 r/Oliveiras 73.

■ ***Hoteles Centro: (€35-55)*** •**Flor Bragança** ✆ 222 082 974 r/Arquitecto Nicolau Nazoni 12. •**Oporto Poets** ✆ 222 026 089 Trv.Ferraz 13.•**França** Praça de Gomes Teixeira,7 ✆ 222 002 791. ***Rua Galeria*** *(adj. Lello books)* ***@Nº82*** •**Nasoni** ✆ 222 083 807 & ***@Nº48*** •**Cristal** ✆ 222 002 100. ***Rua Cedofeita*** (camino) ***@Nº159*** •**Casa Carolina** *€85+!* ✆ 912 088 249. ***@Nº193*** •**Estoril** ✆ 222 002 751.

■ ***Hoteles Central: (€55-95)*** •**Internacional** ✆ 222 005 032 *www.hi-porto.com* r/ Almada 131. •**Grande Hotel Paris** ✆ 222 073 140 r/Fábrica 27 *www.stayhotels.pt/grandehotelparis* •**Paulista** ✆ 222 054 692 Av. dos Aliados 214. •**Aliados** ✆ 222 004 853 r/Elísio de Melo 27 *(adj. Cafe Guranay)*. •*H**** **Grande Hotel do Porto** ✆ 222 076 690 *www.grandehotelporto.com* r/Santa Catarina 197 (adj. café Majestic). Ribera 'downtown' •*H**** **da Bolsa** ✆ 222 026 768 r/Ferreira Borges •*H***** **Carrís** ✆ 20 965 786 r/Infante D. Henrique 1. •*H**** **Riberia do Porto** ✆ 222 032 097 *www.ribeiradoportohotel.com/en* Praça da Ribeira Nº5 or €100+. •*H***** **Pestana** @ Nº1 ✆ 223 402 300.

○ **Monumentos históricos:** ❶ **Cathedral** ***Sé*** + claustro *XII* Terreiro da Sé. ❷ **Casa do Infante** + museo, rua Infante Dom Henrique. ❸ **Igreja de São Francisco** *XIII* + museo €2, Largo de São Francisco. ❹ **Palácio da Bolsa** *XIX* + Claustro €7, Rua de Ferreira Borges. ❺ **Igreja da Misericórdia** *XVIII* + museo. ❻ **Igreja e Torre dos Clérigos** *XVIII,* Torre 75m €2, Rua dos Clérigos. ❼ **Lello & Irmão** *livraria* Rua das Carmelitas, 144. ❽ **Estação de São Bento** *azulejos.*

**The route from Porto to Santiago offers 3 main options.**

❶ **Caminho Central:** ● ● ● 251.2 km and the route chosen by around 60% of all pilgrims. Well waymarked and served with excellent pilgrim hostels and facilities. However, the first stage through Porto is mostly on city pavements and busy roads. The route has been improved by eliminating hazardous areas and waymarking via the Monastery in Vairão which has been beautifully restored as a pilgrim hostel (and museum) and makes a welcome first stage stop-over. From Vairão / Vilarinho onwards the route is a delightful mix of quiet country lanes, agricultural tracks and forest paths that undulate over gentle hills separated by wide river valleys and coastal inlets *rias*.

❷ **Caminho da Costa:** ● ● ● 273.2 km and growing in popularity it now accounts for around 30% of pilgrims. The first stage out of Porto is likewise along busy roads that skirt the airport and waymarks are not consistent. *Note* this refers *only* to the first stage out of Porto; the rest of the Coastal way is a delightful mix of small country lanes and forest paths in the hills above the coast dropping down to stretches of sandy paths and boardwalks by the sea. It crosses over the Minho river estuary into Spain and reconnects with the Camino Central in Redondela.

❸ **Senda Litoral (from Porto):** ● ● ● This makes a good alternative for the first stage out of Porto (33.9 km) excepting in high winds which makes walking difficult (windblown sand). A tourist vibe replaces the camaraderie of the main route but the majority is on boardwalks *paseos de madera* which makes for pleasant walking alongside the sandy coves and beaches. New hostels and several campsites offer pilgrim lodging and the historic town of Vila do Conde makes a good stop-over for this stage from where it is possible to reconnect with the Camino Central via Arcos.

❹ **Senda Litoral (from Vila do Conde):** ● ● ● basically follows the shoreline. It has more of a tourist vibe and wind-blown sand can obliterate paths and makes it difficult to walk in high winds. A new bridge at Foz de Neiva and other improvements to the *Ecovia Litoral Norte* has greatly improved this route. Where the *senda litoral* connects easily with the main *Caminho da Costa* a tick ✓ suggests a reasonable optional alternative for adventurous pilgrims who have a good sense of orientation; otherwise it makes sense to stick with the main waymarked route.

**COSTA:** ● ● ● ▌**Aeroporto** ***(Turismo):*** ●*Hs* AirPorto *[20÷2]* €13-17 ✆ 229 427 397 r/Estrada 244. N-107 Rotonda **Airport** •*H*** **Aeroporto** €46+ ✆ 229 429 334 w*ww.hotelaeroporto.com.pt* r/Pedras Rubras

**LITORAL:** ● ● ● ▌**Foz** •*H*** **Boa Vista** *x70* €78-88 ✆ 225 320 020 *www.hotelboavista.com* Esplanada do Castelo. ▌**Matasinhos:** •*P.* **Leão de Ouro** *x15* €35-45 ✆ 229 380 673 r/ Conde São Salvador, 162 [+150m]. •*Hs* **Fishtail** *x24* €20pp-40 ✆ 229 380 345 *www.fishtail-seahouse.pt* r/Godinho, 224 [+250m]. **Rua Brito Capelo Nº169** [+200m] •*H*** **Porto-Mar** *x33* €56-70 ✆ 229 382 104. **@Nº843** •*Hsr* **D'el Rei** *x20* €30-40 ✆ 229 372 914. **@Nº599** •*P.*Central *x24* €35+ ✆ 229 380 664 *www.pensaocentral.net* ▌**Cabo do Mundo** •**Casa Velha** *x5* €35+ ✆ 965 072 203 r/de Almeiriga Norte 2510. ▌**Lavra** *[+½ km* ▲*Alb.Camping* **Angeiras** ***Orbitur*** *✆ 229 270 571 r/Angeiras.* €8-20 pp*].* ▌**Labruge:** *[+½ km* •*CR* **Smiling Faces** €10-69 ✆ 910 858 047. •*CR* **Praia** *x7* €38-45 ✆ 910 894 591 @Nº439. *+0.5 km* ●*Alb.* **São Tiago** *Mun.[18÷2] €-donativo* ✆ 229 284 686*].* ▌**Vila Chã:** •*P* **Sandra** *x6* €30+ ✆ 919 254 629 adj. ☕*'Tony'. [+¼ km* ●*Alb.Mun.[20÷2]* **São Mamede** €-Donativo ✆ 934 379 460 Trv. do Sol, 40*].* & ▲*Parque* **Campismo Sol** €7+ ✆ 229 283 163 *www.campingvilacha.com* r/do Sol.

🛈**Vila do Conde:** ***Turismo*** ✆ 252 248 473 r/25 April centro + taxi ✆ 252 631 933. ***Centro*:** ●*Alb.* **Santa Clara** *Mun.[25÷3]* €7 ✆ 252 104 717 plaza Mercado. •*Hs* **Bellamar** *[10÷2]* €12 *+9* €38 ✆ 252 631 748 Praça da República No 84 @ No 1 A **Rendilheira** *x10* €65 ✆ 252 615 113. ▌***Ribeira:*** Cais das Lavandeiras*:* •*P* **Patarata** *x10* €40+ ✆ 252 631 894 + adj. •*Hs* **Naval** *Erva Doce x8* €75 ✆ 925 693 470 *navalviladoconde.com*. •*H*** **Brazão** *x36* €39-56 ✆ 252 642 016 *www.hotelbrazao.pt* Av. Dr. João Canavarro (popular with pilgrims). Adj. •*Hs* **Autor** *x6* €70 ✆ 913 361 588 *autorguesthouse.com* ●*Pousada* **HI Vila do Conde** *[56÷5]* €13 *+10* €40+ ✆ 926 739 229 *Pousada* Av. Bento de Freitas, 460. •*CR* **Princesa Do Ave** €30-40 ✆ 252 642 065 Rua Dr António José Sousa Pereira 261. •*Hs* **Venceslau** *x15* €20-50 ✆ 252 646 362 r/Mós 13 (+500m). ▌**Azurara:** •*H**** **Spa Santana** *x75* €64+ ✆ 252 640 460 *www.santanahotel.pt* r/Santana. •*H**** **Villa C Spa** *x43* €85+ ✆ 252 240 420 N-13.

# 14 PORTO – VILARINHO *VILA DO CONDE*

Alb. Mosteiro de Vairão

| | | |
|---|---|---|
| (dotted) | 0.5 | *2%* |
| (light) | 16.8 | *61%* |
| (dark) | 10.3 | *37%* |
| **Stage Total** | **27.6** km (17.2 ml) | |

Total ascent **220**m ±½ *hr*

▲ Alto *m* Igreja Maia 125m *(410 ft)*

< A H > ➲Moreira da Maia **14.9** km. ➲Vairão **24.4** km.

100m PORTO · Araújo · 125m · río Leça · Maia · Moreira · Mosteiró · Gião · VILARINHO · Vairão

0 km · 5 km · 10 km · 15 km · 20 km · 25

**Central:** ● ● ● ▌**Moreira-Maia/N-13:** *[+0.2 km]* •*H*** **Puma** *x36* €40 ✆ 229 482 128 r/Cruz das Guardeiras 776. ▌**Gião** N-306 •*CR* **Casa Mindela** *x6* €49-60 ✆ 914 118 018 (Helena Duarte) *www.casamindela.pt* r/da Joudina 427. ▌**Vairão:** ●★*Alb.* **Mosteiro de Vairão** *Asoc.[72÷12]*+ €-donativo ✆ Eduardo 915 240 661. *Reiki Carla* ✆ 966 431 916. *www.mosteirodevairao.blogspot.com* 🛒*mini-mercado Teixeira 300m.* ❶ **Casa Família Vidal** *Priv.[9÷3]* €12 ✆ 252 661 503 m: 966 766 092 r/Salterio 87. ❷ **Casa da Laura** *Priv.[8÷1]*+ €12 ✆ 917 767 307 r/Estreita 112 adj. ☕ *CJ's* menú. *[+½ km* ❸ **Escuela** ***Polidesportivo*** *Mun. [4÷1]* ✆ 252 661 610 r/D. Ildefonso*]*.

**Senda Litoral:** ● ● ● ▌**Matosinhos:** •*P.* **Leão de Ouro** *x15* €35-45 ✆ 229 380 673 r/ Conde São Salvador, 162 [+150m]. •*Hs* **Fishtail** *x24* €20pp-40 ✆ 229 380 345 *www.fishtail-seahouse.pt* r/Godinho, 224 [+250m]. **Rua Brito Capelo Nº169** [+200m] •*H*** **Porto-Mar** *x33* €56-70 ✆ 229 382 104. **@Nº843** •*Hsr* **D'el Rei** *x20* €30-40 ✆ 229 372 914. **@Nº599** •*P.* **Central** *x24* €35+ ✆ 229 380 664 *www.pensaocentral.net* ▌**Labruge:** [+400m]*Av. Liberdade* •*CR* **Praia** *x7* €38-45 ✆ 910 894 591 @Nº439. •*CR* **Smiling Faces** €10-69 ✆ 910 858 047. *+0.5 km* ●*Alb.* **São Tiago** *Mun.[52÷4] €-donativo* ✆ 229 284 686. ▌**Lavra *Angeiras*** *[+ ½ km Alb.* ▲ **Angeiras *Orbitur*** ✆ *229 270 571 r/Angeiras.* ▌**Vila Chã** *Largo dos Pescadores* W.C. •*P* **Sandra** *x6* €30+ ✆ 919 254 629 adj. ☕ *Tony'.* ●*Alb.Mun.[20÷2]* **São Mamede** €10 ✆ 934 379 460 Trv. do Sol, 40 [+250m]. ▲*Parque* **Campismo Sol** €7+ ✆ 229 283 163 *www.campingvilacha.com* r/do Sol [+200m].

Mosteiro de Santa Maria de Leça
*Detoiur localização de O matrimónio de D. Fernando I e Dna Leonor 1372.*

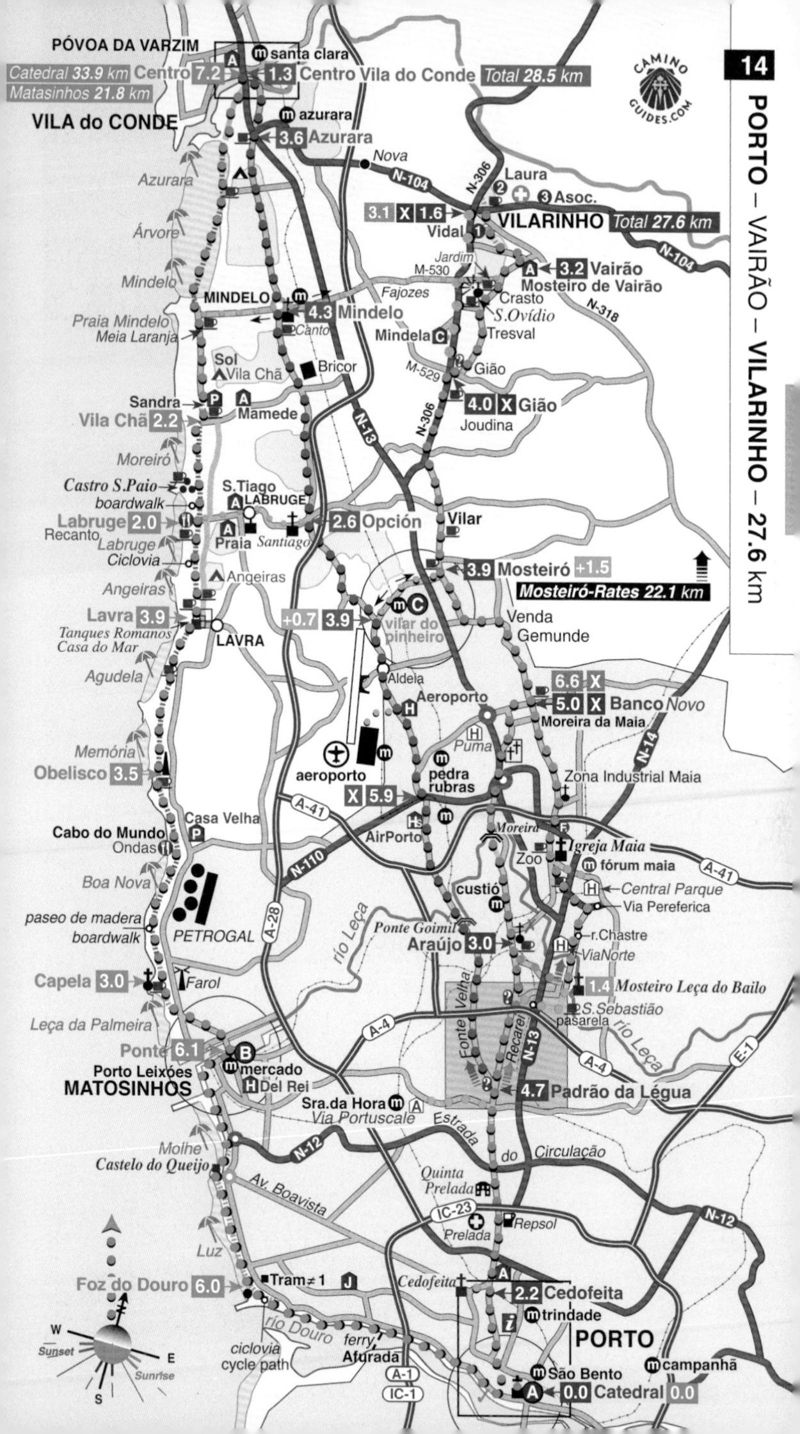

CAMINO GUIDES.COM

PÓVOA DA VARZIM
santa clara
Catedral 33.9 km Centro 7.2 A 1.3 Centro Vila do Conde Total 28.5 km
Matasinhos 21.8 km
VILA do CONDE
azurara
3.6 Azurara
Nova
N-104
N-306
Laura
2 3 Asoc.
Azurara
3.1 X 1.6
VILARINHO Total 27.6 km
Vidal 1
Árvore
Jardim
M-530
A 3.2 Vairão
Mosteiro de Vairão
N-104
Mindelo
MINDELO
Fajozes
Crasto
N-318
4.3 Mindelo
S.Ovídio
Praia Mindelo
Canto
Meia Laranja
Mindela C
Tresval
Sol
Bricor
Vila Chã
M-529
Gião
Sandra
P A
Mamede
4.0 X Gião
Vila Chã 2.2
N-13
N-306
Joudina
Moreiró
Castro S.Paio
S.Tiago
boardwalk
LABRUGE
Labruge 2.0
2.6 Opción
Vilar
Recanto
Praia
Santiago
Labruge
Ciclovia
3.9 Mosteiró +1.5
Angeiras
Angeiras
Mosteiró-Rates 22.1 km
Lavra 3.9
+0.7 3.9
vilar do pinheiro
Venda
Tanques Romanos
Gemunde
Casa do Mar
LAVRA
Agudela
Aldeia
6.6 X
Aeroporto
5.0 X Banco Novo
H
Moreira da Maia
Memória
Puma
N-14
aeroporto
pedra rubras
Zona Industrial Maia
Obelisco 3.5
X 5.9
A-41
Casa Velha
Hs
Moreira
Cabo do Mundo
P
AirPorto
Igreja Maia
Ondas
Zoo
fórum maia
N-110
A-41
Boa Nova
custió
Central Parque
Via Pereferica
paseo de madera
rio Leça
A-28
boardwalk
PETROGAL
Ponte Goimil
r.Chastre
Araújo 3.0
ViaNorte
Capela 3.0
Farol
Fonte Velha
1.4 Mosteiro Leça do Bailo
Recarei
S.Sebastião
Leça da Palmeira
A-4
pasarela
rio Leça
N-13
Ponte 6.1
B
A-4
E-1
Porto Leixões
mercado
MATOSINHOS
Del Rei
4.7 Padrão da Légua
Sra.da Hora
A
Via Portuscale
Estrada
Molhe
N-12
do Circulação
Castelo do Queijo
Av. Boavista
Quinta
Prelada
IC-23
Repsol
N-12
Prelada
Luz
A
Foz do Douro 6.0
Tram ≠ 1
J
Cedofeita
2.2 Cedofeita
trindade
W
rio Douro
ferry
PORTO
Sunset
E
ciclovia
Afurada
cycle path
A-1
São Bento
campanhã
Sunrise
S
IC-1
0.0 Catedral 0.0

## 15 VILARINHO – BARCELOS

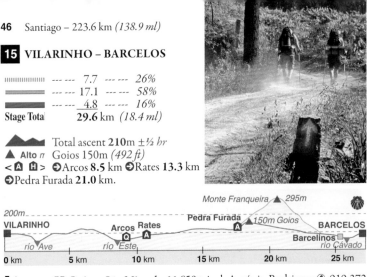

| | | |
|---|---|---|
| --- --- | 7.7 --- --- | *26%* |
| --- --- | 17.1 --- --- | *58%* |
| --- --- | 4.8 --- --- | *16%* |
| **Stage Total** | **29.6** km *(18.4 ml)* | |

Total ascent **210**m ±½ *hr*

▲ Alto *m* Goios 150m *(492 ft)*

< A H > ➲Arcos **8.5** km ➲Rates **13.3** km ➲Pedra Furada **21.0** km.

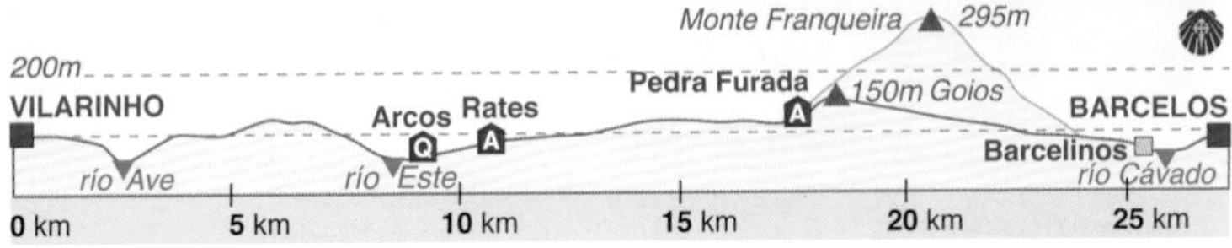


**▌Arcos:** •*CR* **Quinta São Miguel** *x11* €50+ incl. António Rodrigues ✆ 919 372 202 *www.quintasaomiguel.com* •*H* **Villa d'Arcos** €60+ ✆ 252 652 041 r/Alegria 38.
**▌Rates:** ●★*Alb Asoc.* **Rates** *[50÷4]* €-donativo r/S. António 189. •**Casa de Mattos** *x5* €40 ✆ 919 822 398. •**Casa Anabela** *x4* €15-35 incl. ✆ Anabela 919 578 642 *casanabela@gmail.com* r/Padrão da Vila 9. •**Casa da Vila** *x2* €35-50 ✆ Pedro 913 317 842 Rr/Senhor dos Passos 135. *O Pergrino menú* *Macedo* *mini-mercado Da Lurdes.*
**▌Pedra Furada:** ●*Alb.* **Pedra Furada** ***Palhuço*** *Mun.[24÷2]* €8. •**Casa Maria** €45 (floor space *suelo* from €10. ✆ 913 207 459 N-306. *Pedra Furada (Antonio)* *[**Franqueira: +1.4** km •**Quinta da Franqueira** €60-90 ✆ 253 831 606].*

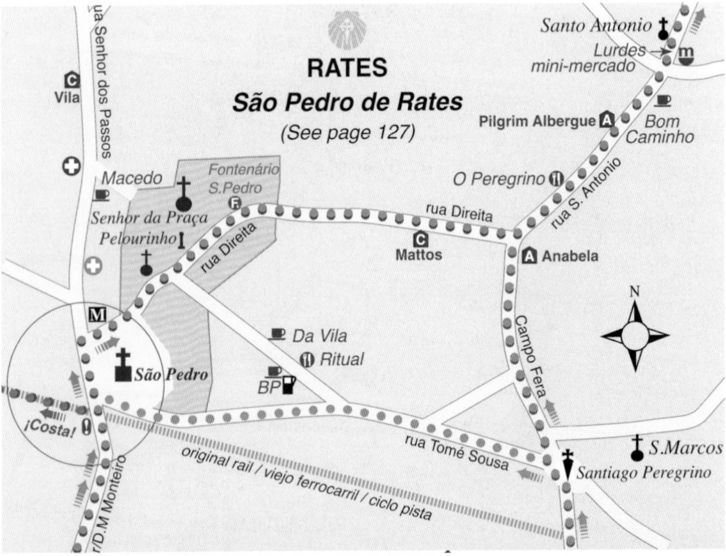

**RATES**
***São Pedro de Rates***
*(See page 127)*

Rua Senhor dos Passos
C Vila
Macedo
Fontenário S.Pedro
*Senhor da Praça*
*Pelourinho*
rua Direita
Mattos
São Pedro
Da Vila
Ritual
BP
¡Costa!
r/D.M Monteiro
rua Tomé Sousa
original rail / viejo ferrocarril / ciclo pista
*Santo Antonio*
Lurdes mini-mercado
Pilgrim Albergue
Bom Caminho
O Peregrino
rua S. Antonio
Anabela
Campo Fera
*S.Marcos*
*Santiago Peregrino*
N

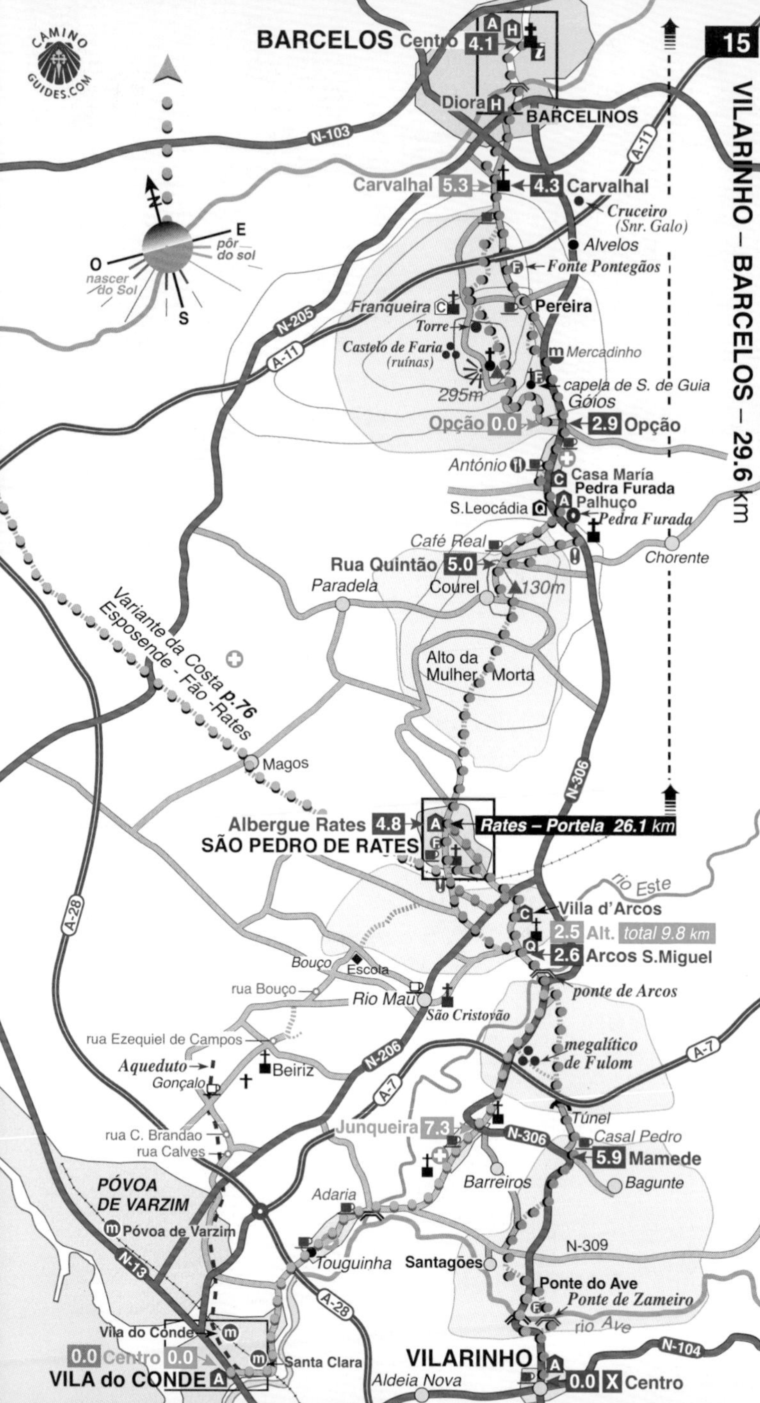

CAMINO GUIDES.COM
15
BARCELOS Centro
4.1
Diora
BARCELINOS
N-103
A-11
VILARINHO – BARCELOS – 29.6 km
Carvalhal 5.3
4.3 Carvalhal
Cruceiro (Snr. Galo)
Alvelos
E
pôr do sol
O
nascer do Sol
S
Fonte Pontegãos
Franqueira
Pereira
Torre
N-205
Castelo de Faria (ruínas)
Mercadinho
capela de S. de Guia
295m
Góios
Opção 0.0
2.9 Opção
António
Casa María
Pedra Furada
Palhuço
S.Leocádia
Pedra Furada
Café Real
Chorente
Rua Quintão 5.0
Paradela
Courel
130m
Alto da Mulher Morta
Variante da Costa p.76
Esposende - Fão -Rates
Magos
N-306
Albergue Rates 4.8
SÃO PEDRO DE RATES
Rates – Portela 26.1 km
rio Este
Villa d'Arcos
2.5 Alt. total 9.8 km
2.6 Arcos S.Miguel
A-28
Bouço
Escola
rua Bouço
Rio Mau
São Cristovão
ponte de Arcos
rua Ezequiel de Campos
megalítico de Fulom
Aqueduto
Beiriz
Gonçalo
N-206
A-7
Túnel
Junqueira 7.3
N-306
Casal Pedro
rua C. Brandao
rua Calves
5.9 Mamede
Barreiros
Bagunte
PÓVOA DE VARZIM
Adaria
Póvoa de Varzim
N-309
N-13
Touguinha
Santagões
Ponte do Ave
A-28
Ponte de Zameiro
rio Ave
Vila do Conde
0.0 Centro 0.0
Santa Clara
VILA do CONDE
VILARINHO
N-104
Aldeia Nova
0.0 X Centro

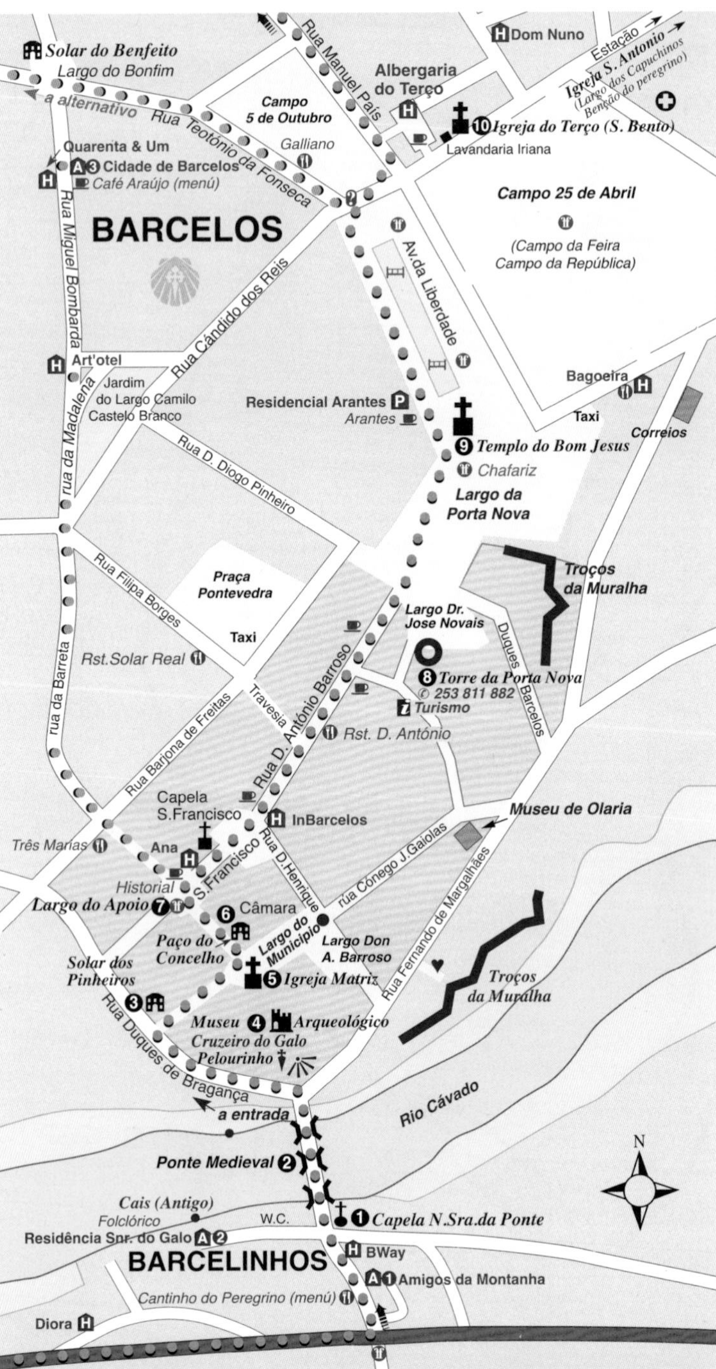

Solar do Benfeito
Largo do Bonfim
a alternativo
Rua Teotónio da Fonseca
Rua Manuel País
Dom Nuno
Estação
Igreja S. Antonio
(Largo dos Capuchinos
Benção do peregrino)
Albergaria
do Terço
Campo
5 de Outubro
10 Igreja do Terço (S. Bento)
Lavandaria Iriana
Galliano
Quarenta & Um
A 3 Cidade de Barcelos
Café Araújo (menú)
Campo 25 de Abril
(Campo da Feira
Campo da República)
BARCELOS
Rua Miguel Bombarda
Av.da Liberdade
Rua Cándido dos Reis
Art'otel
Jardim
do Largo Camilo
Castelo Branco
Residencial Arantes
Arantes
Bagoeira
Taxi
Correios
rua da Madalena
Rua D. Diogo Pinheiro
9 Templo do Bom Jesus
Chafariz
Largo da
Porta Nova
Troços
da Muralha
Rua Filipa Borges
Praça
Pontevedra
Taxi
Largo Dr.
Jose Novais
Duques Barcelos
Rst.Solar Real
8 Torre da Porta Nova
© 253 811 882
Turismo
rua da Barreta
Rua Barjona de Freitas
Travesia
Rua D. António Barroso
Rst. D. António
Capela
S.Francisco
InBarcelos
Museu de Olaria
Três Marias
Ana
S.Francisco
Rua D.Henrique
rua Cónego J.Gaiolas
Historial
Largo do Apoio 7
6 Câmara
Paço do
Concelho
Largo do
Municipio
Largo Don
A. Barroso
Rua Fernando de Margalhães
Solar dos
Pinheiros
5 Igreja Matriz
Troços
da Muralha
3
Rua Duques de Bragança
Museu 4 Arqueológico
Cruzeiro do Galo
Pelourinho
a entrada
Rio Cávado
Ponte Medieval 2
N
Cais (Antigo)
Folclórico
W.C.
1 Capela N.Sra.da Ponte
Residência Snr. do Galo A 2
BWay
BARCELINHOS
A 1 Amigos da Montanha
Cantinho do Peregrino (menú)
Diora

***Medieval** XIV* ❸ ***Solar dos Pinheiros** XV* ❹ ***Paço dos Condes** XV* e ***Museu Arqueológico*** e ***Pelourinho*** ❺ ***Igreja Matriz** XIV.* ❻ ***Câmara e Paços do Concelho*** *Largo do Município (Medieval hospital de peregrinos)* ❼ ***Largo do Apoio** Fonte XVII* ❽ ***Torre da Porta Nova** XV* ❾ ***Templo do S. Bom Jesus da Cruz** XVIII.* ● ***Igreja de Santo António*** Padres Capuchinhos misa de peregrinos 19:00

▌**Barcelinhos:** ● *Alb./Hs.* **Diora** *Casa da Pombas [12÷3]* €10 *x5* €15-30 ✆ Casimiro 960 201 911 www.diorahostel.pt r/São Miguel-O-Anjo, 42. *Alb.*❶ **Amigos da Montanha** *Asoc.[16÷1]* €5 ✆ 253 830 430 Largo dos Penedos, 39. 🍴 *Cantinho do Peregrino* menú €5 (07.00–24:00). •*Hs* **Barcelos Way** €45 ✆ 253 825 090 adj. puente. **Bombeiros** *Alb.*❷ **Residência Senhor do Galo** *Folclórico Asoc. [20÷2]* €5 ✆ 918 967 968 Rua da Carniçaria.

ⓘ **Barcelos:** ***Turismo:*** ✆ 253 811 882 Largo Dr. José Novais & internet. 09.30-18.00. •*Hs* **Casa da Ana** *x6* €60+ ✆ 936 018 008 www.casadaana.pt Rua Visconde Leiria, 37 (S.Francisco). ●*Alb.*❸ **Cidade de Barcelos** *Asoc.[26÷3]*.€-donativo www.alberguedebarcelos.com r/Miguel Bombarda **Nº36** adj. ☕ *Araujo* Emília *menú peregrino €6 adj.@***Nº41** •*Hr* **Kuarenta & Um** *x7* €40+ ✆ 932 117 730 & •*H* **Art'Otel** *x9* €50-60 ✆ 934 024 180 r/Madalena 29. ***Central:*** 🍴/•*H*** **Bagoeira** *x54* €45+ ✆ 253 809 500 Av. Dr. Sidónio Pais, 495. •*H*** **Terço** *x37* €35-45 ✆ 253 808 380 www.hoteldoterco.com r/São Bento. •*R* **Dom Nuno** *x27* €35+ ✆ 253 812 810 r/Dr. Francisco Torres, 141. ***Estação***: •*HsR* **Solar da Estação** €25+ ✆ 933 056 887 Largo Marechal Gomes da Costa.

# 16 BARCELOS – PONTE DE LIMA

| | | |
|---|---|---|
| | 16.5 | *48%* |
| | 15.8 | *45%* |
| | 2.4 | *7%* |
| **Stage Total** | **34.7** km *(21.6 ml)* | |

Total ascent **440**m ±¾ *hr*
▲ Alto *m* Alto da Portela 170 m *(558 ft)*
< A H > ➲Portela **9.8** km ➲Aborim **11.4** ➲Balugães **16.2** ➲Lugar do Corgo **20.0** ➲Vitorino dos Piães **22.5** ➲Facha **25.2** km.

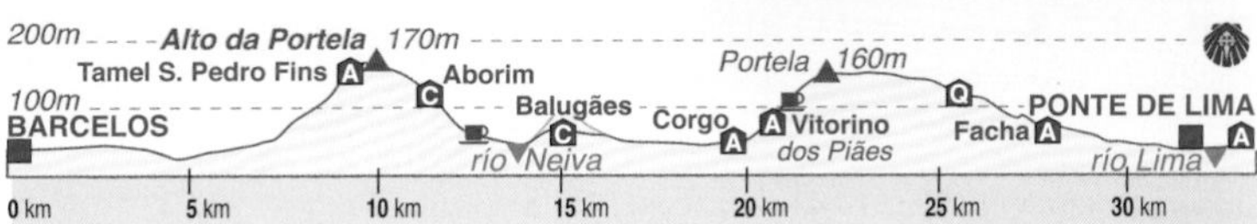


**▌Tamel:** ***(São Pedro de Fins / Portela)*** •**Leonchic** €45 ✆ 932 420 240 +300m. ●*Alb. Mun.[42÷4]* **Casa da Recoleta** €5 ✆ 253 137 075 [m] 935 136 811 adj. Capela Sra. da Portela (photo>)opp. 🍴/☕ *2000.* **▌Aborim:** •**Casa de Santiago** €20pp ✆ 914 463 272 rua de Santiago, 78. *[*● ***Quintiães +1.5** km* •**Casa dos Assentos** €70+ ✆ 919 640 742 (Sra. Julia Machado). *www.casadosassentos.com ]*.

**▌Balugâes:** •*CR* **Quinta da Cancela** *x6* €45+ ✆ 258 763 079 *www.quintacancela.pt [**São Bento +0.3** km* ☕ + ***Cossourado +1.1** km* •*CR* **Casas do Rio** *x6* €50+ ✆ 969 312 585 José Lúis Amaro*]*. **▌Lugar do Corgo:** ●*Alb.* ♥ **Casa da Fernanda** *Priv. [10÷1]* ✆ 914 589 521 Fernanda e Jacinto €35 *media pensión incl. cena comunitaria, com vinho e música!* **▌Vitorino de Piães:** •*CR.* **O Estábulo de Valinhas** *x10* €35 ✆ 910 021 180 + 100m 🍴 *O Lagar.* ●*Alb.* **Casa Sagres** *Priv.*[9÷1] €15 ✆ 962 916 441 **▌Facha Q. Portela** *Priv.[6÷3]*+ €20 (Menú €15) ✆ 964 257 171. •**Casa Santiago** €35 ✆ 919 216 557. ●*Alb.* **O Caminheiro** *[4÷1]* €15 menú €7.50 ✆ 968 408 882. **▌Seara:** *[+0.4 km]* •*Hr.* **Pinheiro Manso** *x20* €30-40 ✆ 258 943 775*]*.

**■ Ponte de Lima:** see next page *próxima página...*

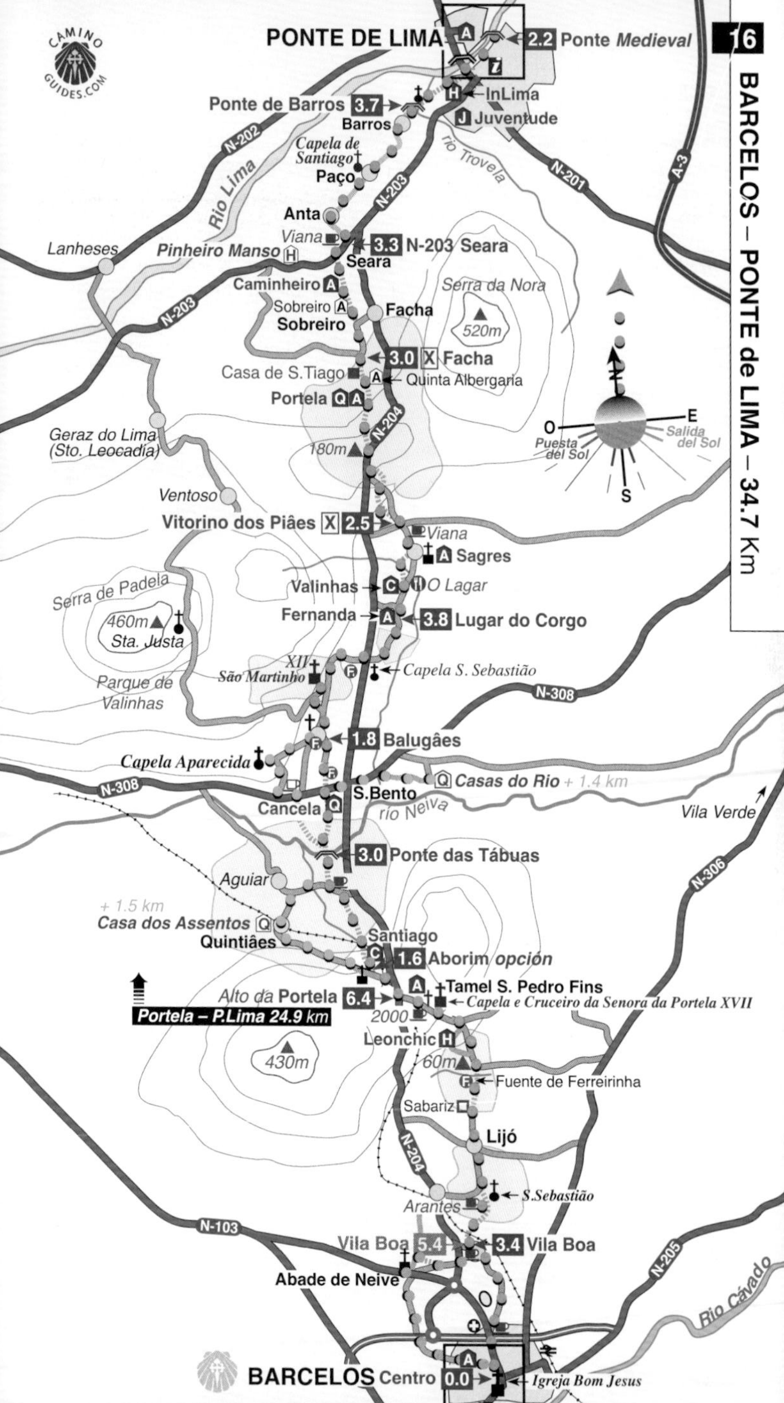

16
BARCELOS – PONTE de LIMA – 34.7 Km
CAMINO GUIDES.COM
PONTE DE LIMA
2.2 Ponte Medieval
InLima
Juventude
Ponte de Barros 3.7
Barros
Capela de Santiago
Paço
Anta
Viana
3.3 N-203 Seara
Seara
Pinheiro Manso
Lanheses
Caminheiro
Sobreiro
Sobreiro
Facha
Serra da Nora
520m
3.0 Facha
Casa de S.Tiago
Quinta Albergaria
Portela
180m
Geraz do Lima (Sto. Leocadia)
Ventoso
Vitorino dos Piães 2.5
Viana
Sagres
Valinhas
O Lagar
Fernanda
3.8 Lugar do Corgo
Serra de Padela
460m
Sta. Justa
XII
São Martinho
Capela S. Sebastião
Parque de Valinhas
1.8 Balugães
Capela Aparecida
Casas do Rio + 1.4 km
S.Bento
Cancela
rio Neiva
Vila Verde
3.0 Ponte das Tábuas
Aguiar
+ 1.5 km
Casa dos Assentos
Quintiães
Santiago
1.6 Aborim opción
Tamel S. Pedro Fins
Capela e Cruceiro da Senora da Portela XVII
Alto da Portela 6.4
Portela – P.Lima 24.9 km
2000
Leonchic
430m
60m
Fuente de Ferreirinha
Sabariz
Lijó
S.Sebastião
Arantes
Vila Boa 5.4
3.4 Vila Boa
Abade de Neive
Rio Cávado
BARCELOS Centro 0.0
Igreja Bom Jesus
O
E
S
Puesta del Sol
Salida del Sol
N-202
N-203
N-201
A-3
N-204
N-308
N-306
N-103
N-205
Rio Lima
rio Trovela

PONTE DE LIMA:

▮ ***Entrance*** *Entrada:* ●**Pousada de Juventude** *[50÷12]* €12 r/João Paulo II ✆ 258 943 797. •*H*******InLima** *x30* €50-70 ✆ 258–900 050 r/Agostinho José Taveira. •*H******Império** *x46* €55+ ✆ 258 009 008 *www.hotelimperiodonorte.com* Rua 5 de Outubro, 97.

▮ ***Central:*** •*CR.***Pinheiro** *x7* €50+ ✆ 258 943 971 r/G. Norton de Matos, 40. •*H* **Mercearia da Vila** *x6* €60 ✆ 925 996 366 adj. parish church *Igreja matriz* r/ Cardeal Saraiva: opp: •*Hs* **Casa Abadia** *Ophis* ✆ 960 403 345 r/Souto 2/3. •*P* **Morais** €20-30 basic *basica* r/Matriz 8 (opp. church entrance). •*CR.***Pereiras** ✆ 258 942 939 r/Fonte da Vila. •*P** **São João** €35 ✆ 258 941 288 adj. 🍴 *Gula* Largo de S. João entrance r/do Rosário 6. •*P* **Beira Rio** €25 ✆ 258 944 044 Passeio 25 de Abril.

▮ ***Suburbs*** *afueras:* •*P* **O Garfo** ✆ 258 743 147 r/Arrabalde S.João Fora Crasto ***+0.5*** km. •*Hs* **Old Village** *[16÷4]* €15 *x2* €40 ✆ 961 574 929 *www.oldvillagehostel.pt* v/Foral Velho de D. Teresa, 1415 (N-203) + ***1.2*** km.

▮ ***Exit*** *Salida:* ●*Alb.* **Casa do Arnado** *Mun.[60÷3]* €5 ✆ m: 925 403 164 (peregrino S.O.S. m: 925 403 162) Largo Dr Alexandre Herculano / Alegria (see photo>). Opp: •**ARC'otel** *x15* €45-60 ✆ 966 506 744. Adj. 🍴 *Petiscas*

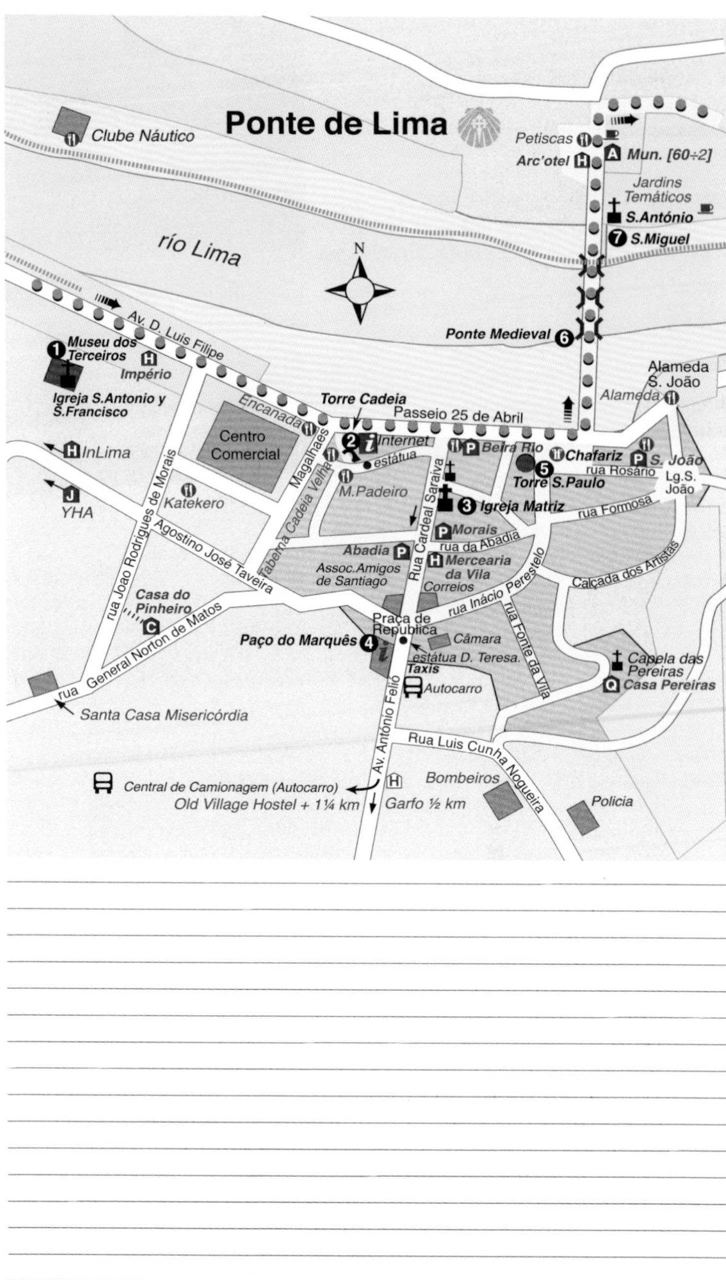
Ponte de Lima
Clube Náutico
río Lima
N
Petiscas
Arc'otel
Mun. [60÷2]
Jardins Temáticos
S.António
7 S.Miguel
Ponte Medieval 6
Av. D. Luis Filipe
1 Museu dos Terceiros
Império
Igreja S.Antonio y S.Francisco
Encanada
Torre Cadeia
Passeio 25 de Abril
Alameda S. João
Alameda
Centro Comercial
2 Internet
estátua
Beira Rio
Chafariz
S. João
rua Rosário
Lg.S. João
5 Torre S.Paulo
InLima
YHA
Katekero
Magalhaes
Taberna Cadeia Velha
M.Padeiro
Rua Cardeal Saraiva
3 Igreja Matriz
rua Formosa
Morais
rua da Abadia
Abadia
Mercearia da Vila
Correios
Assoc.Amigos de Santiago
rua Joao Rodrigues de Morais
Agostino José Taveira
Calçada dos Artistas
rua Inácio Perestelo
Casa do Pinheiro
rua General Norton de Matos
Praça de República
rua Fonte da Vila
Câmara
Paço do Marquês 4
estátua D. Teresa.
Taxis
Autocarro
Capela das Pereiras
Casa Pereiras
Santa Casa Misericórdia
Av. António Feliô
Rua Luis Cunha Nogueira
Central de Camionagem (Autocarro)
Old Village Hostel + 1¼ km
Bombeiros
Garfo ½ km
Policia

# 17 PONTE DE LIMA – RUBIÃES

Ponte romano *Agualonga*

--- --- 10.7 --- --- *58%*
--- --- 7.9 --- --- *42%*
--- --- 0.0 --- --- *0%*
**Stage Total** **18.6** km *(11.6 ml)*

Total ascent **760**m ±*1¼ hr*
▲ Alto *m* Portela Grande 405m *(1,329 ft)*
< A H > ➲Labruja **10.1** km ➲Cabanas **15.8**

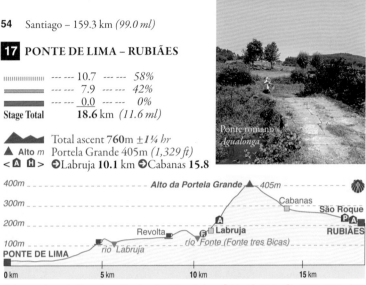

400m Alto da Portela Grande ▲ 405m
300m Cabanas
São Roque
200m
Revolta
Labruja
RUBIÃES
100m
río Labruja
río Fonte (Fonte tres Bicas)
PONTE DE LIMA
0 km 5 km 10 km 15 km

**▌Arcozelo:** ▲*Camping* **Oasis do Caminho** *[10÷1]* €15 ✆ 912 057 420 adj. *Pescaria* r/Borralhos. **▌Labruja:** ❶ Rua dos Valinhos •*B&B* **Quinta Labruja** *x2* €48-68 ✆ 935 268 485 *www.quintalabruja.pt* ❷ ●*Alb.Hs* **Casa da Valada** *Priv.[4÷2]* €20 +*5* €55 ✆ 967 742 694. ❸ ●**Conforto** *[10÷2]* €15 incl. ✆ 935 883 131 *oconforto.wixsite.com/albergue (Note Quinta da Enxurreira is a holiday let).* **▌Cabanas:** •*CR.* **Quinta da Preza** *x6* €60+ ✆ 960 268 724 r/Cabanas, 845. **▌Carreira:** *[+0.2 km]* •***Casa Blanca*** *€15 ✆ Trevor (UK+44) 7867288870 basic hostel priv. €15-30].* **▌Águalonga: N-301** ●*EcoAlb.***BotaRota** *Priv.[10÷1]* €15 +*2* €35 Marianne ✆ +44 7804656388. *[**Detour up right +1.5** km* Águalonga / Trulhe + •*CR **Oliveirinha** x3 €55+✆ 917 600 160 Rua Trulha de Cima **+1** km].* ***Detour down left*** *to •CR **Quinta da Gandra** x5 €45+* ✆ 938 310 855 *[**+0.9** km].*
**■ São Roque:** •*CR* **Casa de Lamas** *Priv.[6÷1]* €15 +*4* €40. ✆ 251 010 282 (Maria Madalena e Josíno) **N-201:** •*Hr* **Repouso do Peregrino** €15pp +*8* €35 incl. ✆ 251 943 692 (Silvia) adj. *farmacia Sousa* •**Constantino** *Priv.[6÷1]* €15pp +25 +*6* €28 ✆ 968 432 059 *(& Constantino adj. Ponte Nova).* •*CR* **Quinta das Leiras** *x5* €25+ incl. pp ✆ 967 813 689 (Helmut & Heidi) *www.quintadaleiras.com* & piscina – adj. •**Casa das Lages** *x3* €15 pp incl. ✆ 964 936 366 (Sophia).
**■ Rubiães:** ●*Alb.* **Escola** *Mun.[34÷2]* €5 ✆ 251 943 472 adj. *São Sebastião.* •*CR.* **S Sebastião** *x8* €15-30 ✆ 251 941 258 (Maria Pereira) adj. ●*Alb.*♥ **O Ninho** *(The Nest) Priv.[17÷4]* €15 ✆ 251 941 002 / 916 866 372 (Marlene & Dª Maria Pequena) garden *jardín.* *Bom Retiro* ✆ 251 941 245 *menú* €7+.

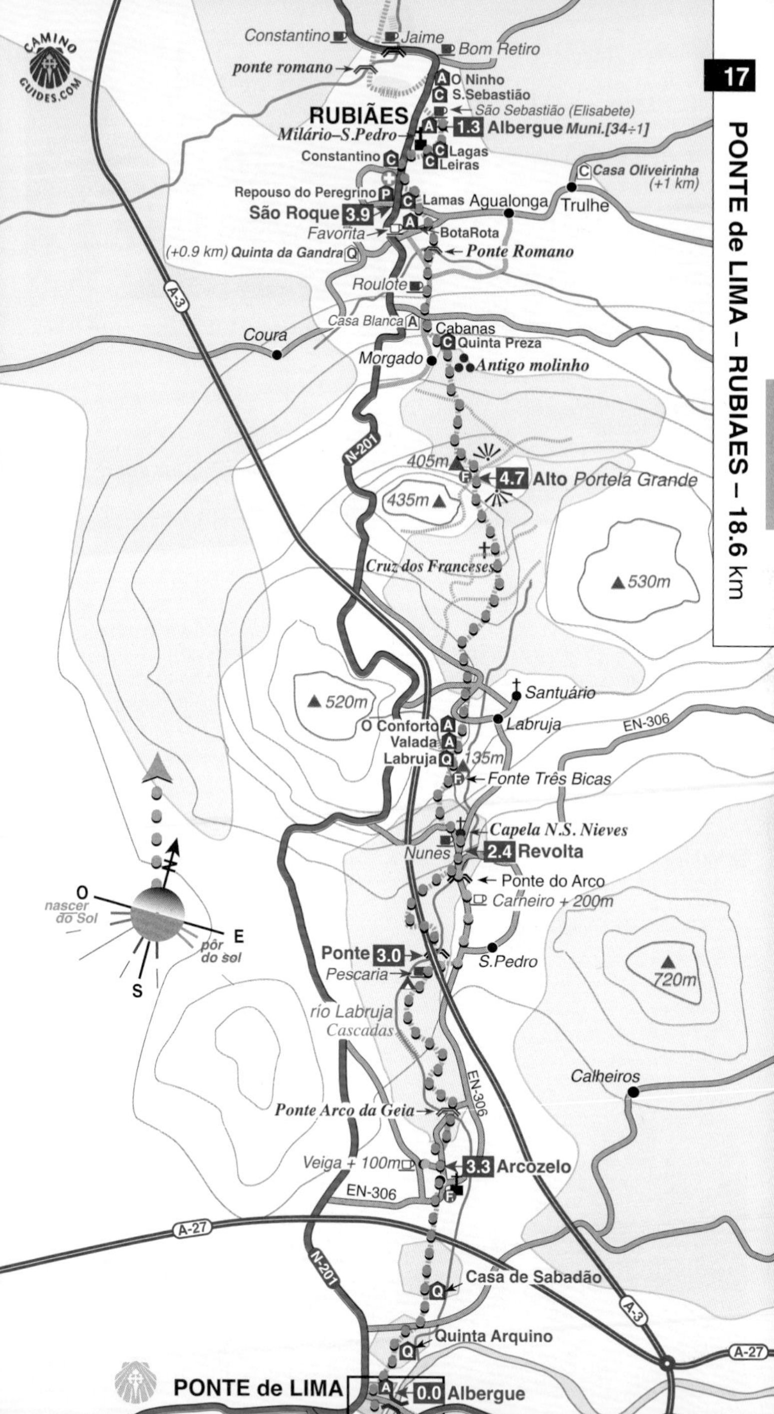
17
PONTE de LIMA – RUBIAES – 18.6 km
CAMINO GUIDES.COM
Constantino
Jaime
Bom Retiro
ponte romano
O Ninho
S.Sebastião
São Sebastião (Elisabete)
RUBIÃES
1.3 Albergue Muni.[34÷1]
Milário–S.Pedro
Constantino
Lagas
Leiras
Casa Oliveirinha (+1 km)
Repouso do Peregrino
Lamas
Agualonga
Trulhe
São Roque 3.9
Favorita
BotaRota
(+0.9 km) Quinta da Gandra
Ponte Romano
Roulote
A-3
Casa Blanca
Cabanas
Quinta Preza
Coura
Morgado
Antigo molinho
N-201
405m
4.7 Alto Portela Grande
435m
Cruz dos Franceses
530m
520m
Santuário
O Conforto
Labruja
EN-306
Valada
Labruja
135m
Fonte Três Bicas
Capela N.S. Nieves
Nunes
2.4 Revolta
Ponte do Arco
Carneiro + 200m
O
nascer do Sol
E
pôr do sol
S
Ponte 3.0
S.Pedro
Pescaria
720m
río Labruja
Cascadas
Calheiros
EN-306
Ponte Arco da Geia
Veiga + 100m
3.3 Arcozelo
EN-306
A-27
N-201
Casa de Sabadão
A-3
Quinta Arquino
A-27
PONTE de LIMA
0.0 Albergue

Ponte romano *Rubiães*

## 18 RUBIÃES – VALENÇA / TUI

| | | |
|---|---|---|
| (path) | 9.6 | *54%* |
| (minor road) | 9.3 | *7%* |
| (main road) | 1.4 | *39%* |
| **Stage Total** | **20.3** km (12.6 ml) | |

Total ascent **200**m ±½ *hr*

▲ Alto *m* S. Bento 270 m *(886 ft)*

<A H> ➲Pecene **4.0** km ➲Fontoura **7.8** km ➲Paços **11.0** ➲Valença **16.9** km.

300m
270m ▲Alto S. Bento
RUBIÃES S.Bento
Pecene
200m
Fontoura
río Coura
100m
Paços
Ponte Romano
VALENÇA
TUI
N-13
Pedreira
río Pedreira
río Minho
0 km
5 km
10 km
15 km

▌**Cossourado**: •*CR.* **Casa da Capela** *x7* €60 ✆ 251 782 005 (Margarida) 917 907 736 quinta adj. capela. ▌**São Bento da Porta Aberta** ●*Alb.* **Cafe Castro** *Priv. [12÷3]* €12.50 ✆ 251 782 210. ▌**Fontoura:** •*CR.* **Quinta do Cruzeiro** *[4÷2]* €30pp *x4* €38-49 ✆ 937 625 011 menú & piscina. ●*Alb.* **Pilger Pause** *Priv. [14÷1]* €13 ✆ Verena **+49** 178 1848 141 Ronald **+49** 1577 0699 249 menú €6. ▌**Paços:** ●*Alb.* **Quinta Estrada Romana** *Priv.[18÷3]* ✆ 251 837 333. €25 incl. menú. ▌**Ponte Pedreira** ●*Alb.* **Quinta do Caminho** *Priv.[18÷1]* €13 *+10* €40 menú €8. Hugo ✆ 251 821 183 www.quintadocaminho.com terraza & piscina. ▌**Valença *Suburbs*** *afueras: [***+0.4** *km* •*H*˙˙ **Valença do Minho** €30+ ✆ 251 824 211 *Av. Miguel Dantas N-13].*

■ **Valença / Tui** see next page *próxima página...*

Catedral *Jardín*

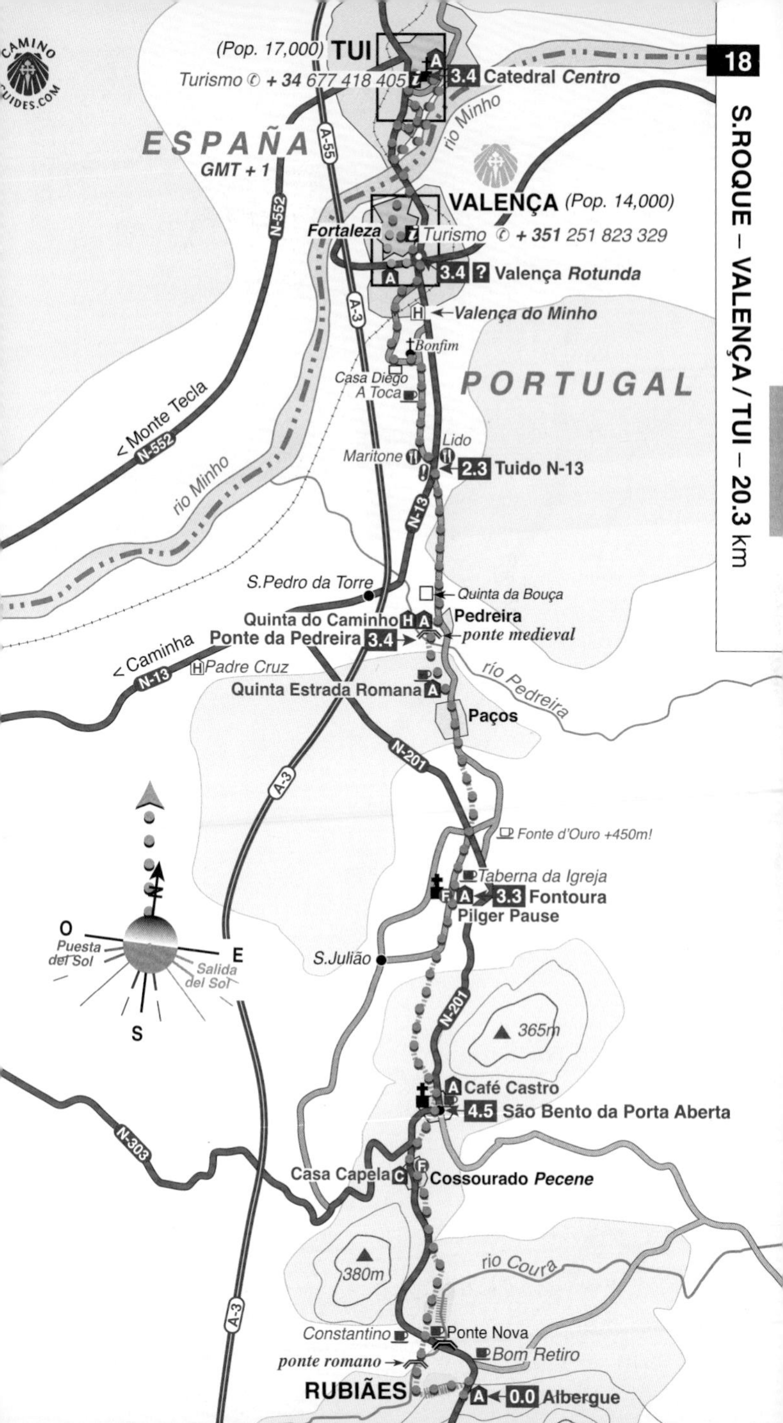

18
S.ROQUE – VALENÇA / TUI – 20.3 km
CAMINO GUIDES.COM
(Pop. 17,000) TUI
Turismo © + 34 677 418 405
3.4 Catedral Centro
rio Minho
ESPAÑA
GMT + 1
A-55
N-552
VALENÇA (Pop. 14,000)
Fortaleza
Turismo © + 351 251 823 329
3.4 ? Valença Rotunda
A-3
Valença do Minho
Bonfim
Casa Diego
A Toca
PORTUGAL
< Monte Tecla
N-552
rio Minho
Lido
Maritone
2.3 Tuido N-13
N-13
S.Pedro da Torre
Quinta da Bouça
Quinta do Caminho
Pedreira
Ponte da Pedreira 3.4
ponte medieval
< Caminha
N-13
Padre Cruz
río Pedreira
Quinta Estrada Romana
Paços
N-201
A-3
Fonte d'Ouro +450m!
Taberna da Igreja
3.3 Fontoura
Pilger Pause
O
Puesta del Sol
E
Salida del Sol
S
S.Julião
N-201
365m
Café Castro
4.5 São Bento da Porta Aberta
N-303
Casa Capela
Cossourado Pecene
380m
rio Coura
A-3
Constantino
Ponte Nova
Bom Retiro
ponte romano
RUBIÃES
0.0 Albergue

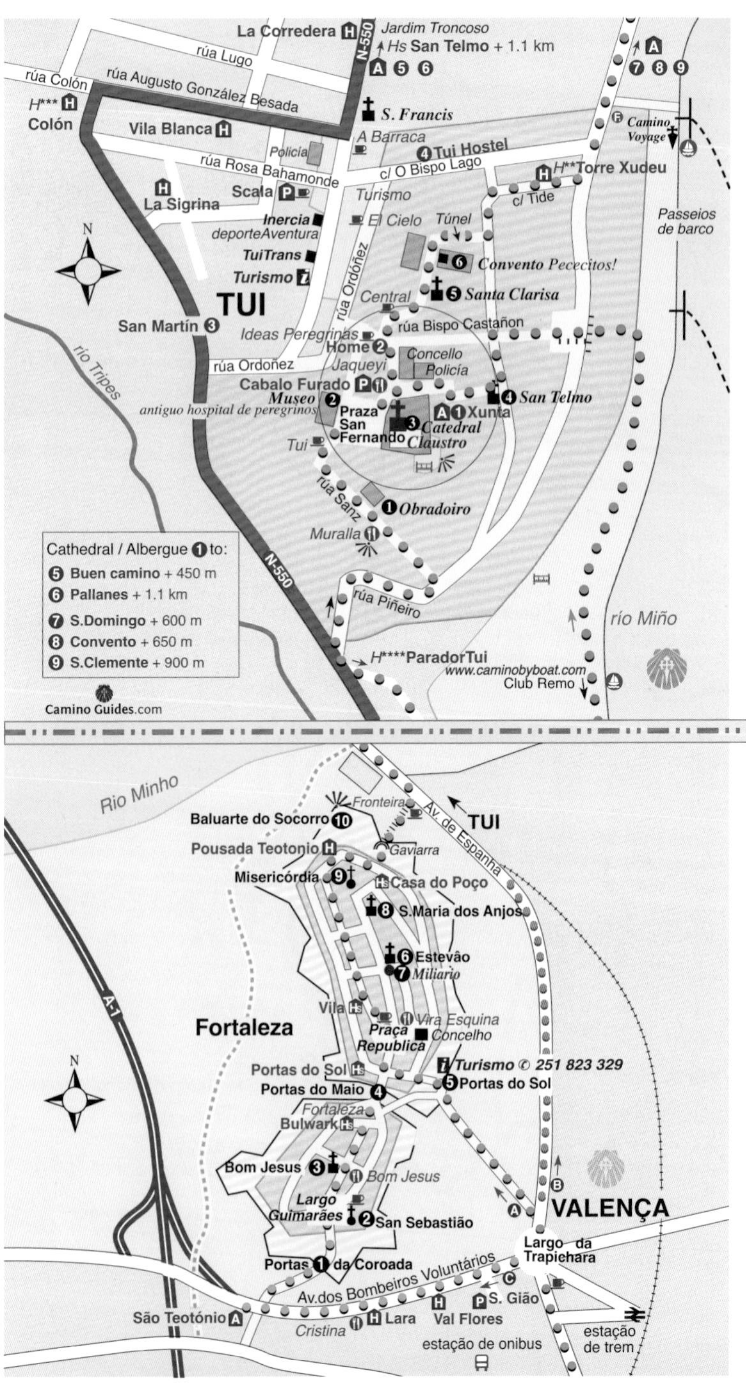

La Corredera
N-550
Jardim Troncoso
Hs San Telmo + 1.1 km
rúa Lugo
rúa Colón
rúa Augusto González Besada
H*** Colón
Vila Blanca
S. Francis
A Barraca
Camino Voyage
Policía
4 Tui Hostel
rúa Rosa Bahamonde
c/ O Bispo Lago
H**Torre Xudeu
La Sigrina
Scala
Turismo
c/ Tide
Passeios de barco
Inercia
deporteAventura
El Cielo
Túnel
TuiTrans
6 Convento Pececitos!
Turismo
rúa Ordoñez
5 Santa Clarisa
Central
TUI
San Martín 3
rúa Bispo Castañon
Ideas Peregrinas
Home 2
río Tripes
Concello
rúa Ordoñez
Jaqueyi
Policía
Cabalo Furado
Museo 2
antiguo hospital de peregrinos
4 San Telmo
1 Xunta
Praza San Fernando
3 Catedral
Claustro
Tui
rúa Sanz
1 Obradoiro
Muralla
Cathedral / Albergue 1 to:
5 Buen camino + 450 m
6 Pallanes + 1.1 km
7 S.Domingo + 600 m
8 Convento + 650 m
9 S.Clemente + 900 m
rúa Piñeiro
río Miño
H****ParadorTui
www.caminobyboat.com
Club Remo
Camino Guides.com
Rio Minho
Fronteira
Av. de Espanha
TUI
Baluarte do Socorro 10
Pousada Teotonio
Gaviarra
Misericórdia 9
Casa do Poço
8 S.Maria dos Anjos
6 Estevão
7 Miliario
A-1
Vila
Fortaleza
Vira Esquina
Praça Republica
Concelho
Turismo © 251 823 329
Portas do Sol
Portas do Maio 4
5 Portas do Sol
Fortaleza
Bulwark
Bom Jesus 3
Bom Jesus
Largo Guimarães
2 San Sebastião
VALENÇA
Largo da Trapichara
Portas 1 da Coroada
Av.dos Bombeiros Voluntários
S. Gião
São Teotónio
Cristina
Lara
Val Flores
estação de onibus
estação de trem

✻ **España** – GMT + 1 / © internacional **+34** (teléfono fijo: 9 / número de móvil: 6)

❶ **TUI** ***Turismo*** Paseo de Calvo Sotelo 16 © 677 418 405 9:30–14:00/ 16:00-19:00. ▌***Albergues Central:*** *Alb.*❶ *Xunta [36÷2]* €8 © 638 276 855. ❷♥**Home** ***Ideas Peregrinas*** *Priv.[10÷2]* €13 *+10* €30+ © 986 076 330 Mónica & Silvana *www.ideas-peregrinas.com* ❸ **Jacob's** *Priv.[19÷4]* €13-15 © 644 557 194 c/Obispo Lago, 5. ❹ **San Martín** *Priv.[19÷5]* €12 © 640 616 473 c/ Coruña, 6. ▌***Suburbs*** *afueras:* ❺ **Buen Camino** *Priv.[20÷1]* €15 incl. © Alba 986 604 052 Av. Concordia. ❻ **Pallanes** *Priv.[20÷2]* €13 *+6* €20-35 © 986 682 446 c/Palláns, 11. ***c/ Antero Rubín: @ Nº20*** ❼ **Santo Domingo** *Priv.[22÷5]* €12-15 © 650 820 685 ***@ Nº30.*** ❽♥**Convento del Camino** *Priv.[19÷2]* €13-15 © 690 328 565 Jorge. ❾ **Villa San Clemente** *Priv.[20÷3]* €15 *+3* €40+ © 678 747 700 c/Canónigo Valiño, 23. ▌***Hotels:*** •**O Novo Cabalo Furado** *x8* €30-60 © 986 604 445 c/Seijas, 3. •*Hs* **La Sigrina** *x10* €45-65 © 654 396 782 *www.lasigrinahostal.es* r/Foxo 8. •*P* **La Corredera** *x14* €40-50 © 629 879 730 *www.pensionlacorredera.com* Paseo de Calvo Sotelo 37. •**Scala** €15+ © 986 601 890 c/Rosa Bahamonde, 5. •*H** **Villa Blanca** *x10* €45-60 © 986 603 525 r/Augusto González Besada, 5. •*H**** **Colón** *x66* €48-60 © 986 600 223 c/Colón. •*H*** **A Torre do Xudeu** *x8* €50-60 © 986 603 535 *www.atorredoxudeo.es* c/Tide 3. ***Tui Outskirts:*** •*H**** **Parador de Tui** *x32* €70+ © 986 600 300. •*Hs*** **San Telmo** *x27* €15-40 © 986 906 116 Av. Concordia,84 adj. rail station estación N-550. •*H**** **Alfonso I** +2.2 km free pick-up *(p.60).*

---

✻ **Portugal** – GMT + 0 / © internacional **+351** (telefone fixo: 2 ou 3 / móvel: 9)

❶ **VALENÇA** ***DO MINHO: Posto de Turismo*** Av. Espanha © 251 823 374. Praça Forte de Valença © 251 823 329. ***Táxis*** © 252 822 121. ***Estação Caminhos do Ferro*** © 252 821 124. Bus ***Autocarro*** © 251 809 588.
▌***Hostels:*** ●*Alb.* **São Teotónio** *Mun. [85÷4]* €5 © 961 168 501 m: 251 826 286 Av. José Maria Gonçalves / Av. Bombeiros Voluntários. •*Hr.* **S. Gião** *x10* €19-27 © 251 030 040. Av. S.Teotónio 17. Av. dos Bombeiros Voluntários. •*H**** **Lara** *x54* €35-40 © 251 824 348. •*H** **Val Flores** *x32* €25-32 © 251 824 106 €30.
▌***Fortaleza:*** ●*Hs* **Bulwark** *[20÷2]* €19 © 251 837 022 *www.hostelbulwark.com* Tv. do Cantinho, 7-11. •*Hr* **Portas do Sol** *x8* €30-70 © 964 607 915 r/Conselheiro Lopes da Silva 51. •*Hs* **Vila** *x7* €45+ © 251 826 080 r/José Rodrigues, 34. •**Casa do Poço** *x7* €60-€80 © 251 010 094 Calçada da Gaviarra, 4 adj. •*H***** **Pousada de S. Teotonio** *x18* €80-90 © 251 800 260.

## 19 TUI – PORRIÑO

| | | |
|---|---|---|
| ▯▯▯▯ | 4.1 | *24%* |
| ▬▬ | 9.5 | *57%* |
| ▬▬ | 3.1 | *19%* |
| **Stage Total** | **16.7** km | *(10.4 ml)* |

Total ascent **340**m ±½ *hr*
▲ Alto *m* Capela La Guia 75 m *(246 ft)*
<Ⓐ Ⓗ> ➲*S.Telmo* ***5.8** km+**1.3*** ➲Orbenlle **9.5** km

100m TUI – S.Telmo Ⓗ – Opción Orbenlle – S.Campio 75m – PORRIÑO
río S.Simón – río Louro – río Louro
0 km – 5 km – 10 km – 15 km

▌**Cruceiro San Telmo N-550** ***detour*** *desvío:* ● ● ● *[**+0.8** km* •**Motel Trébol** *x30* €35 ✆ 986 607 087. ***+1.3** km* •**Hotel Alfonso I** *x64* €35+ ✆ 986 607 060*]*. ▌**Orbenlle**: ●*Alb.* **Casa Alternativo** *Priv.[8÷2]* €25 incl. Dinner *cena* ✆ Dries 622 900 377. ■ **Porriño**: *Alb.*❶ **Peregrinos** *Xunta.[52÷2]* €8 ✆ 986 335 428. ❷ **Camino Portugués** *Priv.[54÷6]* €10-12 ✆ 886 133 252 (Alex) Av. Buenos Aires 40. ❸ **Senda Sur** *Priv.[48÷2]* €10+ *+8* €25+ ✆ 886 129 569 www.sendasur.es r/foz 3. •*H*** **Louro** *x11* €28-48 Raquel ✆ 669 683 476 www.hostallouro.com Av. Buenos Aires, 6 *(above Froiz)* 669 683 476 & 🍴 *Sendasur*. •*P* **Cando** *x4* €28-36 ✆ 986 333 471 r/Progreso, 1 *(above Paso Nivel)*. ▌**Central:** ☕ *A Francachela* & *Alb.* ❹**Camino Santiago** *Priv.[28÷2]* €12 ✆ 623 161 267 r/Servando Ramilo Nº17. ❺ **Rincón** *Priv.[21÷1]* €13 ✆ 886 319 533 r/Cando 3. •*H*** **Parque** *x43* €40 ✆ 986 331 504 www.hotelparqueporrino.es Parque Cristo. •*H* **Azul** *x16* ✆ 986 330 032 www.hotelazul.es c/ Ramirás, 38. •*P*** **Maracaibo** €22-48 ✆ 986 330 901 c/ Manuel Rodríguez, 50. ***Outskirts*** *afueras:* •*H** **Internacional** *x50* €45-58 ✆ 986 330 262 c/ Antonio Palacios 99. •*P** **Puente** €40 ✆ 986 348 094 Av. Domingo Bueno, 67.

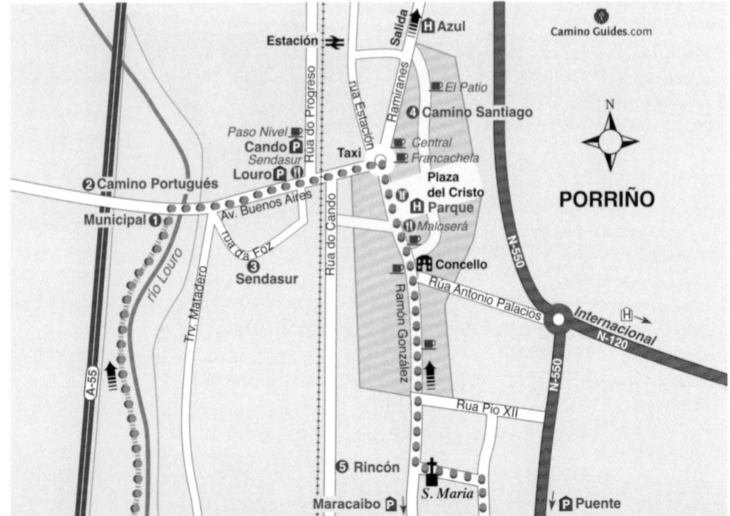

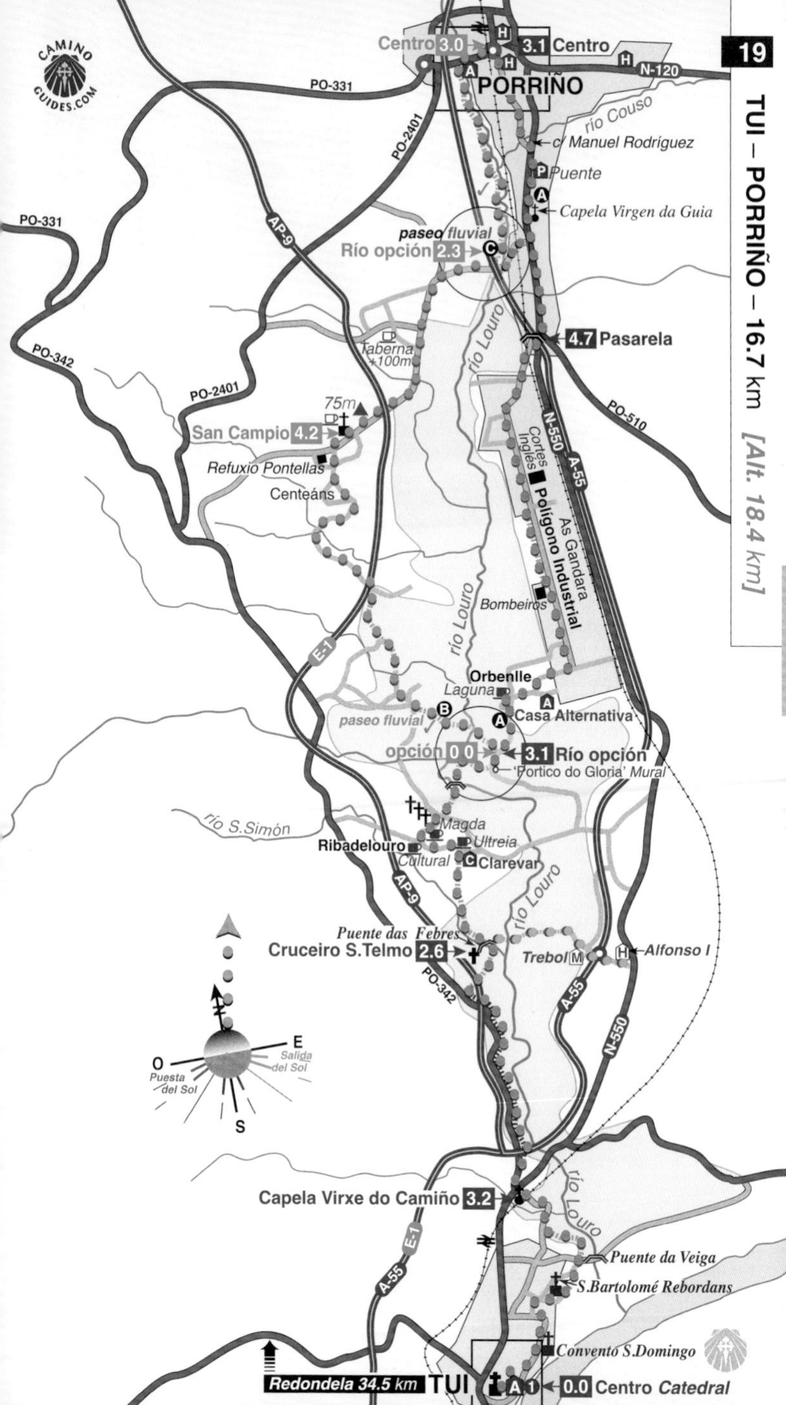

19
TUI – PORRIÑO – 16.7 km [Alt. 18.4 km]
CAMINO GUIDES.COM
Centro 3.0
3.1 Centro
N-120
PORRIÑO
PO-331
PO-2401
río Couso
c/ Manuel Rodríguez
Puente
Capela Virgen da Guia
PO-331
AP-9
paseo fluvial
Río opción 2.3
Taberna +100m
río Louro
4.7 Pasarela
PO-342
PO-2401
PO-510
75m
San Campio 4.2
Refuxio Pontellas
Centeáns
Cortes Inglés
N-550
A-55
As Gandara
Polígono Industrial
Bombeiros
E-1
río Louro
Orbenlle
Laguna
Casa Alternativa
paseo fluvial
opción 0.0
3.1 Río opción
'Portico do Gloria' Mural
río S.Simón
Magda
Ultreia
Ribadelouro
Cultural
Clarevar
AP-9
río Louro
Puente das Febres
Cruceiro S.Telmo 2.6
PO-342
Trebol
Alfonso I
A-55
N-550
E
Salida del Sol
O
Puesta del Sol
S
Capela Virxe do Camiño 3.2
río Louro
E-1
A-55
Puente da Veiga
S.Bartolomé Rebordans
Convento S.Domingo
Redondela 34.5 km
TUI
0.0 Centro Catedral

*Marco Miliário Vía XIX* Monte Cornado

## 20 PORRIÑO – REDONDELA

| | | |
|---|---|---|
| --- --- | 3.1 --- --- | *18%* |
| --- --- | 12.7 --- --- | *74%* |
| --- --- | 1.4 --- --- | *8%* |
| **Stage Total** | **17.2** km (10.7 ml) | |

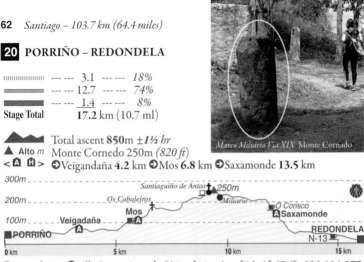

Total ascent **850**m ±*1½ hr*

▲ Alto *m* Monte Cornedo 250m *(820 ft)*

<A H> ➲Veigandaña **4.2** km ➲Mos **6.8** km ➲Saxamonde **13.5** km

300m
Santiaguiño de Antas 250m
200m Os Cabaleiros Miliario O Corisco
Mos Saxamonde
100m Veigadaña
PORRIÑO REDONDELA
N-13
0 km 5 km 10 km 15 km

**▌Veigadaña:** ●*Alb.* **Santa Ana de Veigadaña** *Asoc.[16÷1]* €7 ✆ 986 094 277. **▌Mos** ●*Alb.* **Casa Blanca** *Asoc.[16÷1]* €8 ✆ 986 348 001 opp. •*Alb.* **Flora** *[13÷3]* €10 *x3* €30 *menú* ✆ 986 334 269. **▌Saxamonde:** ●*Alb.* **Corisco** *Priv.[12÷1]+* €12 + €25 ✆ 986 402 166 c/Romano 49. **▌N-550** •*H*˙˙**Brasil 2** *x10 €27+*✆ *986 402 251.* **■ REDONDELA:** *Alb.*❶ **A Rotonda** *Priv.[11÷1]* €17 ✆ 657 805 988. **Rúa Pai Crespo @*Nº55*** ❷ **Santiago de Vilavella** *Priv.[46÷1]* €15 ✆ 673 414 752 & **@*Nº60*** ❸ **A Conserveira** *Priv. [40÷1]* €10 ✆ 676 667 293. •**Alvear Suites** €40+ ✆ 986 400 637. **Centro:** ❹ **Casa da Torre** *Xunta [42÷2]* €8 ✆ 986 404 196 Plaza Ribadavia. ❼ **Alfonso XII** *Priv.[8÷1]* €15 +2 €35 ✆ 986 400 153 r/ Alfonso XII, 22. ***Rua Isidoro Queimaliños Nº44*** •*P* **A Boa Estrela** *x6* €20-40 ✆ 663 292 196 *www.aboaestrela.com* **@Nº35** (corner Praza de Alfóndiga): ❺ **A Casa da Herba** *Priv.[24÷3]* €12-15 +2 €40-50 ✆ 644 404 074 *www.acasadaherba.com* **@Nº33** ❻ *Hs* **Rosa D'Abreu** *Priv.[6÷1]* €15-20 ✆ Rosa 688 422 701. **@Nº10** •**Casa Virginia** house sleeps 8+ from €87-€200 ✆ 660 589 515. **@Nº9** •*Apt.* **O Descansino Pilgrim Rooms** *x3* €30+ ✆ 666 260 651 *www.descansino.com* ***Calle Telmo Bernádez** (opp. Igrexa Santiago)* **@Nº11** ❽ **El Camino** *Priv.*[24÷3] €10-12 ✆ 650 963 676. **&@Nº15** ❾ **Santiago Apóstol** *Par.*[30÷2] €10 ✆ 627 748 802. ❿ **Avoa Regina** *Priv.[32÷2]* €15 ✆ 986 125 297 r/ Picota, 23. 666 260 651.

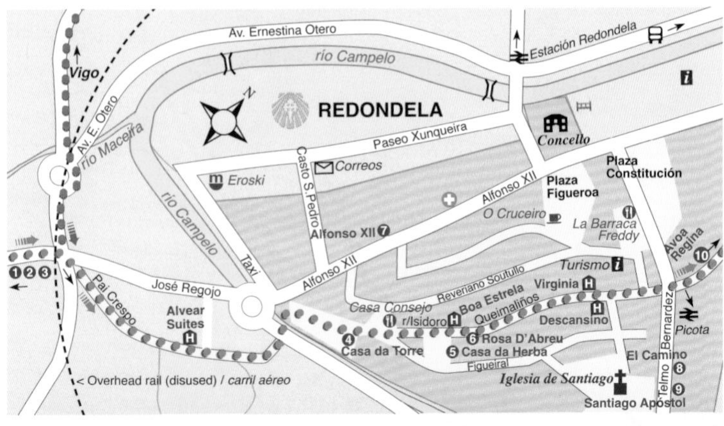

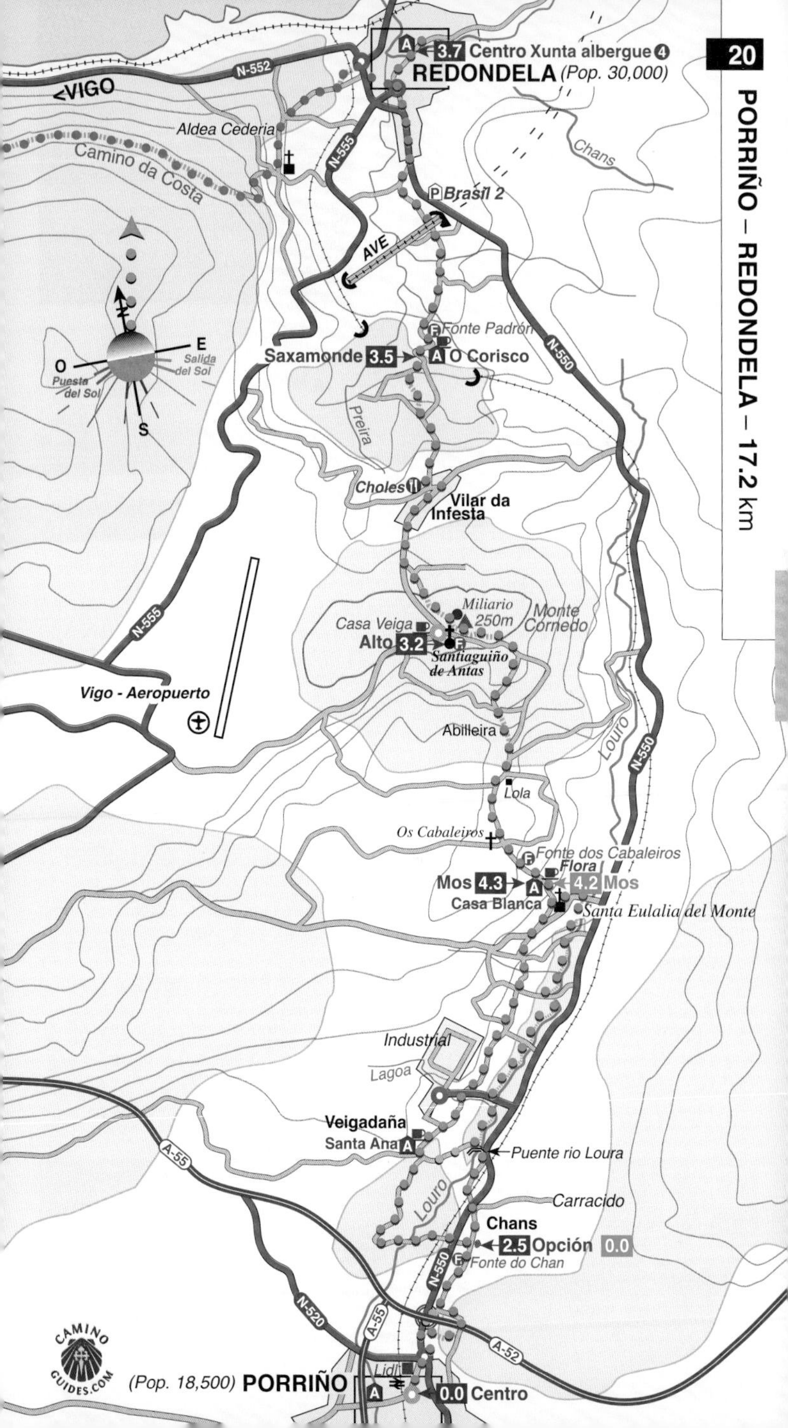

20
PORRIÑO – REDONDELA – 17.2 km
3.7 Centro Xunta albergue 4
REDONDELA (Pop. 30,000)
N-552
<VIGO
Aldea Cederia
Camino da Costa
N-555
Chans
Brasil 2
AVE
Fonte Padrón
Saxamonde 3.5
O Corisco
N-550
E
Salida del Sol
O
Puesta del Sol
S
Preira
Choles
Vilar da Infesta
Miliario 250m
Monte Cornedo
Casa Veiga
Alto 3.2
Santiaguiño de Antas
N-555
Vigo - Aeropuerto
Abilleira
Louro
N-550
Lola
Os Cabaleiros
Fonte dos Cabaleiros
Flora
Mos 4.3
4.2 Mos
Casa Blanca
Santa Eulalia del Monte
Industrial
Lagoa
Veigadaña
Santa Ana
Puente rio Loura
A-55
Louro
Carracido
Chans
2.5 Opción 0.0
Fonte do Chan
N-550
N-520
A-55
A-52
CAMINO GUIDES.COM
Lidl
(Pop. 18,500) PORRIÑO
0.0 Centro

Vella da Canicouva

## 21 REDONDELA – PONTEVEDRA

| | | |
|---|---|---|
| ||||||||||||| | 6.2 | *32%* |
| ═══ | 11.4 | *58%* |
| ▬▬▬ | 2.0 | 10% |
| **Stage Total** | **19.6** km *(12.2 ml)* | |

Total ascent **360**m ±½ *hr*

▲ Alto *m* Alto da Lomba 153 m *(502 ft)*

< A H > ➲Cesantes (Jumbolí) **3.1** km ➲Arcade **6.7** km

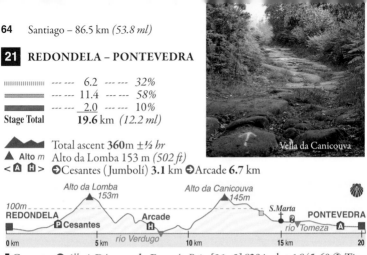

Alto da Lomba 153m · Alto da Canicouva 145m · 100m · REDONDELA · Cesantes · Arcade · río Verdugo · S.Marta · río Tomeza · PONTEVEDRA · 0 km · 5 km · 10 km · 15 km · 20

▌**Cesantes** ●*Alb.* **A Dárşena do Francés** *Priv.[31÷5]* €20 incl. *+1* €45-60 ✆ Tito 663 911 233. ***N-550:*** ☕/•*Hs* **Jumbolí** €33 ✆ 986 495 066 (+200m) ●*Alb.* **O Refuxio Jerezana** *Priv. [24÷3] €12-15 +2 €40* ✆ 601 165 977 *www.orefuxio.org* ● ***Cesantes* +2.5 *km*** •*H* **Antolín** €35+ ✆ 986 459 409 Paseo da Praia & 🍴•*P.* **O Regato** €20+ ✆ 653 794 740. •*CR* **A Vella** €25+ camiño da Vella, 4 ✆ 658 535 935 Jesús. ● ***Soutoxusto:*** •*H* **Santo Apóstolo** *x16* €28-47 ✆ 986 495 136 N-550 & ●*Alb.* **O Recuncho do Peregrino** *Priv. [12÷1]*+ €10 ✆ 617 292 598 Miguel.

■ **Arcade:** *Alb.*❶ **A Xesteira** *Priv. [24÷4]*+ €17+40 ✆ 659 746 772 adj. ❷ **A Filla do Mar** *Priv. [28÷5]* €20 ✆ 986 841 522 *www.albergueafilladomar.com* ❸ **Casa Calvar** *Priv. [26÷2]* €15 ✆ 986 401 754 *www.casacalvar.com* Campo da Feira, 1. •*H*** **Duarte** *x20* €25 ✆ 986 670 057 *www.hotelduarte.com* c/Lameriñas 8 adj. *Alb.*❹ **Lameiriñas** *Priv. [28÷1]* €10-12 ✆ 616 107 820. ❺ **O Lar de Pepa** *Priv. [12÷5]* €10 ✆ 986 678 006 c/Ribeiro 1. •*H*** **Isape** *x18* €30-45 ✆ 986 700 721 r/ Soutomaior,36 (+**0.8** km) opp. *Iglesia de Santiago.* •*H**** **Avenida** *x30* €24-36 ✆ 986 670 100 N-550 (+**0.4** km). ▌**Ponte Sampaio:** ❻*Alb.* **O Mesón** *Priv. [26÷1]* €12 *+2* €65 ✆ 687 462 398 (Tomás).

■ **PONTEVEDRA** ***Suburbs*** *afueras: EP-0002* •*CR* **Casa A Grade** €35 ✆ 696 306 129 Airbnb río Tomeza. •*Hs* **Peregrino** *x15* €35-45 ✆ 986 858 409 *www.hostalperegrino.es* opp. *Alb.*❶ **La Virgen Peregrina** *Asoc.[56÷2]* €8 ✆ 986 844 045 c/ Ramón Otero Pedrayo (adj. Estación de tren). ▌**Rua Gorgullón @Nº70** *Alb.*❷ **GBC** *[40÷2]* €20 ✆ 676 188 664 / **@Nº68** *Alb.*❸ **Aloxa** *Priv.[56÷2]* €12-15 ✆ 986 896 453 *[rear* •*H*** **Alda Estacion** ✆ 886 300 029 *Av.Pombal 76].* / @ **Nº16** *Alb.*❹ **Dpaso** *Priv.[20÷1]* €19 incl. ✆ 653 548 059 *www.dpasohostel.es* ***opp.*** •*H*** **Avenida** 986 857 784 Av.Pombal 46. adj.**@Nº10** *Alb.* ❺ **Nacama** *[42÷1]* €15 ✆ 644 929 243 *www.nacamahostel.es* r/Eduardo Pondal / r/Virxen do Camiño •*H** **Virgen del Camino** ✆ 986 855 900 @Nº55.

Pontesampaio *río Verdugo*

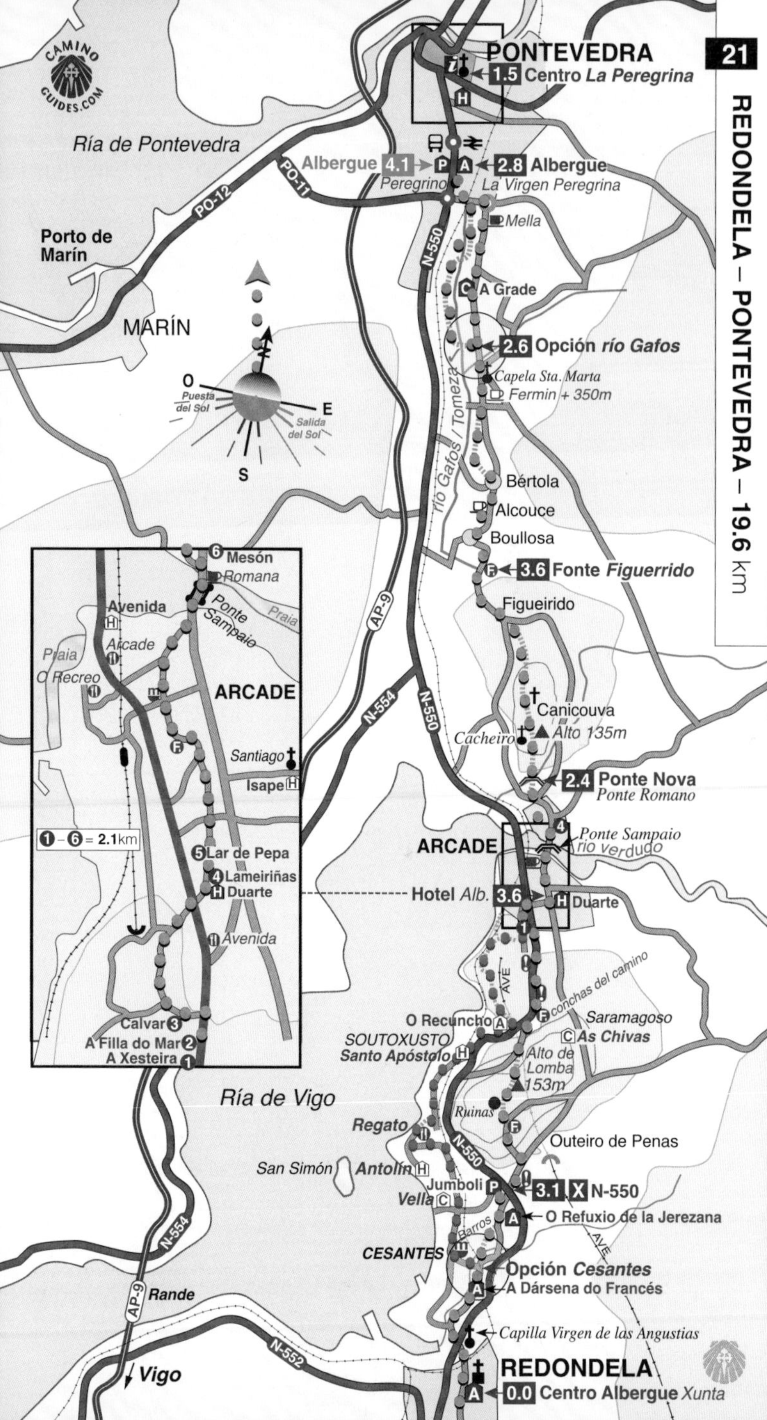

REDONDELA – PONTEVEDRA – 19.6 km
PONTEVEDRA
1.5 Centro La Peregrina
Ría de Pontevedra
PO-12
PO-11
Albergue 4.1
Peregrino
2.8 Albergue
La Virgen Peregrina
Mella
Porto de Marín
MARÍN
N-550
A Grade
2.6 Opción río Gafos
Capela Sta. Marta
Fermin + 350m
O
Puesta del Sol
E
Salida del Sol
S
río Gafos / Tomeza
Bértola
Alcouce
Boullosa
3.6 Fonte Figuerrido
Figueirido
6 Mesón
Romana
Ponte Sampaio
Praia
Avenida
Arcade
Praia
O Recreo
ARCADE
AP-9
N-554
Canicouva
Cacheiro
Alto 135m
Santiago
Isape
2.4 Ponte Nova
Ponte Romano
4
Ponte Sampaio
río Verdugo
ARCADE
1 – 6 = 2.1km
5 Lar de Pepa
4 Lameiriñas
Duarte
Hotel Alb. 3.6
Duarte
Avenida
AVE
conchas del camino
Calvar 3
A Filla do Mar 2
A Xesteira 1
O Recuncho
Saramagoso
As Chivas
SOUTOXUSTO
Santo Apóstolo
Alto de Lomba 153m
Ría de Vigo
Ruinas
Regato
Outeiro de Penas
San Simón
Antolín
Jumboli
3.1 X N-550
Vella
O Refuxio de la Jerezana
Barros
AVE
CESANTES
Opción Cesantes
A Dársena do Francés
Rande
N-552
Capilla Virgen de las Angustias
REDONDELA
Vigo
0.0 Centro Albergue Xunta

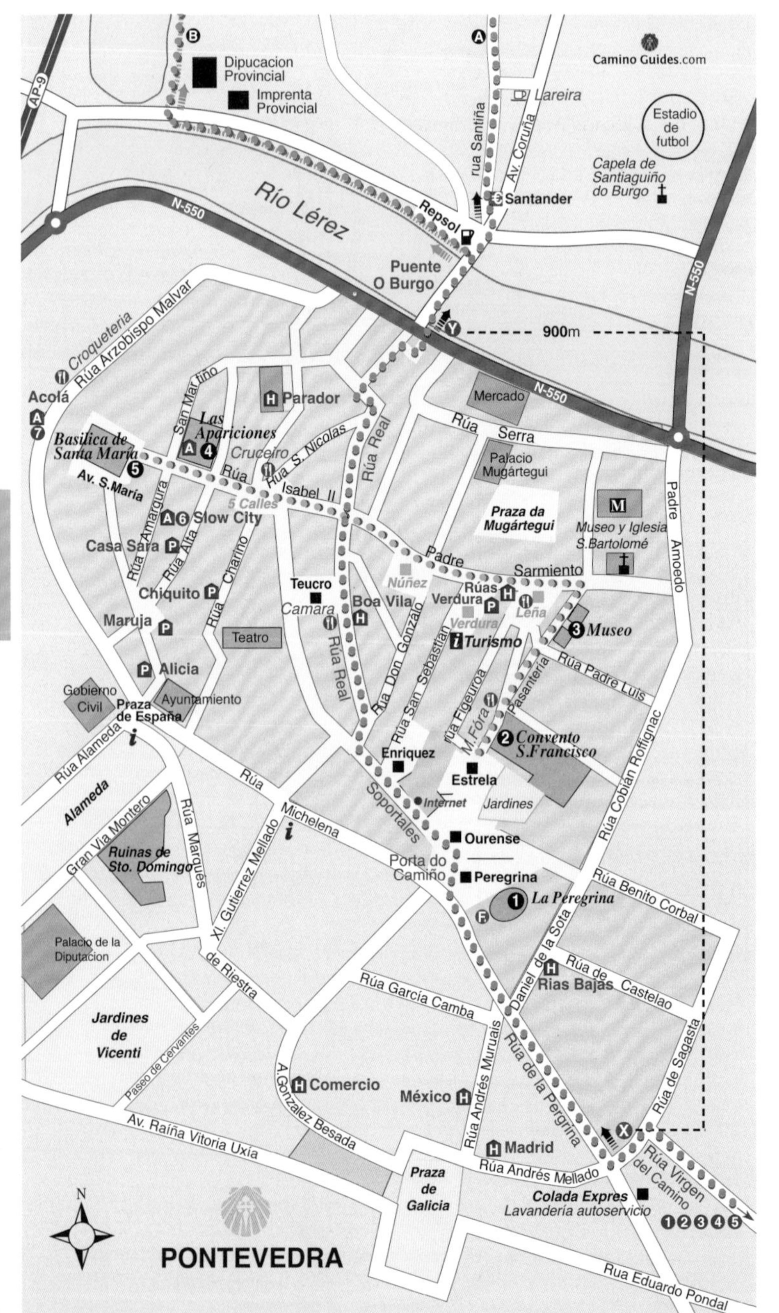

Dipucacion Provincial
Imprenta Provincial
Camino Guides.com
Lareira
Estadio de futbol
rua Santiña
Av. Coruña
Capela de Santiaguiño do Burgo
Santander
Río Lérez
Repsol
N-550
AP-9
Puente O Burgo
900m
Rúa Arzobispo Malvar
Croqueteria
Acolá
Parador
Mercado
Las Apariciones
San Martiño
Basilica de Santa María
Av. S.María
Cruceiro
Rúa S. Nicolas
Rúa Real
Rúa Serra
Palacio Mugártegui
Rúa Isabel II
5 Calles
Slow City
Praza da Mugártegui
Museo y Iglesia S.Bartolomé
Padre Amoedo
Casa Sara
Rúa Amargura
Rúa Alta
Rúa Charino
Padre Sarmiento
Teucro
Camara
Boa Vila
Núñez
Rúas
Verdura
Leña
Chiquito
Maruja
Museo
Teatro
Turismo
Rúa Padre Luis
Alicia
Rúa Don Gonzalo
Rúa San Sebastian
rúa Figeuroa
M. Fóra
Pasantería
Gobierno Civil
Praza de España
Ayuntamiento
Convento S.Francisco
Rúa Cobián Roffignac
Rúa Alameda
Enriquez
Estrela
Alameda
Rúa Michelena
Soportales
Internet
Jardines
Gran Via Montero
Rúa Marqués
Ruinas de Sto. Domingo
XI. Gutierrez Mellado
Ourense
Porta do Camiño
Peregrina
La Peregrina
Rúa Benito Corbal
Palacio de la Diputacion
Daniel de la Sota
Rias Bajas
Rúa de Castelao
de Riestra
Rúa García Camba
Jardines de Vicenti
Paseo de Cervantes
Rúa Andrés Muruais
Rúa de la Pergrina
Rúa de Sagasta
Comercio
México
A.Gonzalez Besada
Av. Raíña Vitoria Uxía
Madrid
Rúa Andrés Mellado
Rúa Virgen del Camino
Praza de Galicia
Colada Expres
Lavandería autoservicio
N
PONTEVEDRA
Rua Eduardo Pondal

**PONTEVEDRA** *Centro:* **Monumentos históricos: ❶ La Peregrina** *XVIII* Praza de la Peregrina. **❷ Convento de San Francisco** Praza de Ourense (*Xardíns de Castro San Pedro*). **❸ Museo de Pontevedra** ***Casa García Flórez*** *(Santiago peregrino XII)* Praza de Leña. **❹ Santuario da Aparicións** rua de Isabel II. **❺ Basílica de Santa María A Grande** *XVI* Av. Santa María.

**❶ Turismo** © 986 090 890 *Casa da Luz* Praza de Verdura. **Taxis** © 986 868 585. **▌Albergues: ❻ Slow City** ***Priv.[6÷1]*** €17 *+2* €40 © 631 062 896 (Jorge) r/ Amargura 5. *Alb.*❼ **Acolá *Priv.[16÷1]*** €17-20 © 678 680 758 r/Arzobispo Malvar 15 (adj.❺ Basílica). •*P.Alb.* **Verdura** *[12÷2]* €20 *+3* €50-80 Praza Verdura,4. **▌Hostels: *(€25-35)* •Fonda Chiquito** © 986 862 192 r/Charino 23. • **Casa O Fidel** © 986 851 234 pulpería Fidel, r/San Nicolás 7. •**Casa Alicia** *x4* © 986 857 079 Av. Santa Mariá 5, adj. Praza España & •*P*'**Casa Maruja** © 986 854 901 *www.pensioncasamaruja.com* •**Casa Sara** *x3* €20-40 Mercedes © 686 970 265 r/Alta 17. ***(€35-55)*** •*H*'' **Room** *(Vedra)* © 986 869 550 c/ Filgueira Valverde, 10. •*H*''' **Rias Bajas** © 986 855 100 c/ Daniel de la Sota Valdecilla, 7. •*H*'' **Ruas** *x22* €39-61 © 986 846 416 *www.hotelruas.net* c/ Sarmiento,20. •*H*'' **Boa Vila** *x10* €40-55 © 986 105 265 *www.hotelboavila.es* r/Real, 4. ***(€100+)*** •**Parador Casa del Barón** © 986 855 800 c/Barón, 19.

Praza da Leña

La Virgen de Peregrina

Rua Don Gonzalo – Rua Sarmiento

Santuario de la Virgen Peregrina

## 22 PONTEVEDRA – CALDAS de REIS

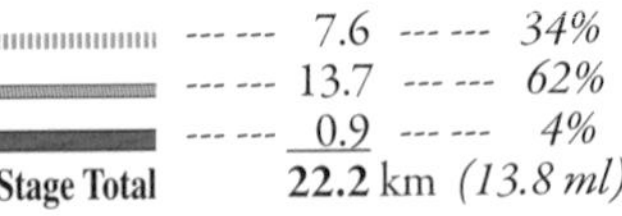

| | | |
|---|---|---|
| ----- ----- | 7.6 ----- ----- | 34% |
| ----- ----- | 13.7 ----- ----- | 62% |
| ----- ----- | 0.9 ----- ----- | 4% |
| **Stage Total** | **22.2** km *(13.8 ml)* | |

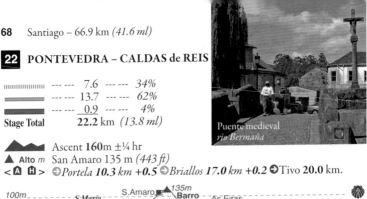

Puente medieval *río Bermaña*

Ascent **160**m ±¼ hr

▲ Alto *m* San Amaro 135 m *(443 ft)*

< A H > *Portela* ***10.3 km +0.5*** *Briallos* ***17.0 km +0.2*** Tivo **20.0** km.

**▌Portela:** *[+* ***0.6*** *km* ●*Alb.* **Portela** *Par.[****16÷2****]* €8 ✆ 655 952 805 Jorge *menú].* **▌Valbon** *[****+150****m]* ●*Alb.***Casa Javier** *[6÷1] €10 + x5* €35+ ✆ *617 058 348 menú.* **▌Briallos:** ●*Alb.* **Briallos** *Xunta.[27÷2]* €8 ✆ *986 536 194.* **▌Tivo:** ☕/●*Alb.* **Vintecatro** *Priv.[18÷4]* €15 *José* ✆ 696 582 014. **■ CALDAS DE REIS:**N-550 *Alb.*❶ **Alecer** *Priv.[12÷5]* €12 ✆ 630 105 582 Av. Doña Urraca. ❷ **A Queimada** *Priv. [72÷4]* €12 ✆ 986 189 194 *www.albergueaqueimada.com* adj. ❸ **Timonel** *Priv.[18÷1]*+ €8-10 ✆ 986 540 840. opp. •*H*****Acuña** *x62* €43-60 ✆ 986 540 010. *Apt.* •**Caldas de Reis** €50 ✆ 698 163 832 adj. •*H*****Dávila** *x26* €45-65 ✆ 986 540 012. **▌*Rua Real* @Nº19** •*H******Via XIX** *x6* €75+ ✆ 986 541 425. **@Nº49** •*H*****Roquiño** €70+ ✆ 886 251 020 c/ Fornos,8. •*H*******Pousada Real** *x11* €55+ ✆ 986 189 910 *www.hotelpousadareal.com* Opp. **@Nº63** *Alb.*❹ **Albor** *Priv.[35÷5]* €15-18 ✆ 600 351 157 *www.alberguealbor.com* ❺ **Caldas de Reis** *Priv.[26÷4]* €814 ✆ 683 605 335 c/ Campo de la Torre 1 adj. •*Hs.* **Torre** €25 ✆ 6656 648 309. •*P.***Río Umia.** €15-30. •*P.* **La Moderna** €20-30 ✆ José 986 540 312. ❻ **Agarimo** *Priv.[17÷5]*+ €18+€35 ✆ 677 333 703. •*H*****Lotus** *x30* €35-55 ✆ 670 466 063 reception *Café Lotus.* ❼ **O Cruceiro** *Priv.[34÷8]* €14 ✆ 986 540 165 *www.ocruceiroalbergue.com* also adj. •*H*****O Cruceiro** €30-52. ❽ **Celenis** *Priv. [44÷1]* €16 ✆ 613 116 894 r/Silgadas, 16. *[+****300****m* •*H*** **Sena** €35 ✆ *986 540 596].* •*P* **As Burgas** *x6* €25-35 ✆ 615 033 297 **@Nº21.** •*P* **Caldas** *x3* €18-48 ✆ Adolfo 607 020 402 **@Nº19** also owns •*H* **Villa Galicia** €20-45 Rua Gaioso, 16. 986 540 012.

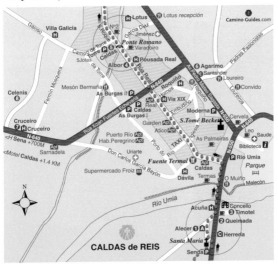

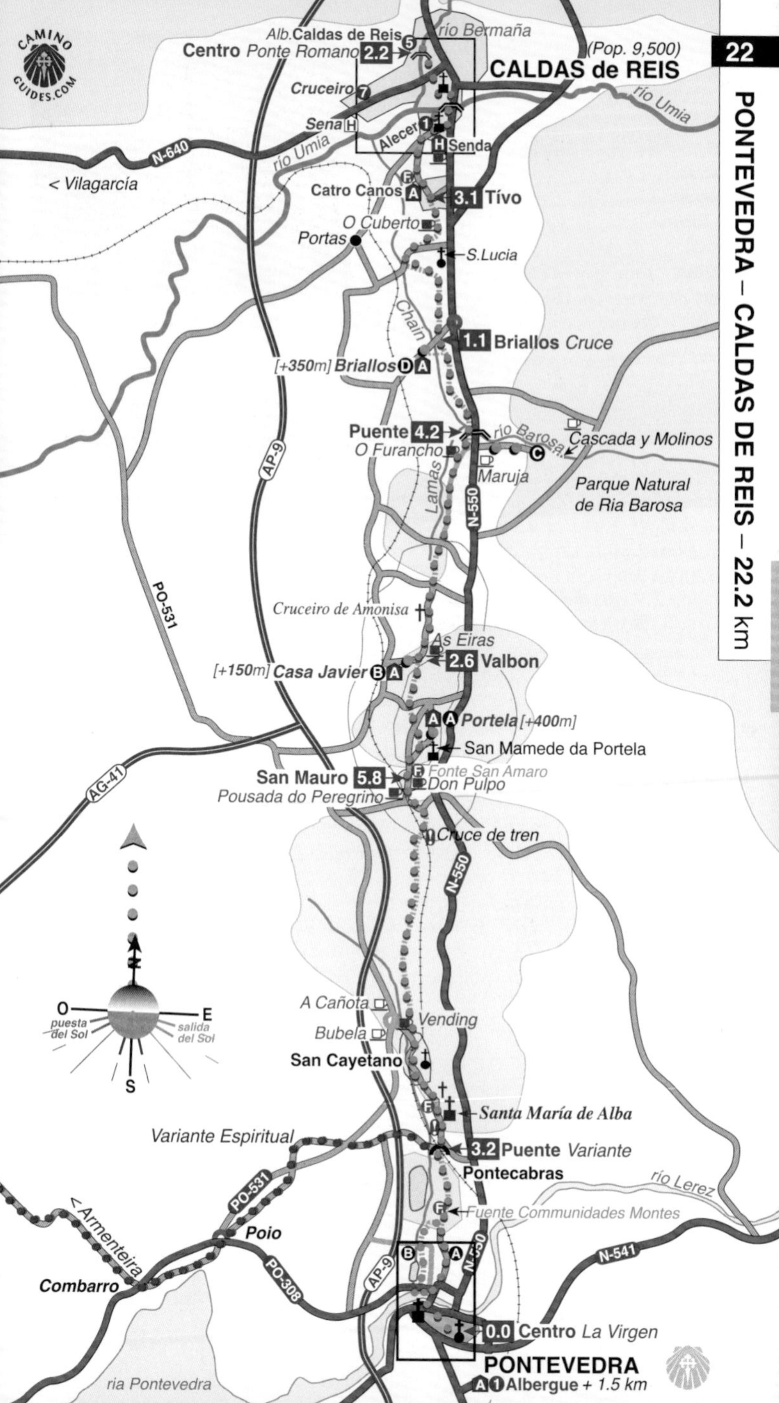

22
PONTEVEDRA – CALDAS DE REIS – 22.2 km
CAMINO GUIDES.COM
Alb. Caldas de Reis 5
río Bermaña
Centro Ponte Romano 2.2
(Pop. 9,500)
CALDAS de REIS
Cruceiro 7
río Umia
Sena H
Alecer 1
H Senda
N-640
río Umia
< Vilagarcía
F
Catro Canos A
3.1 Tívo
O Cuberto
Portas
S.Lucia
Chain
1.1 Briallos Cruce
[+350m] Briallos D A
Puente 4.2
río Barosa
Cascada y Molinos
O Furancho
C
Maruja
Parque Natural de Ria Barosa
Lamas
N-550
AP-9
PO-531
Cruceiro de Amonisa
As Eiras
2.6 Valbon
[+150m] Casa Javier B A
A A Portela [+400m]
San Mamede da Portela
San Mauro 5.8
F Fonte San Amaro
Don Pulpo
Pousada do Peregrino
AG-41
Cruce de tren
N-550
O
E
puesta del Sol
salida del Sol
S
A Cañota
Vending
Bubela
San Cayetano
F
Santa María de Alba
Variante Espiritual
3.2 Puente Variante
Pontecabras
río Lerez
PO-531
F Fuente Communidades Montes
< Armenteira
Poio
B
A
N-550
N-541
PO-308
AP-9
Combarro
0.0 Centro La Virgen
PONTEVEDRA
A 1 Albergue + 1.5 km
ria Pontevedra

## 23 CALDAS DE REIS – PADRÓN

| | | | | |
|---|---|---|---|---|
| --- --- | 8.4 | --- --- | *44%* |
| --- --- | 10.3 | --- --- | *54%* |
| --- --- | 0.4 | --- --- | *2%* |
| **Stage Total** | **19.1** km *(11.9 ml)* | | |

Santiaguiño do Monte

Total ascent **260**m ±½ *hr*

▲ **Alto** *m* Cortiñas 165m *(525 ft)*

< A H > ➲Carracedo **1.0** km ➲Valga **9.6** ➲Pontecesures **16.0** ➲*Herbón* ***16.0 +3.1***

200m Corgullón 165m Carrecedo O Pino Valga 100m CALDAS S.Miguel Pontecesures PADRÓN río Bernesga río Valga Herbón río Ulla 0 km 5 km 10 km 15 km

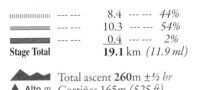

▮ **Carracedo** ***N-550***: *Esperón [****+200****m •P* **Sevi** €20-40 ✆ 986 534 260*]*. ▮ **Valga +*200 m*** ●*Alb.* **Valga** *Xunta.[****78****÷3]* €8 ✆ 638 943 271 (Mª Teresa) ▮ **Pontecesures:** ●*Alb.* **Pontecesures** *Xunta.[****54****÷2]* €5 ✆ 699 832 730 Estrada Escolas, Lugar Infesta. •**A Casa do Rio** *x15* €40+ ✆ 986 557 575 *www.hotelacasadorio.es c/Dr. Victor García.* ▮ ***Herbón 2.9** km:* ●*Alb.***Herbón** *Conv.[****22****÷1]* €-donativo Monasterio Franciscano (AGACS). ■ **PADRÓN**: ❶***Turismo***: ✆ 646 593 319 Av. Compostela ***Pedronía*** *certificado. Alb.*❶ **Camiño do Sar** *Priv. [****20****÷1]* €13-15 ✆ 618 734 373. +100m ❷ **O Pedrón** *Priv. [****43****÷3]* €13 ✆ 881 121 266 ❸ **O da Meiga** *Priv. [****50****÷1]* €13+ ✆ 639 994 048 r/Noirmoutier 16 +200m ❹ **Flavia** *Priv.[****22****÷5]* €12 +7 €25-38 ✆ 981 810 455 Campo da Feira ❺ **A Barca de Pedra** *Priv.[****22****÷5]* €15-18. ✆ Rebeca 679 199 770 *www.abarcadepedra.es* c/ Vidal Cepeda 6. ***Centro***: ❻ **Rossol** *Priv.[****18****÷1]* €13-16 ✆ 981 810 011 *www.alberguerossol.com Plaza Rodriguez Cobián.* ❼ **Murgadán** *Priv. [****32****÷1]* €14 *x3* €45 ✆ 638 298 437 r/Corredoira da Barca, 5. ❽ **Corredoiras** *Priv.[****18****÷1]* €14-17 ✆ 981 817 266 c/ Corredoira da Barca, 10. ❾ **D'Camiño** *Priv. [****15****÷3]* €15+ ✆ 615 046 723 *www.baralberguedcamino.com* r/Peregrinos, 3. ❿ **Padrón** *Xunta.[****46****÷1]* €8 ✆ 673 656 173. **Hoteles:** •*H*****Chef Rivera** *x17* €35-46 +🍴 ✆ 981 810 413 *www.chefrivera.com* r/ Enlace Parque. •*P*** **Casa Cuco** ✆ 981 810 511 Av. Compostela. •*P******Jardín** *x7* €35+ ✆ 981 810 950 *www.pensionjardin.com* adj. Jardín Botanico /Av. da Estación. •*H*****Rosalia** *x21* €25-40 ✆ 981 812 490 *www.hotelrosalia.es* r/ Maruxa Villanueva *(adj. estación de tren & museo de Rosalia de Castro)*. •*P*****Grilo** *x9* €19-39 ✆ 981 810 607 Av. Camilo José Cela (N-550).

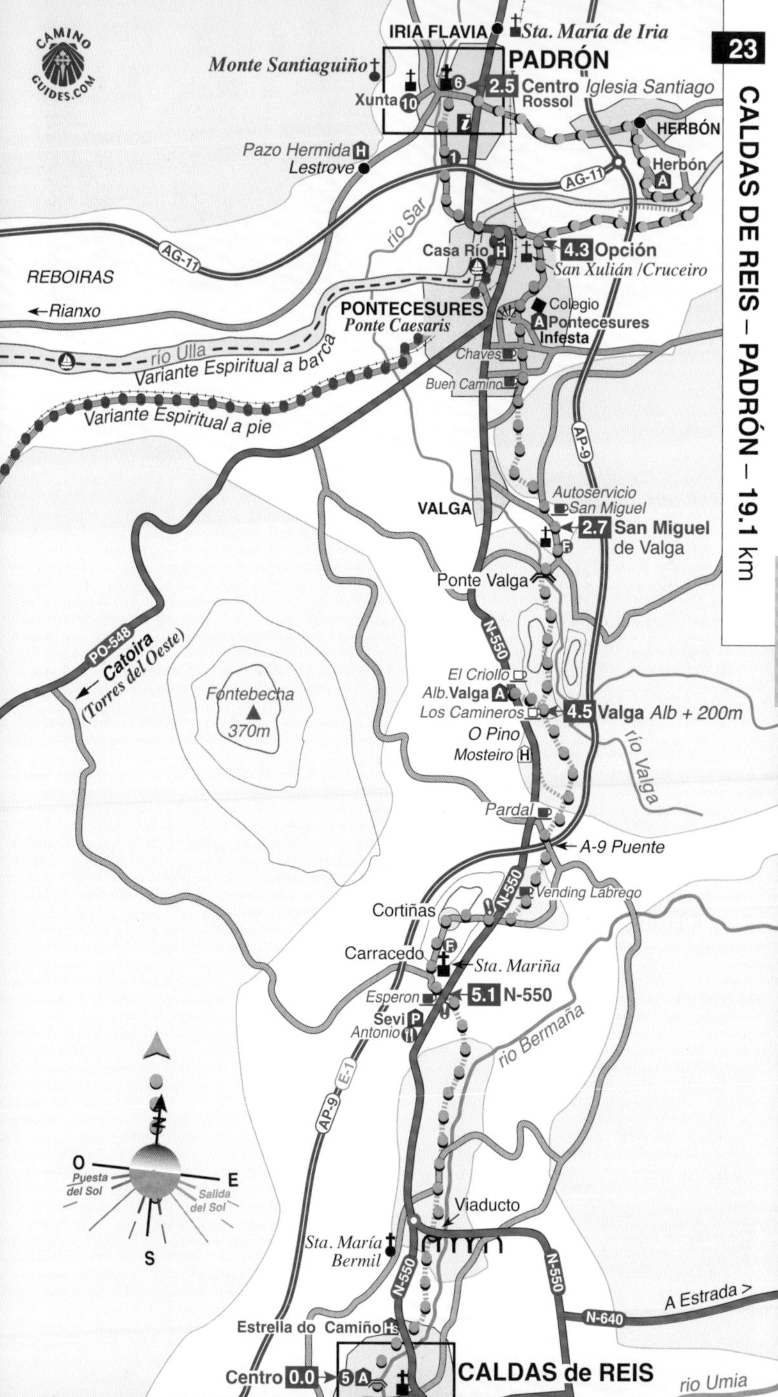
CAMINO GUIDES.COM
CALDAS DE REIS – PADRÓN – 19.1 km
IRIA FLAVIA
Sta. María de Iria
PADRÓN
Monte Santiaguiño
6
2.5 Centro Iglesia Santiago
Rossol
Xunta 10
HERBÓN
Herbón
Pazo Hermida
Lestrove
1
AG-11
río Sar
Casa Río
4.3 Opción
San Xulián /Cruceiro
REBOIRAS
←Rianxo
PONTECESURES
Ponte Caesaris
Colegio
Pontecesures
Infesta
Chaves
Buen Camino
río Ulla
Variante Espiritual a barca
Variante Espiritual a pie
AP-9
Autoservicio
San Miguel
VALGA
2.7 San Miguel de Valga
Ponte Valga
N-550
PO-548
Catoira
(Torres del Oeste)
Fontebecha
370m
El Criollo
Alb. Valga
Los Camineros
4.5 Valga Alb + 200m
O Pino
Mosteiro
río Valga
Pardal
A-9 Puente
Vending Labrego
Cortiñas
Carracedo
Sta. Mariña
Esperon
5.1 N-550
Sevi
Antonio
río Bermaña
AP-9 E-1
O
Puesta del Sol
E
Salida del Sol
S
Viaducto
Sta. María Bermil
A Estrada >
N-640
Estrella do Camiño
Centro 0.0
5
CALDAS de REIS
río Umia

## 24 PADRÓN – SANTIAGO

| | | |
|---|---|---|
| | 8.2 | *32%* |
| | 13.8 | *54%* |
| | 3.6 | *14%* |
| **Stage Total** | **25.6** km *(15.9 ml)* | |

Total ascent **340**m ±½ *hr*
▲ Alto *m* Monte Agro 260m *(853 ft)*
<Ⓐ Ⓗ> ➲Iria **1.0.** ➲Escravitude **6.4** km.
➲Picaraña **9.5** km. ➲Faramello / Teo **10.8** km. ➲Miladoiro **18.6** km.

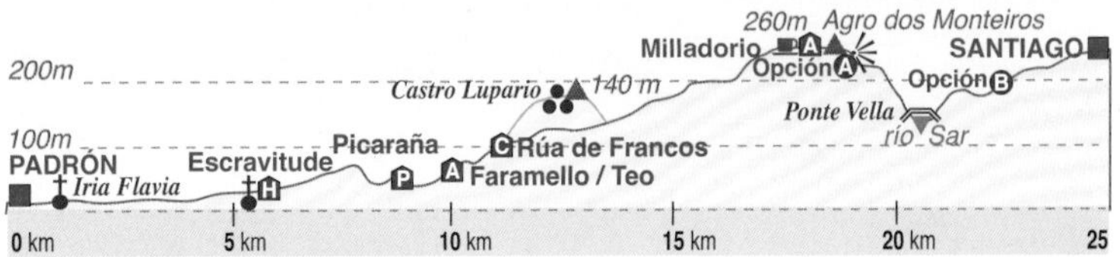


▮ **Padron / Iria Flavia:** ● *Alb.* **Sant-Yago** *Priv.[10÷1]* €15 ✆ 686 961 793 Trav. Iría, 131. ● *Alb.* **Cruces de Iria** *Priv.[16÷2]* €12 ✆ 981 811 723 Hector adj. ***Iglesia Santa María***. N-550 •*H**** **Scala** *x190* €40-75 ✆ 981 811 312. ▮ **Escravitude:** *[+0.2 km •CR **Meixida** x5 €45-60 ✆ 981 811 113].* 🍴/● *Alb.* **O Lagar de Jesús** €16 ✆ José 881 060 708 *www.olagardejesus.com* + garden *jardín* adj. Iglesia •*H** **Grande da Capellania** *x7* €46-51 ✆ 981 509 854. 🍴/•*P** **Buen Camino** €15-30 ✆ 616 228 775. ● *Alb.* **Cruces Inn** *Priv.[22÷2]* €13+ ✆ 646 596 573 Lugar de Cruces. ▮ **Picaraña Abaixo.** *[+0.4 km N-550* 🍴/•***HK*** *x5* €18-35 ✆ *981 803 210].* ▮ **Areal** *[+200m* •*P** **Areal** *x3* €15-24 ✆ 650 194 760. ▮ **Picaraña:** •*P**** **Pividal** *&* 🍴. *Milagrosa / Alfonso x14* €25-40 ✆ 981 803 119. •*P** **Glorioso** *x6* €20-33 ✆ 981 803 181. ▮ **Faramello** 🍴/❶ **La Calabaza del Peregrino** *Priv.[36÷4]* €14 ✆ 981 194 244. ***Teo +150m*** *Alb.* ❷ **Teo** *Xunta.[20÷2]+ €8.* ▮ **Parada de Francos** •*CR* **Parada de Francos** *x10* €60-80 ✆ 981 538 004 *www.paradadefrancos.com* opp. 🍴 *Carboeiro. [**I Biduido: Raíces +0.4** km: •**Casa do Cruceiro** x7 €62-69 ✆ 981 548 596].* ▮ **Milladoiro** ● *Alb.* **Milladoiro** *Priv.[62÷3]* €14 ✆ 981 938 382 c/Buxo,6 adj. ☕ *Joy **+300m** Rúa Pardiñeiros / Rúa Anxeriz •H** **Payro** €40 ✆ 881 975 176].*

■ **SANTIAGO** see next page *próxima página...*

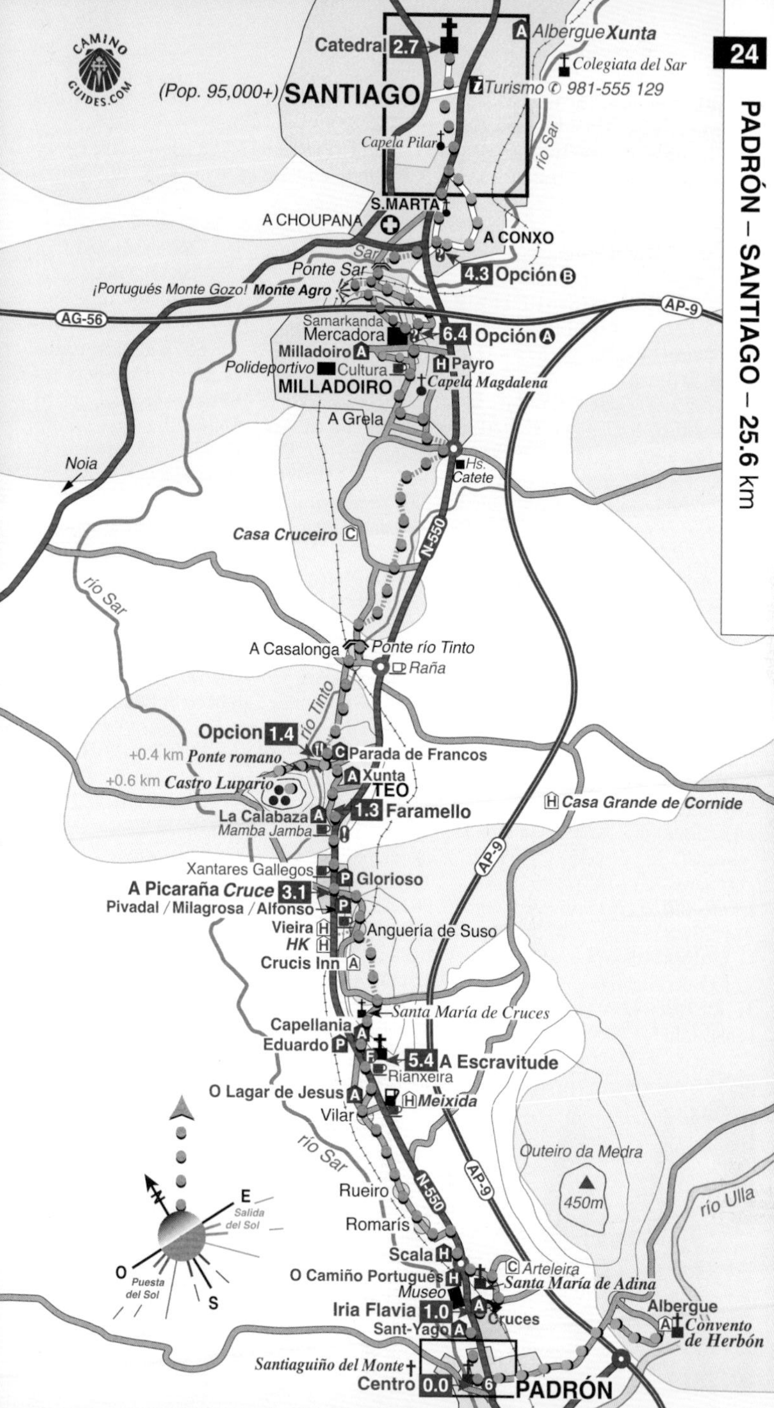
24
PADRÓN – SANTIAGO – 25.6 km
CAMINO GUIDES.COM
Catedral 2.7
(Pop. 95,000+) SANTIAGO
Albergue Xunta
Colegiata del Sar
Turismo © 981-555 129
Capela Pilar
río Sar
S.MARTA
A CHOUPANA
A CONXO
Sar
Ponte Sar
4.3 Opción B
¡Portugués Monte Gozo! Monte Agro
AG-56
AP-9
Samarkanda
Mercadora
6.4 Opción A
Milladoiro
Payro
Polideportivo
Cultura
MILLADOIRO
Capela Magdalena
A Grela
Hs. Catete
Noia
Casa Cruceiro
N-550
río Sar
A Casalonga
Ponte río Tinto
Raña
río Tinto
Opcion 1.4
+0.4 km Ponte romano
Parada de Francos
+0.6 km Castro Lupario
Xunta
TEO
La Calabaza
1.3 Faramello
Mamba Jamba
Casa Grande de Cornide
AP-9
Xantares Gallegos
Glorioso
A Picaraña Cruce 3.1
Pivadal / Milagrosa / Alfonso
Vieira
HK
Anguería de Suso
Crucis Inn
Santa María de Cruces
Capellania
Eduardo
5.4 A Escravitude
Rianxeira
O Lagar de Jesus
Meixida
Vilar
río Sar
Outeiro da Medra
N-550
AP-9
450m
río Ulla
Rueiro
Romarís
E
Salida del Sol
O
Puesta del Sol
S
Scala
Arteleira
O Camiño Portugués
Santa María de Adina
Museo
Iria Flavia 1.0
Cruces
Albergue
Convento de Herbón
Sant-Yago
Santiaguiño del Monte
Centro 0.0
6
PADRÓN

● **Turismo** *Centro*: r/ Vilar 63 © 981 555 129 *May-Oct: 09:00-19.00 (winter 17:00)*
● **Tur Galicia** Praza de Mazarelos (Tues-Sat)10:00 - 17:00.
● **Pilgrim Services** Rúa Nova 7 (adj. catedral) © 912 913 756 left luggage €3.
● **Laundromat:** 09:00-22:00 **SC18** Rúa San Clemente 18 © 673 753 869.

■ *Albergues: **€10-€20** (depending on season / beds per dormitory)* ❶–❾ *(Camino Francés).* ▮ **Rúa Concheiros Nº48** ❿ **El Viejo Quijote** *Priv.[20÷2]* © 881 088 789. **Nº36** ⓫ **La Estrella** *Priv.[24÷6]* © 617 882 529. **Nº10** ⓬ **Porta Real** *Priv.[20÷6]* © 633 610 114. ▮ **Belvís +500***m* ⓭ **Seminario Menor** *Conv. [173÷12]+81* © 881 031 768 *www.alberguesdelcamino.com* Av. Quiroga Palacios *(see photo >)*. ▮ **c/ S.Clara** ⓮ **La Salle** *Priv.[84÷14]* © 981 585 667 ▮ **c/ Basquiños Nº45** ⓯ **Basquiños** *Priv.[8÷1]* © 661 894 536 **Nº67** ⓰ **Meiga Backpackers** *Priv.[28÷5]* © 981 570 846. ■ **Centro Histórico:** ⓱ **O Fogar de Teodomiro** *Priv.[20÷5]+* © 981 582 920 Plaza de Algalia de Arriba 3. ⓲ **The Last Stamp** *Priv.[62÷10]* © 981 563 525 r/ Preguntorio 10. ⓳ **Azabache** *Priv.[20÷5]* © 981 071 254 c/Azabachería 15. ⓴ **Km.0** *Priv.[50÷10]* (€ 18-26) © 881 974 992 *www.santiagokm0.es* r/ Carretas 11 (new renovation by pilgrim office) ㉑ **Blanco** *Priv.[20÷2]+* +€35-55 © 881 976 850 r/ Galeras 30. ㉒ **Mundoalbergue** *Priv. [34÷1]* © 981 588 625 c/ San Clemente 26. ㉓ *Roots & Boots (closed temp.) Priv. [48÷6] © 699 631 594 r/Campo Cruceiro do Galo.* ■ ***Otros:*** ㉔ **La Estación** *Priv. [24÷2]* © 981 594 624 r/ Xoana Nogueira 14 (adj. rail station **+2.9** km). ㉕ **Compostela Inn** *Priv.[120÷30]+* © 981 819 030 off *AC-841 (adj. H Congreso +6.0 km).* ■ ***Hoteles €30–60:*** •*Hs* **Santiago** © 608 865 895 r/Senra 11. •*Hs* **Moure** © 981 583 637 r/dos Loureiros. •*H* **Fonte S. Roque** © 981 554 447 r/ do Hospitallilo 8. •*Hs* **Estrela** © 981 576 924 Plaza de San Martín Pinario 5. •*Hs* **San Martín Pinario** *x127* © 981 560 282 *www.hsanmartinpinario.com* Praza da Inmaculada. •**Pico Sacro** r/San Francisco 22 © 981 584 466. •*H** **Montes** © 981 574 458 *www.hotelmontes.es* r/ Raíña 11. **Rúa Fonseca Nº1** •*P* **Fonseca** © 603 259 337. **Nº5** •*Hs* **Libredon** 981 576 520 & •*P* **Barbantes /Celsa** ©981 583 271 on r/ Franco 3. **Rúa Vilar Nº8** •*H****Rua Vilar © 981 519 858. **Nº17** •*H*** **Airas Nunes** © 981 569 350. **Nº65** •*Hs*** **Suso** © 981 586 611 *www.hostalsuso.com*. **Nº76** •*Hs* **Santo Grial** © 629 515 961. •*Hs* **Alameda** © 981 588 100 San Clemente 32. ▮ ***€60–90:*** •*H* **A Casa Peregrino** © 981 573 931 c/ Azabachería. •**Entrecercas** © 981 571 151 r/Entrecercas. **Porta de Pena Nº17** •*H* **Costa Vella** © 981 569 530 (+Jardín) **Nº5** •*P* **Casa Felisa** © 981 582 602 (+Jardín). •**MV Algalia** © 981 558 111 Praza Algalia de Arriba 5. •*H****Pazo De Altamira © 981 558 542 r/ Altamira, 18. ▮ ***€100+*** •*H**** **San Francisco** Campillo de San Francisco © 981 581 634. •*H**** **Hostal de los Reyes Católicos** Plaza Obradoiro © 981 582 200.

○ ***Centro Histórico:*** ❶ Convento de Santo Domingo de Bonaval XIII^th^ *(panteón de Castelao, Rosalía de Castro y museo do Pobo Galego).* ❷ Mosteiro de San Martín Pinario XVI^th^ *y museo* ❸ Pazo de Xelmirez XII^th^ ❹ Catedral XII^th^ –XVIII^th^ *Portica de Gloria, claustro, museo e tesouro* ❺ Hostal dos Reis Católicos XV^th^ *Parador* ❻ Pazo de Raxoi XVIII^th^ *Presendencia da Xunta* ❼ Colexio de Fonseca XVI^th^ *universidade y claustro* ❽ Capela y Fonte de Santiago ❾ Casa do Deán XVIII^th^ *Oficina do Peregrino (original).* ❿ Casa Canónica *museo Peregrinaciónes.* ⓫ Mosteiro de San Paio de Antealtares XV^th^ *Museo de Arte Sacra.* ⓬ S.Maria Salomé XII^th^.

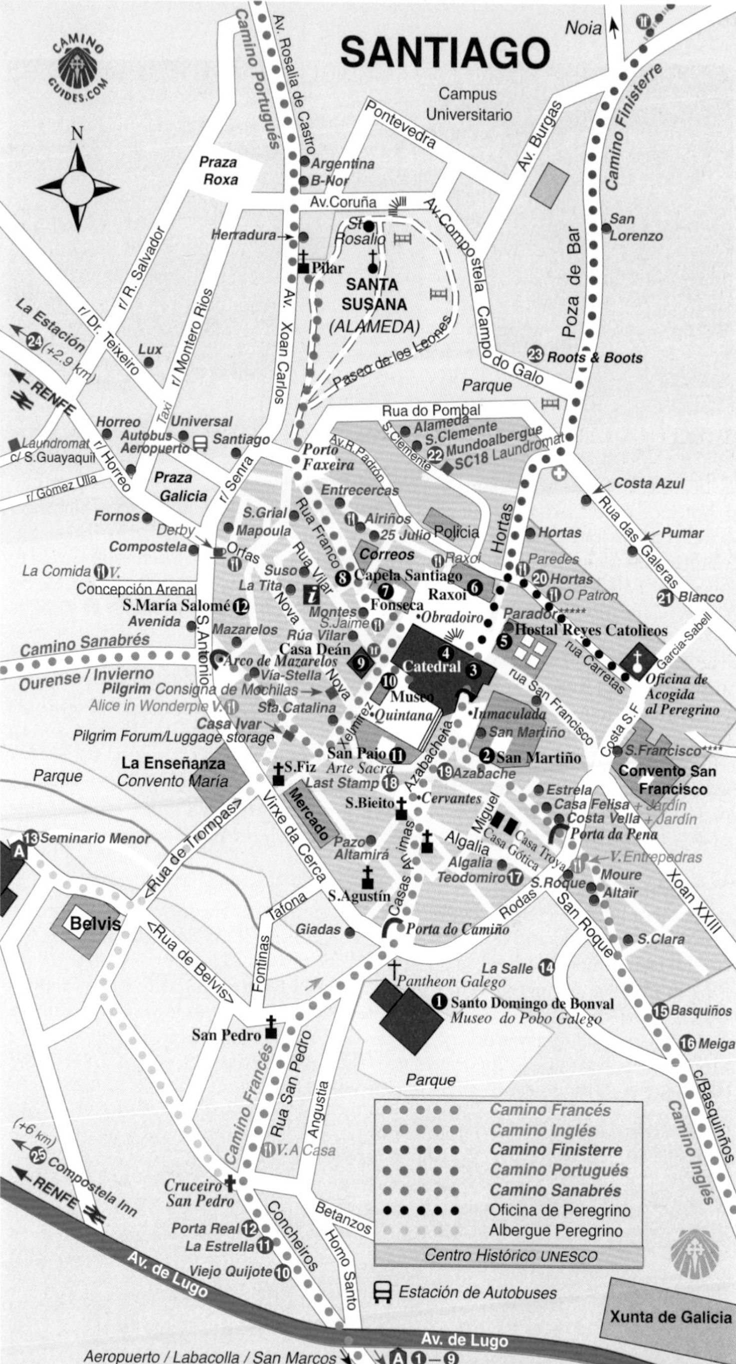
SANTIAGO
CAMINO GUIDES.COM
N
Noia
Campus Universitario
Pontevedra
Av. Burgas
Camino Finisterre
Camino Portugués
Av. Rosalia de Castro
Argentina
B-Nor
Praza Roxa
Av.Coruña
Av.Compostela
San Lorenzo
Herradura
St. Rosalio
Pilar
SANTA SUSANA
(ALAMEDA)
Av. Xoan Carlos
Paseo de los Leones
Campo do Galo
Poza de Bar
r/ R. Salvador
r/ Dr. Teixeiro
r/ Montero Rios
La Estación
24 (+2.9 km)
RENFE
Lux
23 Roots & Boots
Parque
Rua do Pombal
Horreo
Universal
Autobus Aeropuerto
Santiago
Taxi
Laundromat
c/ S.Guayaquil
r/ Horreo
r/ Gómez Ulla
Praza Galicia
r/ Senra
Porto Faxeira
Av.R.Padrón
S.Clemente
Alameda
S.Clemente
22 Mundoalbergue
SC18 Laundromat
Costa Azul
Entrecercas
S.Grial
Rua Franco
Airiños
25 Julio
Policia
Hortas
Hortas
Pumar
Rua das Galeras
Fornos
Derby
Mapoula
Compostela
Orfas
Correos
Raxoi
Paredes
La Comida V.
Suso
Rua Vilar
8 Capela Santiago
20 Hortas
21 Blanco
Concepción Arenal
La Tita
7 Fonseca
6 Raxoi
O Patron
S.María Salomé 12
Nova
Montes
S.Jaime
Obradoiro
Parador *****
Avenida
Mazarelos
Rúa Vilar
5 Hostal Reyes Catolicos
Garcia-Sabell
Camino Sanabrés
S. Antonio
Casa Deán
4
rua Carretas
Arco de Mazarelos
9
Catedral 3
Oficina de Acogida al Peregrino
Ourense / Invierno
Vía-Stella
10
rua San Francisco
Pilgrim Consigna de Mochilas
Museo
Alice in Wonderpie V.
Sta.Catalina
Xelmírez
Quintana
Inmaculada
Costa S.F
Casa Ivar
San Martiño
Pilgrim Forum/Luggage storage
Azabachería
Costa Vella
S.Francisco****
La Enseñanza
San Paio 11
2 San Martiño
Convento San Francisco
Parque
Convento María
S.Fiz
Arte Sacra
19 Azabache
Last Stamp 18
Estrela
Rua de Trompas
Virxe da Cerca
Mercado
S.Bieito
Cervantes
Miguel
Casa Felisa + Jardín
Costa Vella + Jardín
13 Seminario Menor
Porta da Pena
A
Pazo Altamirá
Casas Ánimas
Casa Gótica
Casa Troya
V. Entrepedras
Algalia
Algalia
Moure
Teodomiro 17
S.Roque
Altaïr
Xoan XXIII
Belvis
S.Agustín
Rodas
San Roque
Tafona
Rua de Belvis
Giadas
Porta do Camiño
S.Clara
Fontinas
La Salle 14
Pantheon Galego
1 Santo Domingo de Bonval
Museo do Pobo Galego
15 Basquiños
San Pedro
16 Meiga
Parque
Camino Francés
Rua San Pedro
Angustia
c/Basquiños
Camino Inglés
(+6 km)
25 Compostela Inn
V.A Casa
RENFE
Cruceiro San Pedro
Porta Real 12
La Estrella 11
Viejo Quijote 10
Concheiros
Betanzos
Homo Santo
Av. de Lugo
Av. de Lugo
Camino Francés
Camino Inglés
Camino Finisterre
Camino Portugués
Camino Sanabrés
Oficina de Peregrino
Albergue Peregrino
Centro Histórico UNESCO
Estación de Autobuses
Xunta de Galicia
Aeropuerto / Labacolla / San Marcos
A 1 – 9

Camino da Costa

## PORTUGUESE COASTAL ROUTES: ❶ *Caminho da Costa* ❷ *Senda Litoral*

2 beautiful routes now being discovered by an increasing number of pilgrims. Choice of routes between the 'main' ***Caminho da Costa*** ● ● ● ● which runs parallel to the coast along a mix of country roads and woodland paths. This is the traditional way with familiar yellow arrows and a sense of camarderie so beloved of pilgrims. **273.2** km from Porto Cathedral to Santiago – *[**325.2** km to include the camino Espiritual (**288.3** km if taking the boat from Arousa to Padron* ● ● ● ●*].*

The ***Senda Litoral*** ● ● ● ● basically follows the shoreline although difficulties arise where a path ends at an impassable obstruction such as a river estuary. A new pedestrian bridge at Foz de Neiva *(part of the Ecovia Litoral Norte improvements)* has greatly improved this route. It has more of a tourist vibe and wind-blown sand can obliterate paths and signs and it is difficult to walk in high winds. Where the *senda litoral* connects easily with the main *Caminho da Costa* a tick ✓ suggests a reasonable optional alternative for adventurous pilgrims who have a good sense of orientation; otherwise it makes sense to stick with the main waymarked route.

The addition of these routes is not welcomed by everyone. There are those with investment in the *Camino Central* who are concerned at the increasing popularity of the coastal route and claiming it has no historical basis... and those along the coastal route who endeavour to promote it as their own. But no one need worry for the camino is generous in its embrace and nobody has a monopoly on the caminos which are there to help us create a more loving and inclusive world. Gratitude is due to the voluntary work of pilgrim associations and individuals who have promoted & waymarked the routes over the years so that today we need only the barest information to get us safely to our destination.

Senda Litoral

Luis Freixo based in Vigo has been waymarking routes along the coast for many years and his detailed maps can be found at ***caminador.es*** Another useful offline mapping app. for the area can also be downloaded from ***maps.me*** In these early formational years of the coastal routes feedback helps towards their improvement. Thanks to David Hamilton for the warning of the danger of crossing the río Nieve in flood and Ian Omnet for permission to reproduce the photograph above. Spate rivers are very unpredictable and we need to assess risks honestly in these situations. While the maps are not designed for going 'off route' in this case steps were retraced to the road bridge that was fortuitously included on the map which allowed rejoining the waymarked coastal route at Santiago do Neiva...

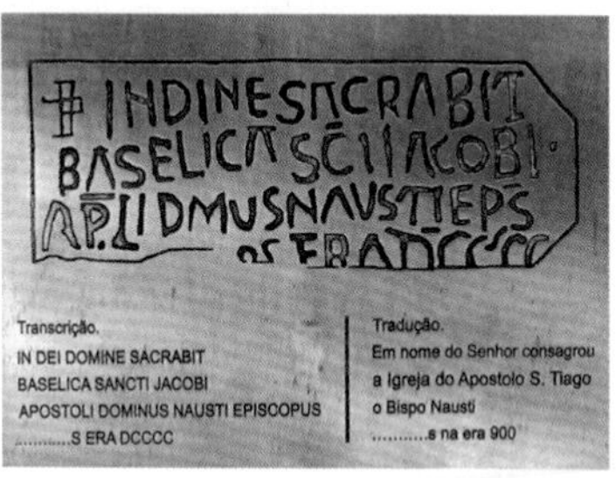


...and this neatly answers those who argue that the coast is not an authentic camino. When renovating the *Igreja Santiago de Castelo do Neiva (see p.210)* directly on on the *Camino da Costa* the earliest evidence ever found in Portugal commemorating Santiago was unearthed. A stone carved in the year 900 and dedicated to Sancti Jacobi was found in the wall. Placed there within a few short decades from the discovery of the great saint's tomb and it lies there still... don't miss it!

Little else needs to be said. It is the experience of walking these lovely routes that will inform. Check *updates at* ***www.caminoguides.com*** for the most recent corrections and additions.

*Bom caminho...*

# 15a VILA do CONDE – ESPOSENDE
## *Póvoa de Varzim* *Marinhas*

Campos de Masseira

| | | |
|---|---|---|
| --- --- | 5.6 --- --- | *23%* |
| --- --- | 18.2 --- --- | *75%* |
| --- --- | 0.4 --- --- | *02%* |
| **Stage Total** | **24.2** km *(15.0 ml)* | |

Total ascent **440**m ±¾ *hr*
▲ Alto *m* Apulia 20m *(65 ft)*
< A H > ➲Póvoa Varzim **3.9** km ➲Praia S. Andrés **9.2** km
➲*Praia Estela* ***14.8 km +0.5*** ➲*Apulia* ***17.8 km +0.6*** ➲*Fão* ***21.5 km +0.2***

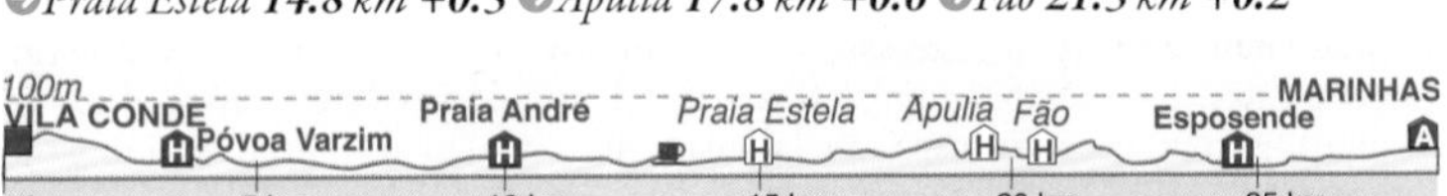


**Camino da Costa:** ● ● ● ● ▌**Póvoa de Varzim: Turismo:** Praça Marquês de Pombal ✆ 252 298 120. ●*Alb.***São José de Ribamar** *Par.[36÷4]* €-donativo ✆ 252 622 314 Av. Mouzinho de Albuquerque Nº32 & @Nº54 •*H*** **Avenida** *x22* €38-48 ✆ 252 683 222. •*Hs* **Sardines & Friends** *[6÷1]* €14 +*7* €35 ✆ 962 083 329 r/Ponte 4. •*H*** **Luso Brasileiro** *x62* €40+ 252 690 710 r/ Dos Cafés 16. •*H**** **Grande Hotel** *x88* €65+ ✆ 252 290 400 Largo do Passeio Alegre, 20. ▌**A Ver O Mar:**•*H* **Santo Andre** *x80* €58± ✆ 252 615 666 Av. de S. André. ▌**Aguçadoura** *[+**350**m •CR.* **Aguçadoura** *x4* €15pp ✆ 252 010 865 *r/ Guizos 120].* ▌**Apúlia:** *(see senda Litoral below).* ▌**Fão:** •*Hs* **Spot** *[8÷2]* €14 +*6* €30+ ✆ 934 324 426 r/ dos Veigas 14. •*Alb./Pousada)* **Foz do Cavado** €20± ✆ 253 982 045 Alameda Bom Jesus. *[**+1.2** km **Ofir** incl. •H**** **Parque do Rio** €40-80 ✆ 253 981 521 www.parquedorio.pt ].*

■ **ESPOSENDE:** ●*Alb.* **Sleep&Go** *[12÷2]* €11 +*2* €36 ✆ 932 005 800 Av. São Martinho. •*H** **Mira Rio** €40± ✆ 253 964 430 r/ Ponte D. Luis Filipe. ***Centro:*** ❶*Alb.***Eleven** *Priv.[12÷2]* €16 + *x1* €45 ✆ 962 651 485 + *menú* www.hosteleleven.pt r/Narciso Ferreira, 57. Concello ***Turismo*** ✆ 253 960 100. ❷ *Hs* **Esposende** *x5* €20-55 ✆ 932 832 818 r/ Conde Agrolongo **Nº29** &@**Nº22** ❸ *Hs* **InnEsposende Sports** *[6÷1]* €14 +*10* €29-44 ✆ 932 466 542 www.innesposende.com ❹ *Hs* **Eskama** *x5* €30-€45 ✆ 916 952 098 Largo Dr. Fonseca Lima 4. ❺ *H**** **Zende** *x25* €30+ ✆ 253 969 090 Av. Dr. Henrique Barros Lima 23. ❻ **Clube Pinhal da Foz** €45-55 ✆ 253 961 098 r/Pinhal da Foz. ❼ *H**** **Suave Mar** *x88* €44-50 ✆ 253 969 400.

**Senda Litoral:** ● ● ● ● *[**+300**m Campismo **Rio Alto (Orbitur)** €8-16+ ✆ 252 615 699.* ▌**Apúlia:** *[**+600**m **Av. Praia Nº45*** •*H**** **Apulia Praia** *x44* €40+ ✆ 253 989 290.***Nº67*** ●*Alb.***Santiago da Costa** *Priv.[9÷4]* €12 ✆ 961 885 803.

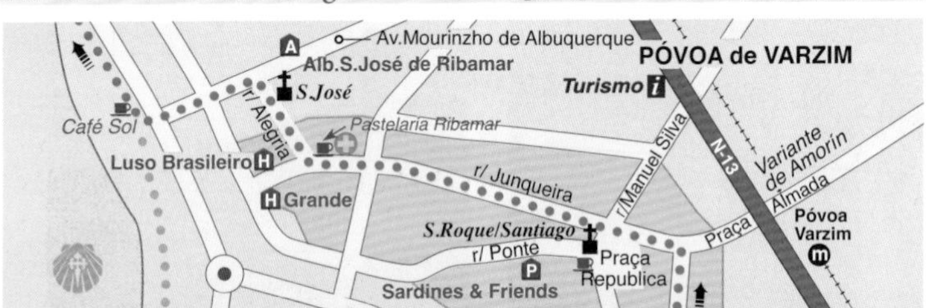

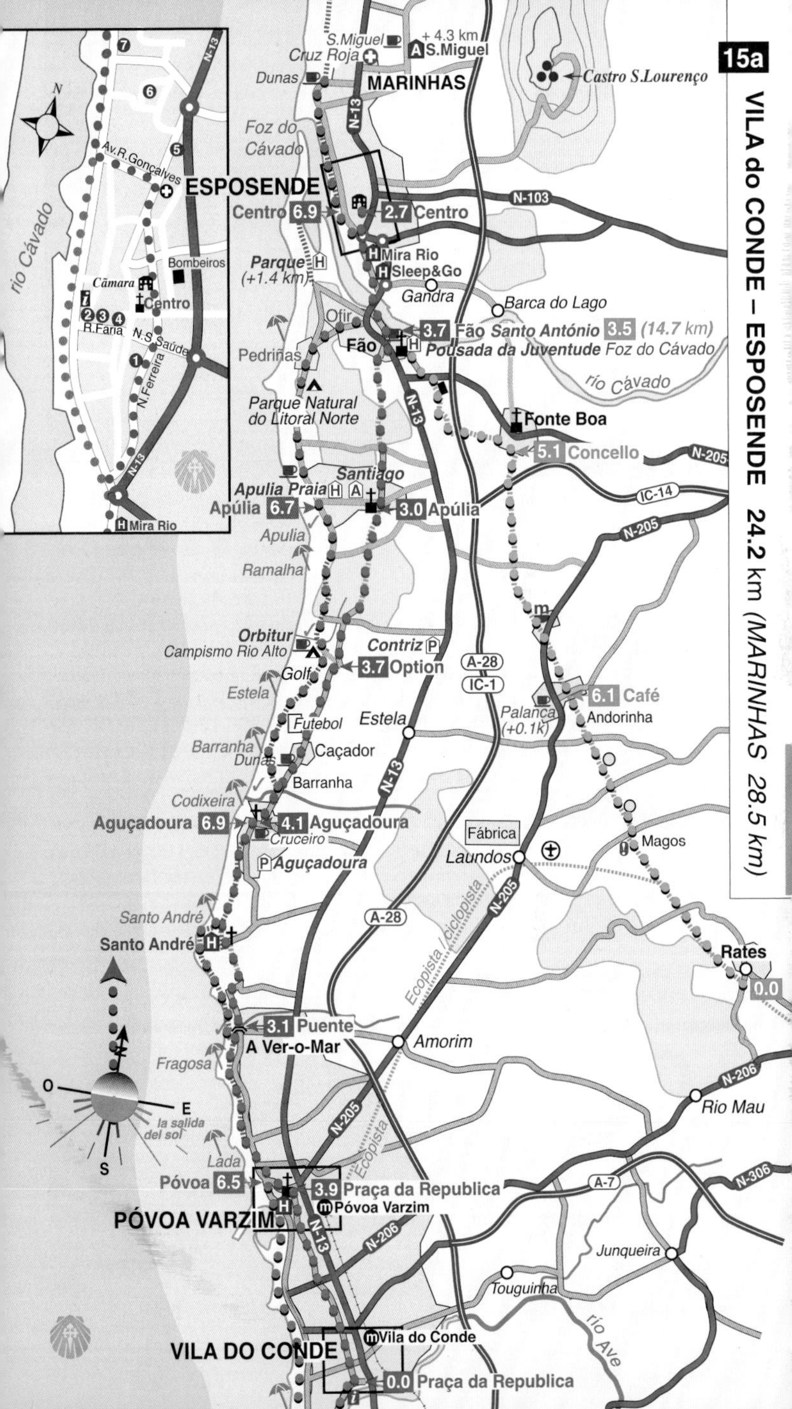

15a
VILA do CONDE – ESPOSENDE 24.2 km (MARINHAS 28.5 km)
S.Miguel
+ 4.3 km
S.Miguel
Cruz Roja
Dunas
MARINHAS
Castro S.Lourenço
Foz do Cávado
N-13
N-103
ESPOSENDE
Centro 6.9
2.7 Centro
Mira Rio
Sleep&Go
Parque
(+1.4 km)
Gandra
Barca do Lago
Ofir
3.7 Fão Santo António 3.5 (14.7 km)
Fão
Pousada da Juventude Foz do Cávado
Pedriñas
río Cávado
Parque Natural do Litoral Norte
Fonte Boa
5.1 Concello
N-205
Santiago
Apulia Praia
Apúlia 6.7
3.0 Apúlia
IC-14
Apulia
Ramalha
Orbitur
Campismo Rio Alto
Contriz
Golf
3.7 Option
A-28
IC-1
Estela
Futebol
Estela
6.1 Café
Palanca
(+0.1k)
Andorinha
Barranha
Caçador
Dunas
Barranha
Codixeira
Aguçadoura 6.9
4.1 Aguçadoura
Cruceiro
Aguçadoura
Fábrica
Laundos
Magos
Ecopista / ciclopista
Santo André
Santo André
Rates
0.0
3.1 Puente
A Ver-o-Mar
Amorim
Fragosa
O
E
S
la salida del sol
N-206
Rio Mau
Lada
Póvoa 6.5
3.9 Praça da Republica
Póvoa Varzim
PÓVOA VARZIM
Ecopista
A-7
N-306
Junqueira
Touguinha
río Ave
Vila do Conde
VILA DO CONDE
0.0 Praça da Republica
rio Cávado
Av.R.Gonçalves
Bombeiros
Câmara
Centro
R.Faria
N.S Saúde
N.Ferreira
Mira Rio

## 16a ESPOSENDE – VIANA do CASTELO

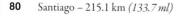

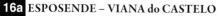

| | | | | |
|---|---|---|---|---|
| ‖‖‖‖‖‖‖ | --- --- | 7.8 | --- --- | *30%* |
| ▬▬ | --- --- | 15.6 | --- --- | *61%* |
| ▬▬ | --- --- | 2.2 | --- --- | *9%* |
| **Stage Total** | | **25.6** km | *(15.9 ml)* | |

Total ascent **300**m *±½ hr*

▲ Alto *m* Vila do Conde 8m *(853 ft)*

< A H > ➲Chafé **17.5** km ➲Darque **22.9** km.

*Río Nieve*

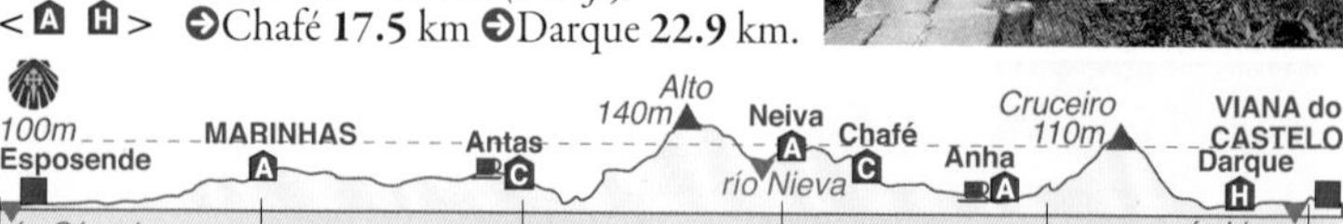


**COSTA: ▌Antas:** •*CR* **Antas** *x4* €17pp+ ✆ 962 319 979 r/Barão Maracanã, 4. **▌Castelo do Neiva:** ●*Alb.* **Don Nausti** *Mun.[20÷2]* €6-10 *+1* €20 ✆ 962 471 251. **▌Chafé:** •*CR.* **Campo do Forno** *x3* €28 ✆ 934 122 695. •*CR* **Casa da Reina** €60+ ✆ 258 351 882 c/Pardinheiro, 122. **▌Anha:** *[+500m* ●*Alb.* ***Carolina*** *Priv. [8÷2]* €15 ✆ *969 004 514 Av. 9 Julho].* •*H**** **Paço d'Anha** €30-60 ✆ 258 322 459 **▌Darque:** ***N-13*** •*H*****Cais** *x23* €40+ ✆ 258 331 031. •*P.* **Don Augusto** €40 ✆ 258 322 491. **▌VIANA DO CASTELO:** ●*Alb.* **São João da Cruz** *Conv.[26÷2]* €6-10 +€25 ✆ 258 822 264 r/Carmo 1. ●**Pousada de Juventude** *Mun.[40÷2]* €11-13 ✆ 258 838 458 r/Limia. •*H*****Do Parque** *x120* €30+ ✆ 258 828 605 Praça da Galiza. •*H*****Calatrava** *x15* €50+ ✆ 258 828 911 r/Manuel Fiúza 157. ***Centro:*** ➊**Turismo** ***Praça da Liberdade*** ✆ 258 098 415. •*H******Fábrica do Chocolate** *x18* €80+ ✆ 258 244 000 r/Gontim, 70. •*Hs* **Enjoy Viana** *x8* €30-39 ✆ 914 668 475 r/M.Romaria, 53. •*H*****Laranjeira** *x30* €52+ ✆ 258 822 261 r/ Cândido dos Reis 45. •*P.***Dona Emília** *x6* €38+ ✆ 917 811 392. •*Hs* **Senhora do Carmo** *x10* €23-35 ✆ 927 811 099 r/Grande 72. •*H**** **Margarida Da Praça** €57+ ✆ 258 809 630 Largo 5 Outubro Nº58 & @ Nº68 •*H*****Jardim** *x20* €40-50 ✆ 258 828 915. •*Hs* **Avenida** *x10* €23-35 ✆ 927 811 099 Av. Combatentes, 49. **▌*Santuário de Santa Luzia*** ●*Alb.* **S.Lucia** *Conv.[38÷5]* €15-25 ✆ 258 823 173 •*H******Pousada** *x80* €120+! ✆ 2588 00 370.

**LITORAL: ▌Belinho ▲ Os Belinhenses** ✆ 933 612 546. **▌Amorosa** •*H*****Areias Claras** €35+ ✆ 258 351 014 r/Praia. **▌Darque ▲ Orbitur** €8+ ✆ 258 322 167 r/ Diogo Álvares adj. •*H******FeelViana.** •*H*****Cais** *x46* €120+! ✆ 258 330 330.

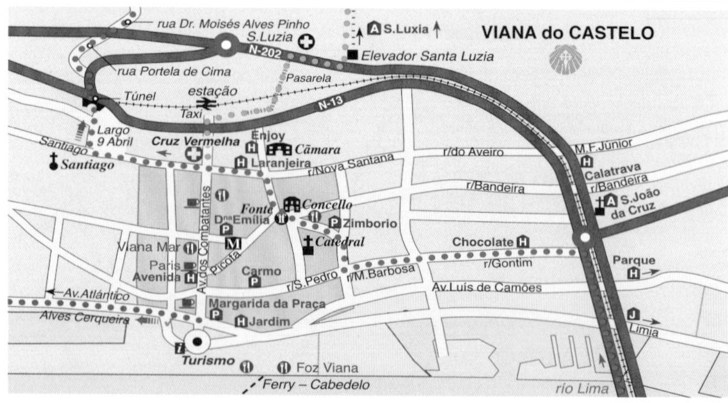

25.2 -v- 25.6 Centro 2.0
VIANA do CASTELO
Ferry
río Lima
(Summer Verano) Ferry
Cabedelo
Darque 3.8
3.2 Darque
Cais Nova
Don Augusto
Cais Postilhão
A-28
N-13
GR.1
INATEL
N-13-3
Darque
Cabedelo
Cruceiro
Alto 113m
Rodanho 3.2
pasarela
Paço d'Anha
Carolina
Rodanho
O Nosso (Terraza)
3.4 Anha
Ecovia Litoral Norte
GR.1
Noval
N-13
Casa Reina
Forno
Amorosa 2.6
Av.Atlántico
3.5 Chafé
Areias Claras
Ecovia Litoral Norte >
Snr. Crasto
Campo de fútbol
Calvario
S.Romão
A-28
Praia de Castelo de Neiva 3.0
Pedra Alta
Junqueira
Joana
Porto de Pesca
Ladeiras
N-13-3
GR.1 Palheiros de Sargaço
Castelo de Neiva
Igreja 1.8
Santiago de Castelo do Neiva IX
PR.14
Ecovia Litoral Norte >
D.Nausti
Guadalupe
N-13
PR.13
Moldes
Foz de Neiva
3.6 Pasarela
N-103
Pasarela !Nueva! 4.4
Quim
Reguenga
río Neiva
Guilheta
Foz do Neiva
Os Belinhenses
Laje
PR.1
Antas
Rua Painça
Ecovia Litoral Norte >
Kabul
Antas
Torre
S.Amaro
Gabriela
O
Puesta del sol
E
Salida del sol
S
Belinho
Rua Praia
Escola Belinho
3.8 Belinho 'Bom Caminho'
Outeiro
Barros
Mar
Cruzeiro da Praia 4.1
A-28
Praia S.Bartolomeu
Rio deMinhos
Aguas do Norte
Praia Río Minhos
MARINHAS
Barzin
CEPÂES
4.3 Albergue S.Miguel
Ecovia Litoral Norte >
Castro S.Lourenço
N-13
Ecovia Litoral 2.3
Dunas
< rua Agrela
CAMINO GUIDES.COM
Suave Mar
ESPOSENDE
N-103
Centro 0.0
0.0 Centro

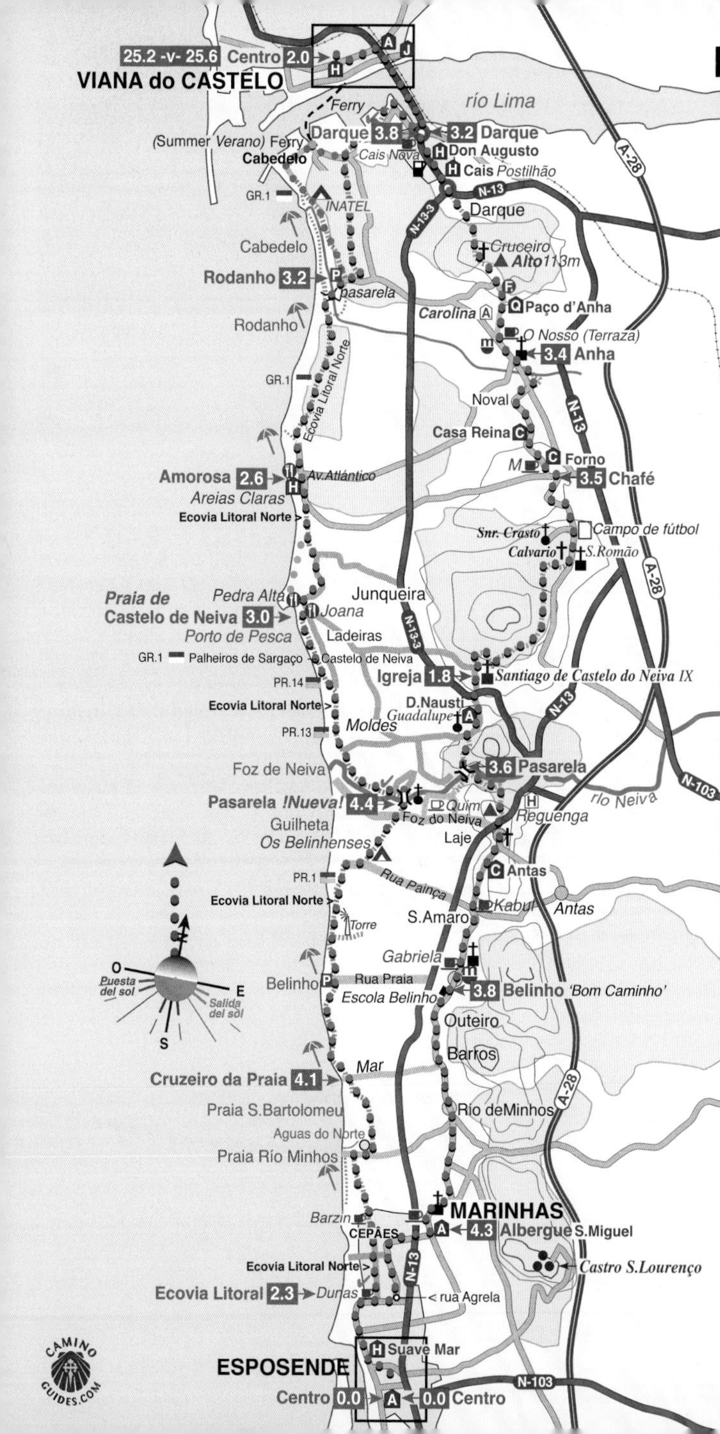

## 17a VIANA do CASTELO – CAMINHA

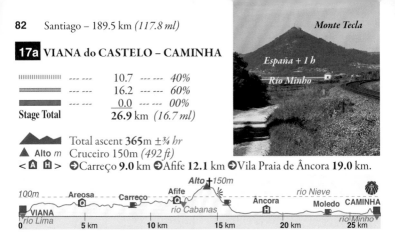

| | | | |
|---|---|---|---|
| | 10.7 | 40% | |
| | 16.2 | 60% | |
| | 0.0 | 00% | |
| **Stage Total** | **26.9** km *(16.7 ml)* | | |

Total ascent **365**m ±¾ *hr*

▲ Alto *m* Cruceiro 150m *(492 ft)*

< A H > ➲Carreço **9.0** km ➲Afife **12.1** km ➲Vila Praia de Âncora **19.0** km.

● Costa: ▌**Carreço:** *[N-13* ***+400m*** *•Alb/CR* **Rada** *Priv.[6÷1]* €14 *+3* €30+ ✆ *966 211 969 Tv. Vinha Nova].* •*CR* **Nato** *x8* €65-75 incl. ✆ 258 834 041 r/Moreno 130. ●*Alb.***Casa do Adro** *Priv.[20÷2]* €14 *+2* €40 ✆ 966 557 617. ●*Alb.***Casa do Sardão** *[20÷2]* €12 Hugo Lopes ✆ 961 790 759 Av. do Paço 769. ▌**Vila Praia de Âncora:** ❹*H*** **Meira** *x54* €60-70 ✆ 258 911 111 r/ 5 Outubro. ❶*Apt.***Quinta Vila Praia** *x20* €40+✆ 258 950 050 ***r/Cândido dos Reis*** @**Nº23** &@**Nº32** ❷**Baixinho** *x8* €60. ❸**Quim Barreiros** *x26* €40 ✆ 258 959 100 ***Av. Ramos Pereira*** *(beach front)* @**Nº115** & @**Nº 353** ❺*Alb.Hs* **D'Avenida** *[18÷3]* €10 *+20* €40 ✆ 258 407 764 ❻*P.* **Farol do Portinho** *x6* €24 ✆ 258 911 542 r/Laureano Brito, 82. 🍴/❼*P** **Abrigo Portinho** *x7* €30 ✆ 258 911 577 r/Pescadores 22. ▌**Moledo:** •*P.* **Xicotina** *x3* €20-40 ✆ *912 279 889.* •*Hs* **Caracóis e Borboletas** *x6* €35 ✆ 258 722 104. •*Apt* **Aldeamento do Camarido** €65 ✆ 258 722 130.

■ **CAMINHA:** ***Agonia*** •*P* **Litos** *x6* €30+ ✆ 938 452 300. ●*Alb.* **Bom Caminha** *[14÷2]* €15 *+3* €45 ✆ 963 528 441 (Vani). ❶***Turismo*** ✆ 258 921 952. Ferry: ❶ Principal ✆ 986 611 526 / ❷ **Taxi Mar** (Marco) ✆ 915 955 827. ❸ **Mário Gonçalves** ✆ 963 416 259. •*H**** **Design & Wine** *x23* €50+ ✆ 258 719 040 & •*Hs* **Caminha** *x4* €45+ ✆ 968 939 660 •*P* **Galo D'Ouro** *x10* €30-40 ✆ 258 921 160 r/Corredoura 15. •*H* **Muralha** *x7* €50 ✆ 258 728 199 r/Barão S.Roque 69. •*P** **Arca Nova** *Priv.[20÷1]* €14+*12* €20-40 ✆ 935 390 402 Largo Sidónio Pais. ●*Alb.* **Caminha** *Asoc.[30÷2]* €6 ✆ 914 290 431 Av Padre Pinheiro.

● ***Litoral:*** •*H*** **Compostela** *x41* €40 ✆ 258 981 465 Afife N-13 ***+300m].*** **Caminha: +2.4** km •*Camping* **Orbitur** €8-14 ✆ 258 921 295 Praia do Foz do Minho. **+1.5** km N-13. •*H**** **Porta do Sol** *x110* €100+ ✆ 258 710 360.

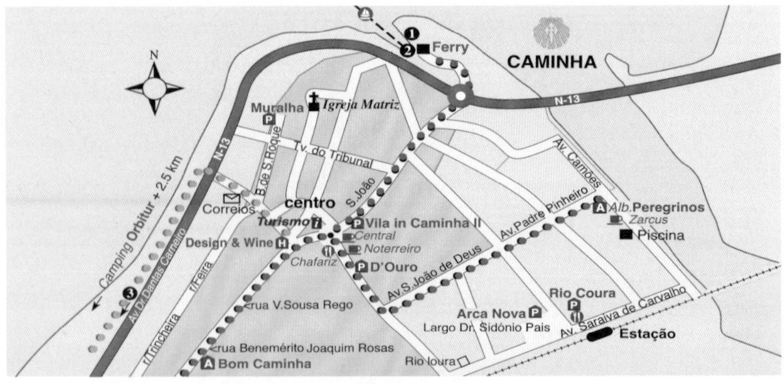

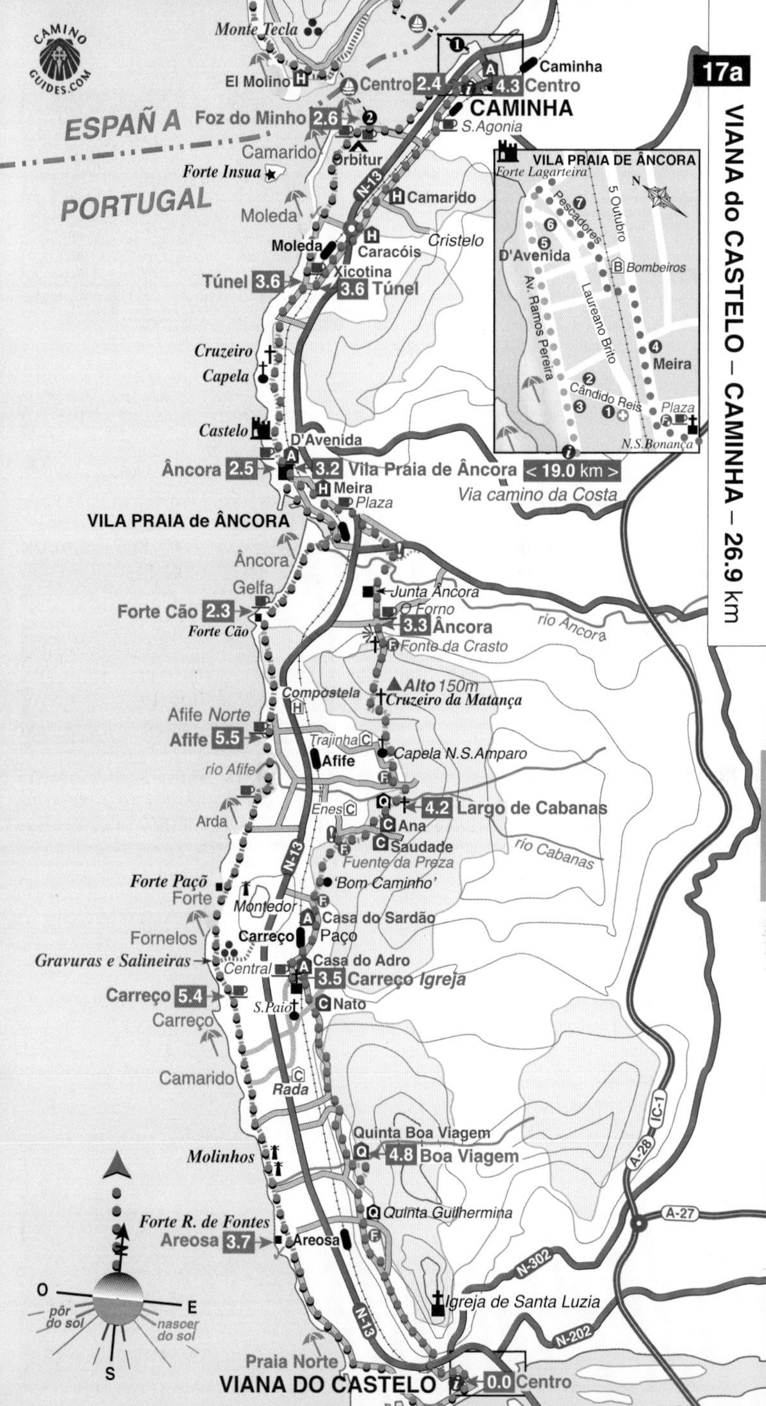
17a
VIANA do CASTELO – CAMINHA – 26.9 km
CAMINO GUIDES.COM
ESPAÑ A
PORTUGAL
Monte Tecla
El Molino
Centro 2.4
4.3 Centro
Caminha
CAMINHA
S.Agonia
Foz do Minho 2.6
Camarido
Orbitur
Forte Insua
N-13
Camarido
Moleda
Moleda
Caracóis
Cristelo
Xicotina
Túnel 3.6
3.6 Túnel
Cruzeiro
Capela
Castelo
D'Avenida
Âncora 2.5
3.2 Vila Praia de Âncora
< 19.0 km >
Via camino da Costa
Meira
Plaza
VILA PRAIA de ÂNCORA
VILA PRAIA DE ÂNCORA
Forte Lagarteira
Pescadores
5 Outubro
D'Avenida
Bombeiros
Laureano Brito
Av. Ramos Pereira
Meira
Cândido Reis
Plaza
N.S.Bonança
Âncora
Gelfa
Forte Cão 2.3
Forte Cão
Junta Âncora
O Forno
3.3 Âncora
rio Ancora
Fonte da Crasto
Alto 150m
Compostela
Cruzeiro da Matança
Afife Norte
Afife 5.5
Trajinha
Capela N.S.Amparo
Afife
rio Afife
Arda
Enes
4.2 Largo de Cabanas
Ana
Saudade
rio Cabanas
Fuente da Preza
'Bom Caminho'
Forte Paçô
Forte
Montedor
Casa do Sardão
Fornelos
Carreço
Paço
Gravuras e Salineiras
Central
Casa do Adro
3.5 Carreço Igreja
Carreço 5.4
S.Paio
Nato
Carreço
Camarido
Rada
Quinta Boa Viagem
4.8 Boa Viagem
IC-1
A-28
Molinhos
Quinta Guilhermina
A-27
Forte R. de Fontes
Areosa 3.7
Areosa
N-302
O
E
pôr do sol
nascer do sol
S
Igreja de Santa Luzia
N-202
Praia Norte
VIANA DO CASTELO
0.0 Centro

## 17b CAMINHA – VALENÇA / TUI

Ecovia *río Minho*

| | | | | |
|---|---|---|---|---|
| | --- --- | 10.9 | --- --- | *40%* |
| | --- --- | 16.5 | --- --- | *60%* |
| | --- --- | 0.0 | --- --- | *00%* |
| **Stage Total** | | **29.9** km | | *(18.6 ml)* |

Total ascent **150**m ±*¼ hr*
▲ Alto *m* Valença 95m *(310 ft)*
<A H> ➲V.N. Cerveira **14.4** km.
➲*Loivo / Segirém alt.* ***12.0*** *km.*

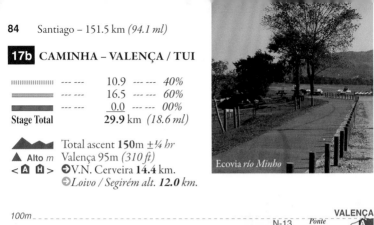

100m
VALENÇA
N-13
Caminha — Lanhelas — V.N. Cerveira — Montorrosa — *Ponte Veiga Mira*
*río Minho* — *río Minho*
0 km — 5 km — 10 km — 15 km — 20 km — 25 km

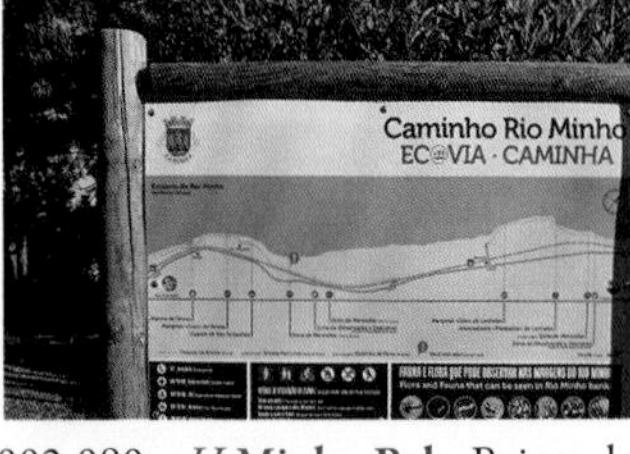


▌***Seixas:*** *•Rs* ***São Pedro €50*** *© 258 727 486 r/ Parede Alta 14.* [**+0.4** km] *via* rua do Praia *– N-13 •Q* ***Villa Idalina €65*** *© 258 724 367.*
▌***Lanhelas:*** ☕ *Alvarinho* r/S.Joao da Sa.

■ **Vila Nova de Cerveira:** ●**Pousada de Juventude** *Muni. [44÷2]*+ €8 (+£35) ©251 709 933 Rua Alto das Veigas (N-13). •**Casa do Cais** €55 © 934 874 367. •*H***** **INATEL Cerveira** r/ do Forte de Lovelhe €85 © 251 002 080. •*H* **Minho Belo** Bairro de Lourido €35 © 251 794 690. *[*● ***Detour:*** *+1km •CR* ***Gwendoline*** *€12-30 menú €6 © 963 528 441 (Lawrence & Vani) rua da Reguinha 136, Loivo. + •****Pilgrim's Rest*** *© 927 441 126 rua de Segirem 359].*

■ **Valença / Tui** p.59

CAMINHA – VALENÇA – 29.9 km

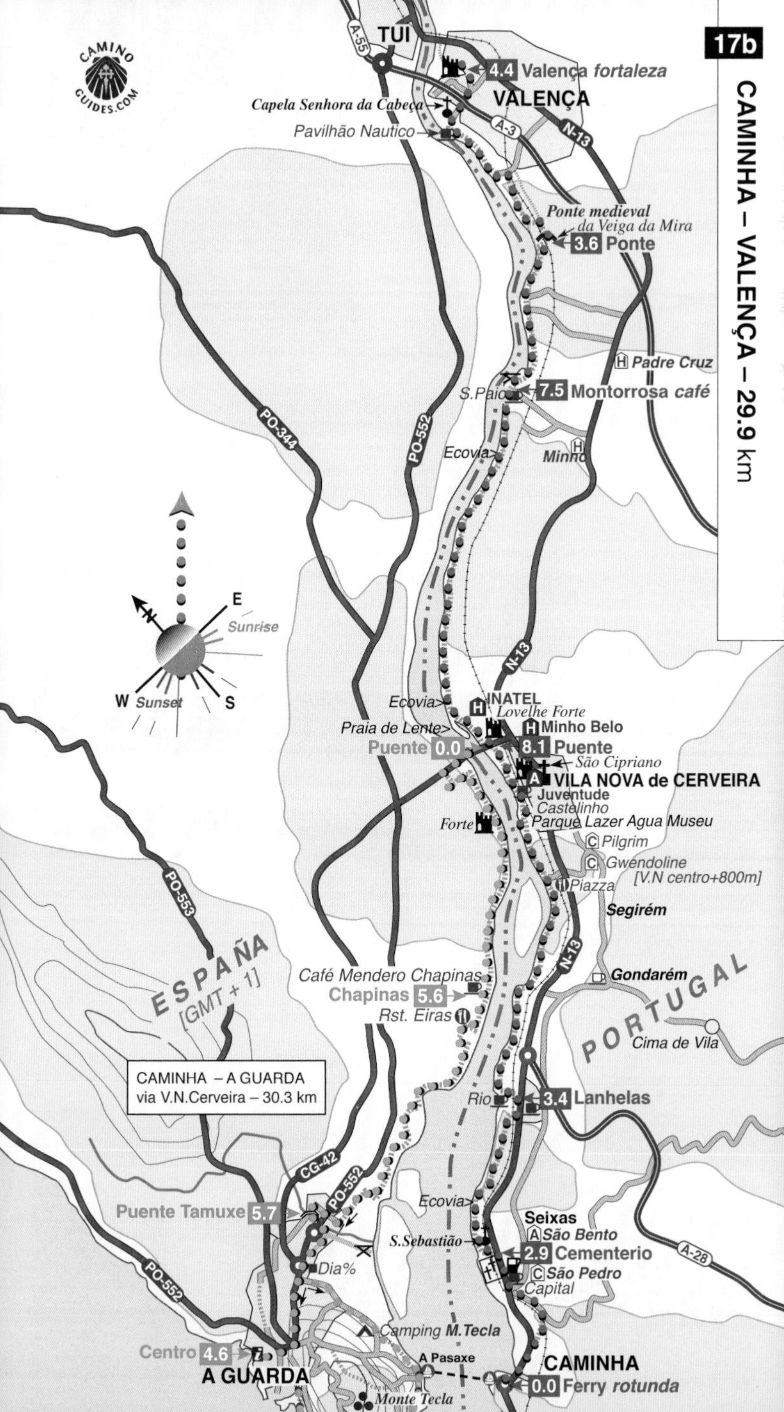
CAMINO GUIDES.COM
TUI
A-55
4.4 Valença fortaleza
VALENÇA
Capela Senhora da Cabeça
Pavilhão Nautico
A-3
N-13
Ponte medieval da Veiga da Mira
3.6 Ponte
Padre Cruz
S.Paio
7.5 Montorrosa café
Ecovia
Minho
PO-344
PO-552
E
Sunrise
W
Sunset
S
N
N-13
INATEL
Ecovia
Lovelhe Forte
Praia de Lente
Minho Belo
Puente 0.0
8.1 Puente
São Cipriano
VILA NOVA de CERVEIRA
Juventude
Castelinho
Forte
Parque Lazer Agua Museu
Pilgrim
Gwendoline
[V.N centro+800m]
Piazza
Segirém
PO-553
ESPAÑA
[GMT + 1]
Café Mendero Chapinas
Chapinas 5.6
Rst. Eiras
Gondarém
PORTUGAL
Cima de Vila
CAMINHA – A GUARDA
via V.N.Cerveira – 30.3 km
Rio
3.4 Lanhelas
CG-42
PO-552
Ecovia
Puente Tamuxe 5.7
Seixas
São Bento
S.Sebastião
2.9 Cementerio
São Pedro
Capital
A-28
Dia%
PO-552
Camping M.Tecla
Centro 4.6
A GUARDA
A Pasaxe
CAMINHA
0.0 Ferry rotunda
Monte Tecla

## 18a CAMINHA – PORTO MOUGÁS

*Via **A Guarda & O Serrallo***

Ferry *río Minho*

| | | |
|---|---|---|
| ---- --- | 10.1 | --- --- *44%* |
| ---- --- | 13.1 | --- --- *56%* |
| ---- --- | 0.0 | --- --- *00%* |
| **Stage Total** | **23.2** km *(14.4 ml)* | |

Total ascent **240**m ±½ *hr*

▲ Alto *m* Monte Tecla 100m *(328 ft)*

<A H> A Guarda **3.8** km. Oia **16.7** km. O Serrallo **20.3** km.

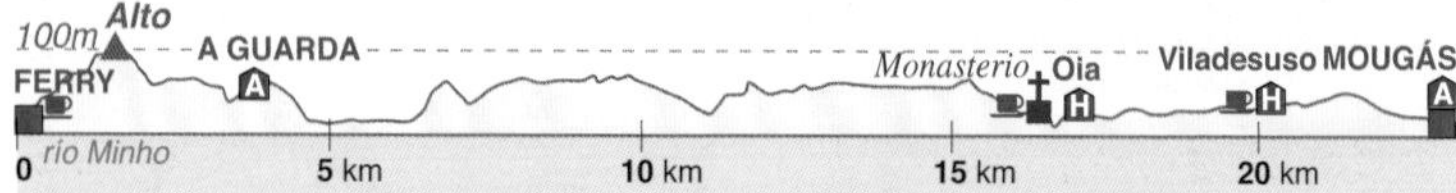


**A Pasaxe** •*Camping **Santa Tecla*** [**+1.4** km] Rua Baixada O Rio Miño *bungalow x10* €40 ✆ 986 613 011. **Senda Litoral:** ● ● ● ● ✓ *H*** **El Molino** €45 ✆ 986 627 233 Playa de Camposancos +300m •*H*** **Novo Muiño** *x20* €70 ✆ 986 627 169. **A Guarda:** **Turismo:** Oficina Municipal ✆ 986 614 546 Plaza Relo. ●*Alb.* **Peregrinos** *[36÷2]* €6 ✆ Concello da Guarda 986 610 025 m: 696 986 515 Rua Puerto Rico, 7. •*H* **Celta** €60 ✆ 986 610 445 Calle Rua De Galicia, 53. •*H*** **Vila da Guarda** €30 ✆ 986 61 11 21 Calle Tomiño, 8. •*H*** **Bruselas** €25 ✆ 986 614 521 Rúa Ourense. •*H*** **Eli-Mar** €35 ✆ 986 613 000 Rúa Vicente Sobrino, 12. •*H**** **Convento de San Benito** €60 ✆ 986 611 166 Plaza de San Benito. •*H** **Brisamar** €35+ ✆ 986 613 901 Calle Donantes de Sangre, 72. •*H*** **Hostal Del Mar** €18+ ✆ 986 610 638 Irmáns Noia (Praia Area Grande). **Oia:** •*CR* **Casa Puertas** €50+ ✆ 986 362 144 Vicente Lopez,7. •*H** **A Raíña** €35+ ✆ 986 362 908 Rúa A Riña. **Real Monasterio de Oia** *(restauración hotel monumento?)*. **Viladesuso-Oia:** •*H**** **Glasgow** €50+ ✆ 986 361 552. •*H**** **Costa Verde** €40+ ✆ 986 361 561. •*CR Budiño de Serraseca* €60+ ✆ 986 361 856 *A Serra Seca Viladesuso (+2 km)*. **Mougás:** ●*Alb.* **Aguncheiro** *Priv.[20÷3]*+ €10-30 ✆ 665 840 774 (Javier y Jorge).

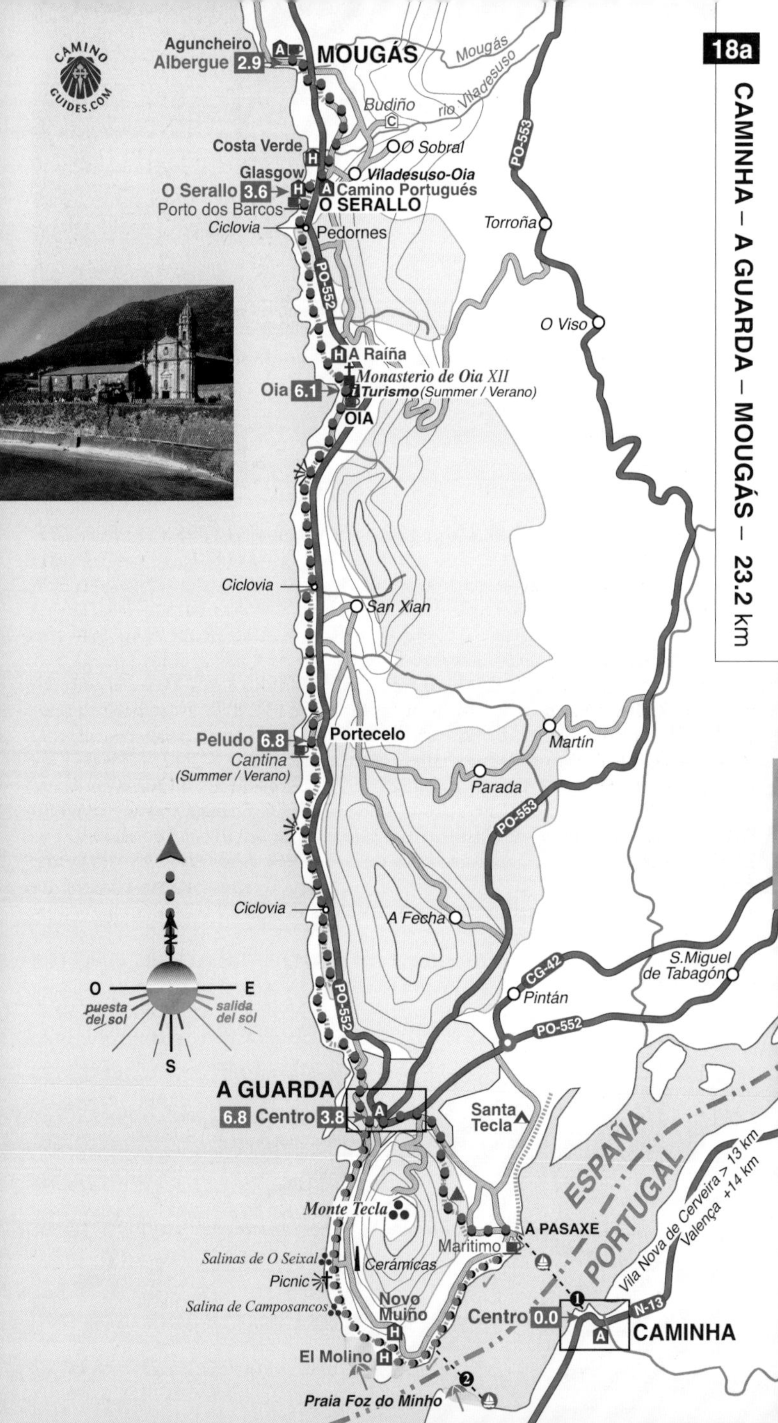

18a
CAMINHA – A GUARDA – MOUGÁS – 23.2 km
CAMINO GUIDES.COM
Aguncheiro
Albergue 2.9
MOUGÁS
Mougás
río Viladesuso
Budiño
PO-553
Costa Verde
O Sobral
Glasgow
Viladesuso-Oia
O Serallo 3.6
Camino Portugués
Porto dos Barcos
O SERALLO
Ciclovia
Pedornes
Torroña
PO-552
O Viso
A Raíña
Monasterio de Oia XII
Oia 6.1
Turismo (Summer / Verano)
OIA
Ciclovia
San Xian
Peludo 6.8
Portecelo
Martín
Cantina
(Summer / Verano)
Parada
PO-553
O
E
S
puesta del sol
salida del sol
Ciclovia
A Fecha
S.Miguel de Tabagón
CG-42
Pintán
PO-552
PO-552
A GUARDA
6.8 Centro 3.8
Santa Tecla
ESPAÑA
PORTUGAL
Vila Nova de Cerveira > 13 km
Valença +14 km
Monte Tecla
A PASAXE
Maritimo
Salinas de O Seixal
Cerámicas
Picnic
Salina de Camposancos
Novo Muiño
Centro 0.0
N-13
CAMINHA
El Molino
Praia Foz do Minho

# 19a MOUGÁS – A RAMALLOSA *Via BAIONA*

--- --- 2.3 --- --- *14%*
--- --- 14.0 --- --- *86%*
--- --- 0.0 --- --- *00%*
**Stage Total** **16.3** km *(10.1 ml)*

Total ascent **260**m ±½ *hr*
▲ Alto *m* Portela 130m *(427 ft)*
< A H > ➲Pedra Rubia **2.0** km. ➲A Ermida **4.1** km ➲Baiona **11.2** km.

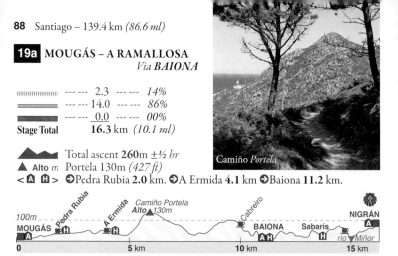

Camiño *Portela*

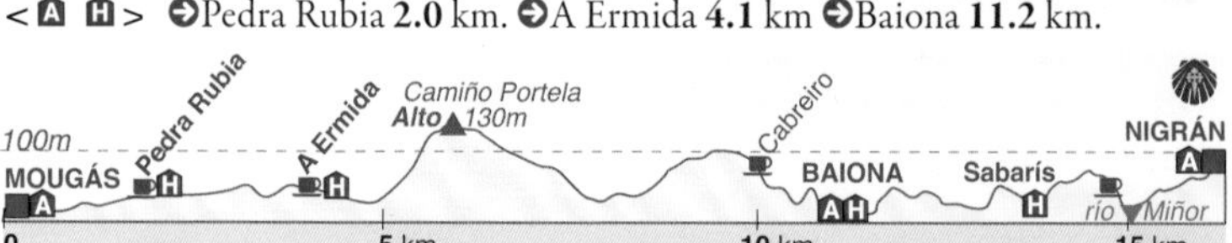


**Camino da Costa:** ● ● ● ● ▮ **Mougás:** ▲ **O Muiño** €30 ✆ 986 361 600 (PO-550). *H** **Soremma** €35-€65 ✆ 986 356 067 Las Mariñas (PO-550). ▲ **Mougás** €36-€51 ✆ 986 385 011 As Mariñas-Mougás. •*H* **O'Peñasco** / *R Bodas* ✆ 986 361 565 c/ As Mariñas (PO-550). ■ **BAIONA:** *Alb.*❶ **Baionamar** *Priv.[24÷2]* €15 ✆ 986 138 025 c/ Venezuela, 6. ❷ **Estela do Mar** *Priv.[20÷1]* €15 ✆ 986 133 213 (Ivana) *esteladomar.com* Laureano Salgado, 15. •*H*** **Rompeolas** €40 ✆ 615 140 220 Av. Joselín. •*H** **Parador de Baiona** €150+ ✆ 986 355 000 Av. Arquitecto JesúsValverde, 3. •*H** **Carabela La Pinta** €30+ ✆ 986 355 107 c/ Carabela la Pinta. •*H** **Pinzón** €30+ ✆ 986 356 046 Rúa Elduayen, 21. •*H*** **Tres Carabelas** €60+ ✆ 986 355 441 c/ de Ventura Misa, 61. •*H*** **Anunciada** €40+ ✆ 986 356 018 c/ de Ventura Misa, 58. •*H*** **Pazo de Mendoza** €65+ ✆ 986 385 014 Elduayen, 1. *H* **Cais** €45 ✆ 986 355 643 c/ del Alférez Barreiro, 3. •*Hs*** **Santa Marta Playa** €30 ✆ 986 356 045 Camino del Molino 4. ▮ **Sabarís.** ●*Alb.* **Playa de Sabarís** *Priv.[20÷1]* €15 ✆ 986 152 380 Rúa Porta do Sol, 55. **A RAMALLOSA Nigrán:** ●*Alb.Hospedería* **Pazo Pias** *Priv.[40÷20!]*+ €10-40 ✆ 986 350 654 Camiño da Cabreira,21 A Ramallosa. 🍴 Antipodas Calle de la Romana Alta 4.

**Senda Litoral:** ● ● ● ● ✓ ***Rúa das Areas @Nº13*** •*H**** **Casa do Marqués** €45 ✆ 986 353 150 & ***Nº28*** •*Hs*** **El Viejo Galeón** €35 ✆ 986 350 207. •*H** **Avenida** €40 ✆ 986 354 728 Av. Julián Valverde Nº41 + Nº40. •*H** **Arce Baiona** €30 ✆ 986 386 060. •*H** **Vasco da Gama** ✆ 986 353 350 Av. José Pereira Troncoso, 18.

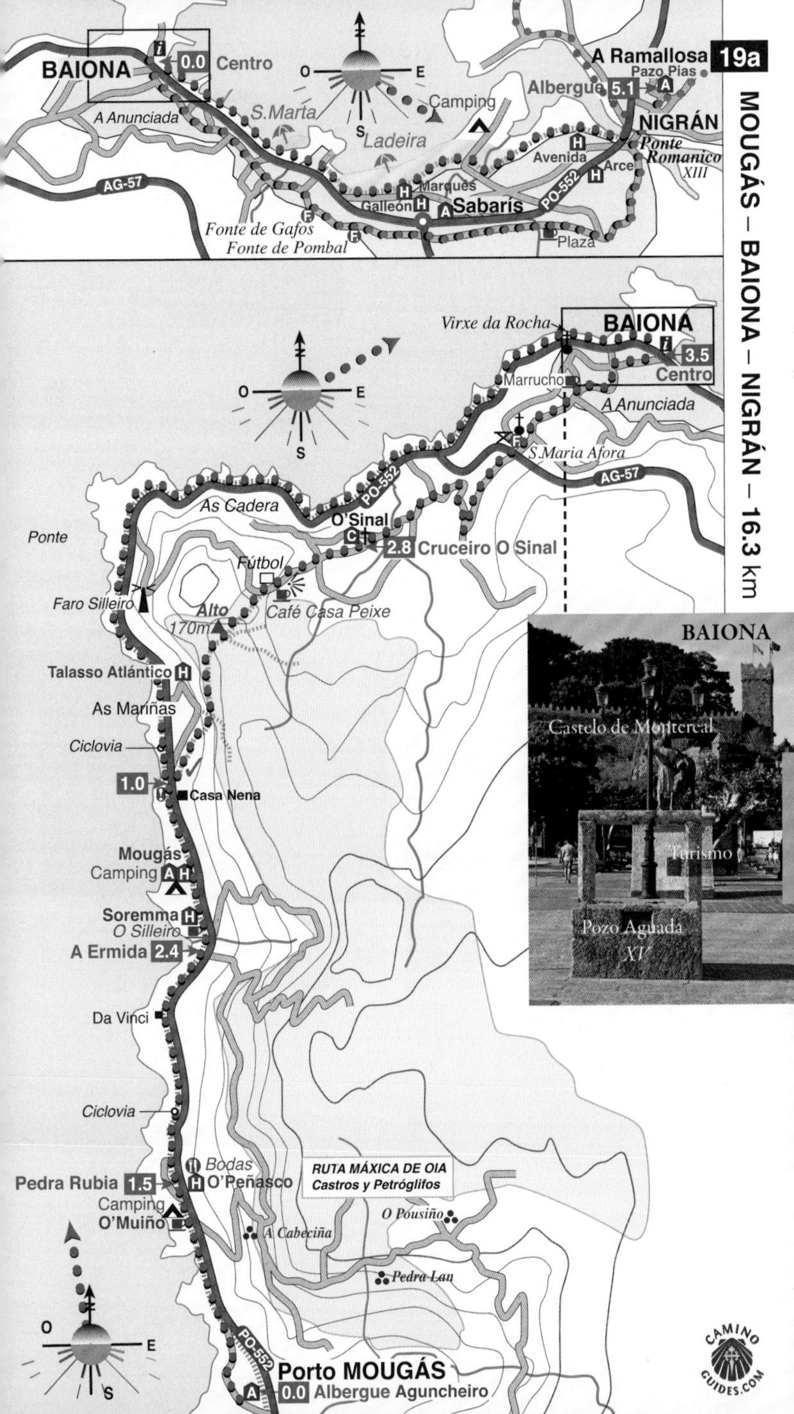

19a
MOUGÁS – BAIONA – NIGRÁN – 16.3 km
BAIONA
0.0 Centro
A Anunciada
S.Marta
Ladeira
Camping
A Ramallosa
Pazo Pias
Albergue 5.1
NIGRÁN
Ponte Romanico XIII
Avenida
Arce
Marques
Galleón
Sabarís
PO-552
AG-57
Fonte de Gafos
Fonte de Pombal
Plaza
Virxe da Rocha
BAIONA
3.5 Centro
Marrucho
A Anunciada
S.Maria Afora
AG-57
PO-552
As Cadera
O'Sinal
2.8 Cruceiro O Sinal
Ponte
Fútbol
Faro Silleiro
Alto 170m
Café Casa Peixe
Talasso Atlántico
As Mariñas
Ciclovia
1.0
Casa Nena
Mougás
Camping
Soremma
O Silleiro
A Ermida 2.4
Da Vinci
Ciclovia
Bodas
Pedra Rubia 1.5
O'Peñasco
Camping O'Muiño
RUTA MÁXICA DE OIA
Castros y Petróglifos
O Pousiño
A Cabeciña
Pedra Lan
PO-552
Porto MOUGÁS
0.0 Albergue Aguncheiro
BAIONA
Castelo de Monterreal
Turismo
Pozo Aguada XV
CAMINO GUIDES.COM

## 20a A RAMALLOSA *NIGRÁN* – VIGO

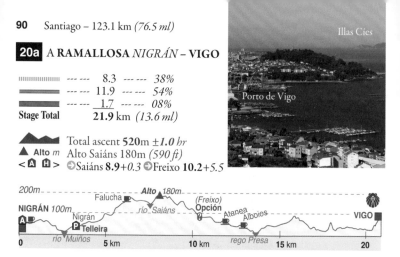

| | | |
|---|---|---|
| ⁞⁞⁞⁞⁞⁞ | 8.3 | *38%* |
| ▬ | 11.9 | *54%* |
| ▬ | 1.7 | *08%* |
| **Stage Total** | **21.9** km *(13.6 ml)* | |

Total ascent **520**m ±***1.0*** *hr*
▲ Alto *m* Alto Saiáns 180m *(590 ft)*
<A H> Saiáns **8.9**+*0.3* Freixo **10.2**+*5.5*

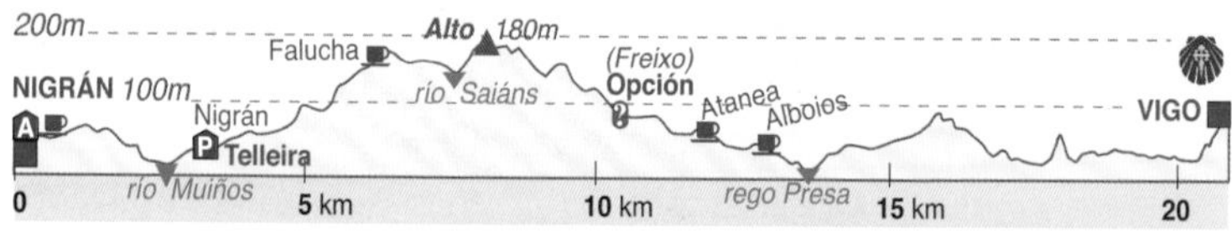


▌**Saiáns** ●*Alb.***San Xurxo** *Asoc.[8÷1]* €8 ✆ 986 491 918 r/Eira Vella, 4 (+800m Litoral & + 300m Costa).■ **Vigo** *Parque de Castrelos:* **Pazo Quiñónes de León** *(Museo Municipal)* ✆ 986 295 070. **Igrexa de Santa María de Castrelos** *románico XIII.* **Vigo Balaídos** •*H****NH* **Hesperia** €40 ✆ 986 296 600 Av. da Florida 60. ▌**Freixo** ●●● ●*Alb.***O Freixo** *[8÷1]* €-donativo ✆ 680 756 664.▌**Senda Litoral:** ●●● ✓ •*H*** **Playa De Vigo** €40 ✆ 986 202 020 Av de Samil 95. •*H* **Playa Santa Baia** €30+ ✆ 986 241 548 Av. Atlántida 121 adj. Museu do Mar +220m.

Alb. y Pazo Pías

Alb. Freixo

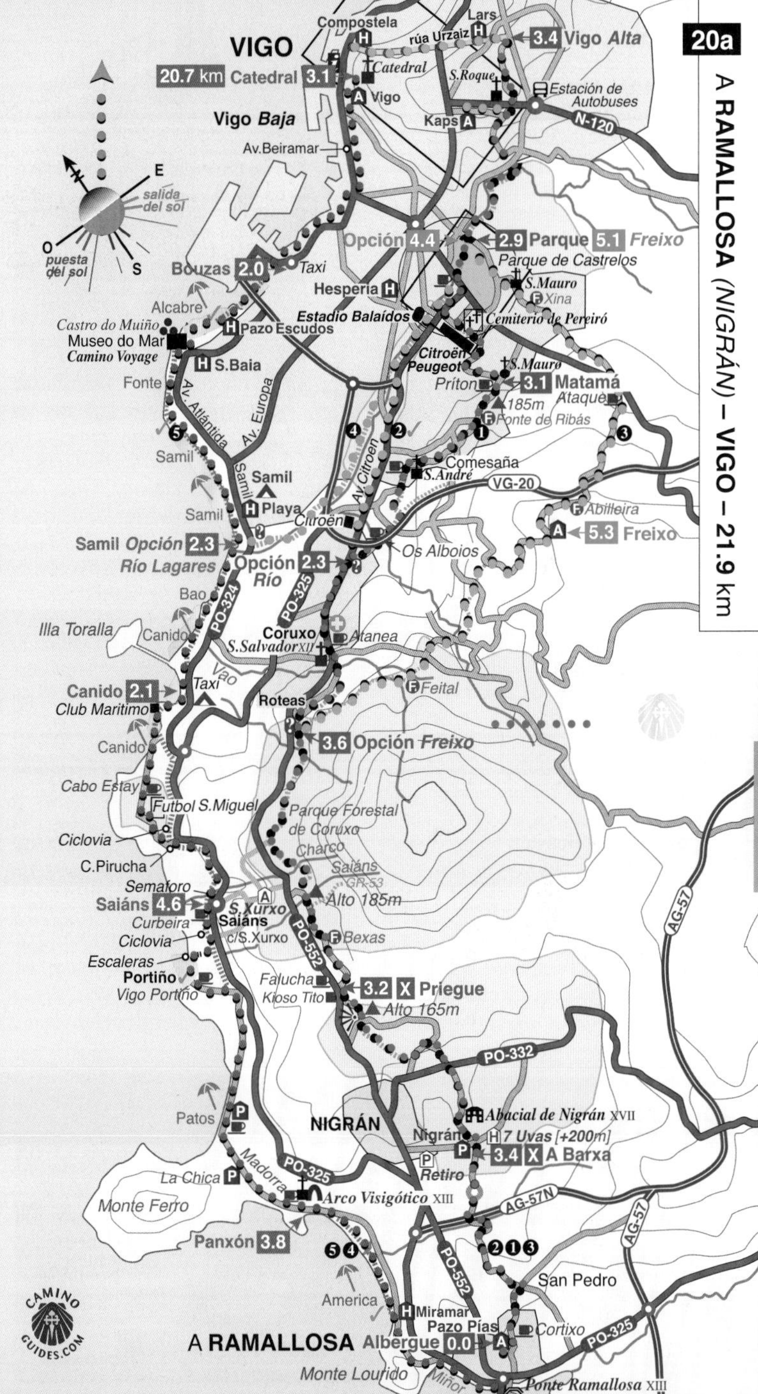

A RAMALLOSA (NIGRÁN) – VIGO – 21.9 km
VIGO
20.7 km Catedral 3.1
Vigo Baja
Compostela
rúa Urzaiz
Lars
3.4 Vigo Alta
Catedral
S.Roque
Estación de Autobuses
Vigo
Kaps
N-120
Av.Beiramar
E
salida del sol
O
puesta del sol
S
Opción 4.4
2.9 Parque 5.1 Freixo
Parque de Castrelos
Bouzas 2.0
Taxi
Hesperia
S.Mauro
Xina
Estadio Balaídos
Cemiterio de Pereiró
Alcabre
Castro do Muiño
Museo do Mar
Camino Voyage
Pazo Escudos
S.Baia
Citroën Peugeot
S.Mauro
Fonte
Príton
3.1 Matamá
Ataque
185m
Fonte de Ribás
Av. Atlántida
Av. Europa
Av. Citroen
Samil
Comesaña
S.André
Samil
Playa
VG-20
Abilleira
Samil
Citroën
5.3 Freixo
Samil Opción 2.3
Río Lagares
Opción 2.3
Río
Os Alboios
Bao
PO-324
PO-325
Illa Toralla
Canido
Coruxo
Atanea
S.Salvador XII
Vao
Canido 2.1
Club Maritimo
Taxi
Roteas
Feital
3.6 Opción Freixo
Canido
Cabo Estay
Futbol S.Miguel
Parque Forestal de Coruxo
Ciclovia
Charco
C.Pirucha
Saiáns
GR-53
Semaforo
Saiáns 4.6
S.Xurxo
Saiáns
Alto 185m
Curbeira
Ciclovia
c/S.Xurxo
PO-552
Bexas
Escaleras
Portiño
Vigo Portiño
Falucha
Kioso Tito
3.2 X Priegue
Alto 165m
AG-57
PO-332
Patos
NIGRÁN
Abacial de Nigrán XVII
Nigrán
7 Uvas [+200m]
3.4 X A Barxa
Madorra
PO-325
Retiro
La Chica
Arco Visigótico XIII
Monte Ferro
AG-57N
Panxón 3.8
PO-552
AG-57
San Pedro
America
Miramar
Pazo Pías
Cortixo
PO-325
A RAMALLOSA Albergue 0.0
Monte Lourido
Miñor
Ponte Ramallosa XIII
CAMINO GUIDES.COM

▮ **Vigo** ***Alta Lodging:*** •*Hs* **Kaps** *[24÷4]* €17+*14* €30 ✆ 986 110 010 *www.hostelvigo.com* Emilia Pardo Bazán 12. •*H**** **Tryp Los Galeones** *x50* €55+ ✆ 902 144 440 Av de Madrid 21. •**Pepe** ✆ 648 538 956 c/Badajoz 13. •*Hs* **Los Tres Luces** *x15* €40 ✆ 986 420 477 Venezuela 61. •*Hs* **Pio V** *x6* €25 ✆ 986 410 060 c/ Alcalde Vázquez Varela 46. ***Calle México*** *@**Nº22*** •*H*** **Celta** *x40* €29-33 ✆ 986 414 699 &*@**Nº7*** •*H*** **Casablanca** *x9* €35 ✆ 986 482 712. •*Hs*** **Lar Atlántica** *x18* €35 ✆ 616 706 948 Rúa Urzaiz, 83/1ºA. ▮ ***Hotels:*** *€35-75:* •*H**** **Oca Ipanema** ✆ 986 471 344 Vázquez Varela 31. ***Rúa Lepanto*** *@**Nº4*** •*Hs Int.* **Lapplandia** ✆ 605 457 792. *@ **Nº16*** •*Hs*** **Casais** ✆ 886 112 956. *@**Nº18*** •*H*** **Panton** *x40* €29-34 ✆ 986 224 270. *@**Nº26*** •*H*** **Lino** ✆ 986 447 004. •*H**** **Occidental** *México* €75+ ✆ 986 431 666 Vía Norte **Nº10** & *@* **Nº9** •*H** **Solpor** *x8* €27-33 ✆ 986 416 036. **Iglesia de los Picos** *Inmaculada Concepción* ✆ 986 274 622 barrio del Calvario.

▮ **Vigo** ***Baja:*** **Casco antiguo:** ●*Alb.* **Vigo** *Xunta.[**96**÷7]* €8 Praza do Berbés, 5. ●*Hs.* **R4** *Priv.[22÷1]* €20 ✆ 986 699 727 r/Real, 4. *Hs.* **Real** *x9* €20-25 ✆ 699 621 449 r/Real, 22. •*H*** **Compostela** €35+ ✆ 986 228 227 r/García Olloqui 5 *(Praza da Compostela).* •*Hs*** **La Colegiata** €25-40 ✆ 986 220 129 Plaza Iglesia 3. •*H*** **Puerta del Sol** *x25* €39-45 ✆ 986 222 364 Porta do Sol, 14. •*Hs* **Continental** €25-45 ✆ 986 220 764 Bajada la Fuente 3. •*H** **Aguila** €20+ ✆ 986 431 398 c/ Victoria 6. •*H** **Nautico** €25 ✆ 986 122 440 c/ Luis Taboada 28. •*H*** **Del Mar** *x32* €35-45 ✆ 986 436 811 r/ Luis Taboada, 34. •*H*** **Atlantico** €40 ✆ 986 220 530 r/ García Barbón, 35 (opp. Igrexa Santiago). *[Note missionary brothers **Hermanos Misioneros** Av. de Galicia no longer accept pilgrims].*

▮ **Vigo BAJA** ❶**Turismo Vigo** ✆ 986 224 757 Estación Marítima C/ Cánovas del Castillo 3. ○ ***El barrio histórico de Vigo:*** ❶ **Concatedral** ***Colexiata de Santa María de Vigo*** neoclásico *XIX (***104.4** km to Santiago).* ❷ **Casa de Arines** *Ceta XV* (Instituto Camões) calle Real. ❸ **Ayuntamiento** *antiguo* Praza da Constitución. ***Marítima:*** ❹ Monumento a Xulio Verne *(20.000 leguas de viaje submarino; que menciana la Ría de Vigo).* ❺ **O Castro** *XVII (y Parque Monte del Castro).* ❻ Neo Gothic **Igrexa de Santiago** *XIX* Rúa García Barbón *(***103.2** km to Santiago Cathedral entitling the bona fide pilgrim to apply for a Compostela).*

Monumento a Xulio Verne

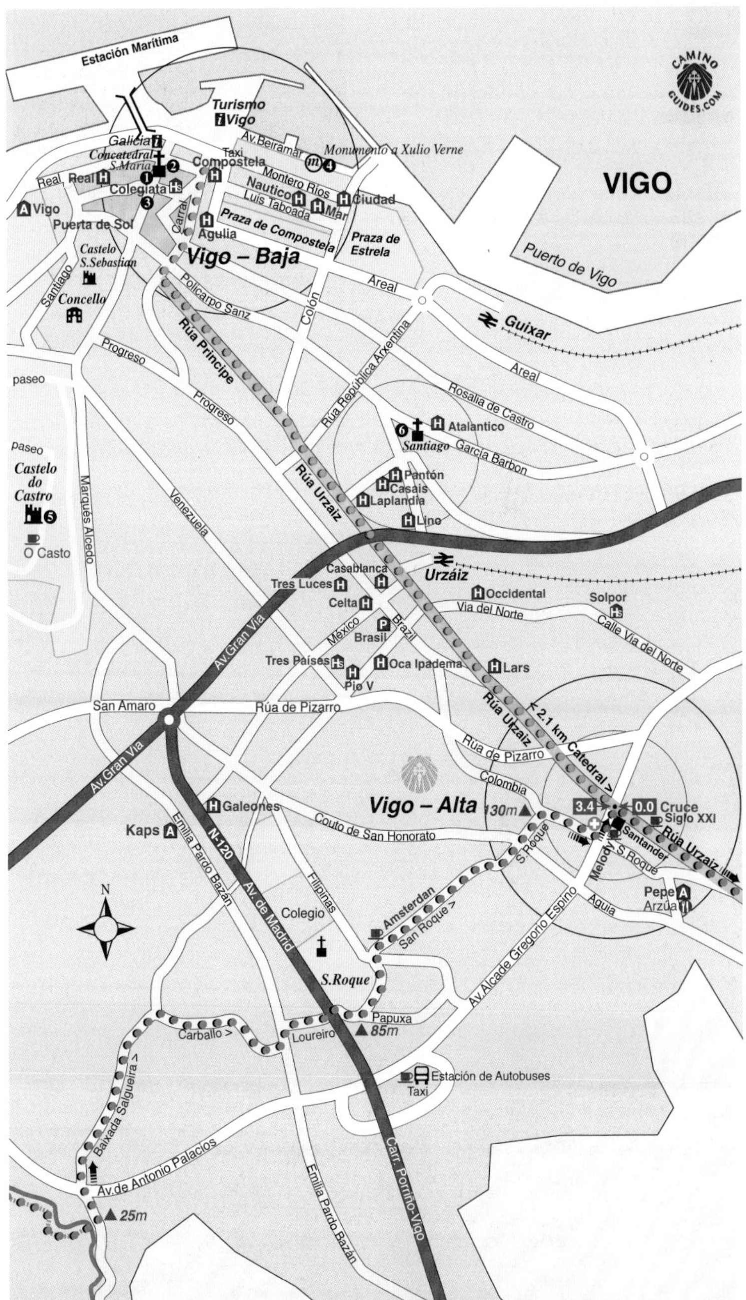

VIGO
Estación Marítima
Turismo Vigo
Galicia
Concatedral S.María
Monumento a Xulio Verne
Av.Beiramar
Taxi
Compostela
Real
Colegiata
Montero Ríos
Nautico
Luis Taboada
Mar
Ciudad
Vigo
Puerta de Sol
Carral
Agulia
Praza de Compostela
Praza de Estrela
Castelo S.Sebastian
Vigo – Baja
Puerto de Vigo
Areal
Santiago
Concello
Policarpo Sanz
Colón
Rúa Principe
Rúa República Arxentina
Guixar
Progreso
paseo
Rosalia de Castro
Atalantico
Santiago
García Barbon
Castelo do Castro
Marqués Alcedo
Venezuela
Rúa Urzaiz
Pantón
Casais
Laplandia
Lino
O Casto
Casablanca
Urzáiz
Tres Luces
Celta
Occidental
Solpor
Via del Norte
Calle Via del Norte
México
Brasil
Brazil
Av.Gran Via
Tres Países
Oca Ipadema
Lars
Pio V
San Amaro
Rúa de Pizarro
Rúa Urzaiz
2.1 km Catedral >
Colombia
Vigo – Alta
130m
3.4
0.0 Cruce
Siglo XXI
Galeones
Couto de San Honorato
Santander
Rúa Urzaiz
S.Roque
Melody
Kaps
Emilia Pardo Bazán
N-120
Av. de Madrid
Filipinas
Amsterdan
San Roque >
Pepe
Arzúa
Aguia
Av.Alcade Gregorio Espino
N
Colegio
S.Roque
Papuxa
Carballo >
Loureiro
85m
Estación de Autobuses
Taxi
Baixada Salgueira >
Av.de Antonio Palacios
25m
Emilia Pardo Bazán
Carr. Porriño-Vigo

## 21a VIGO – REDONDELA

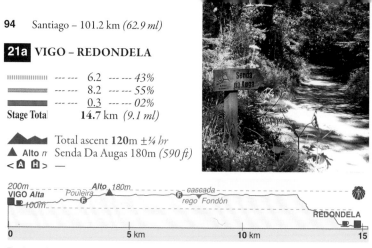

| | | | |
|---|---|---|---|
| | --- --- | 6.2 | --- --- *43%* |
| | --- --- | 8.2 | --- --- *55%* |
| | --- --- | 0.3 | --- --- *02%* |
| **Stage Total** | | **14.7** km | *(9.1 ml)* |

Total ascent **120**m ±¼ *hr*

▲ Alto *m* Senda Da Augas 180m *(590 ft)*

<A H> —

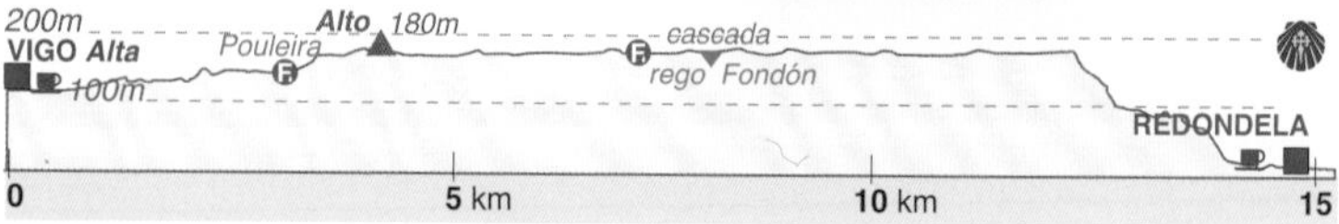

200m VIGO Alta 100m Pouleira Alto 180m cascada rego Fondón REDONDELA 0 5 km 10 km 15

**▌Chapela:** •*Hs* **Bahía de Chapela** Av. Redondela 14 (adj. Ponte de Rande ria Vigo – free pickup *transporte gratuito*) ✆ 986 452 780. ■ **Redondela** *(p.62)*

Stage *Etapa* **21 Redondela – Pontevedra** *p.64*

< ***Albergue de Torres REDONDELA.*** Unión de ***Camino da Costa*** y ***Camino Central.***

21a

VIGO – REDONDELA – 14.7 km

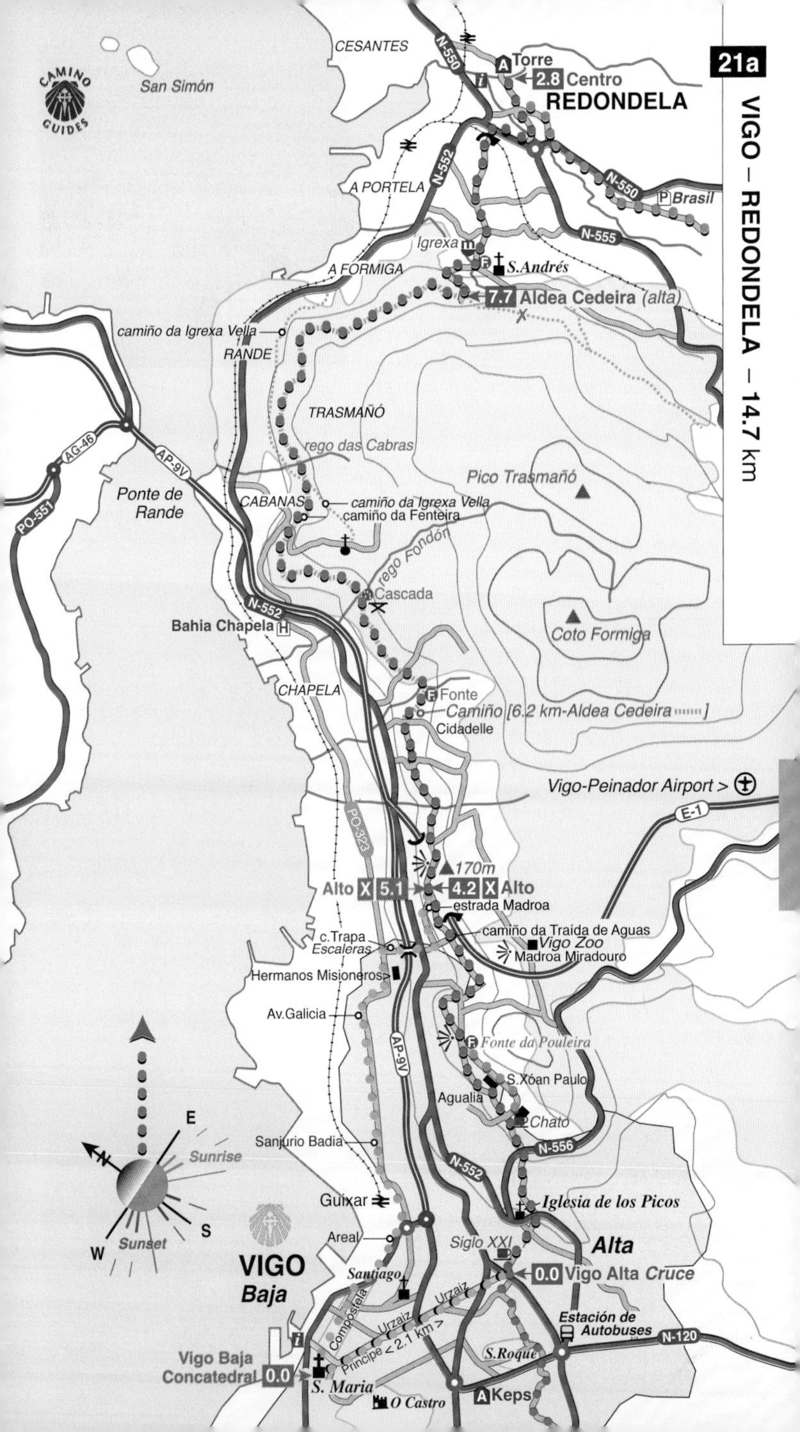

## 22a PONTEVEDRA – ARMENTEIRA

Santiago – 108.3 km *(67.3 ml)*

| | | |
|---|---|---|
| (dotted) | 8.9 | *42%* |
| (grey) | 11.8 | *55%* |
| (dark) | 0.7 | *03%* |
| **Stage Total** | **21.4** km *(13.3 ml)* | |

Total ascent **1,280**m *±2¼ hr*
▲ Alto *m* Outeiro Do Cribo 455m *(1,490 ft)*
<A H> ➲Campaño **5.9** km. ➲Poio **8.2** km. ➲Combarro **11.3** km.

Combarro *Praia*

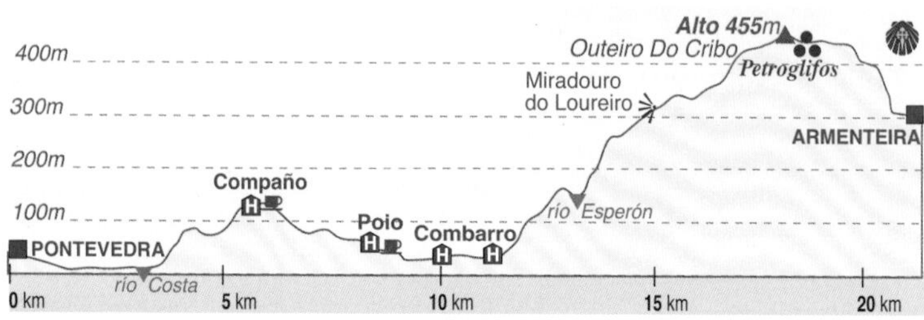


**▮ Campañó:** •*H*** **Campaniola** *x30* €36 ✆ 986 872 711 *www.campaniola.es* +café.
**▮ Poio:** •*H* **Monasterio Poio** €35 ✆ 986 770 000 rúa Convento, 2. *[+½ km •H* **San Juan I** *(+ II)* €25 ✆ 986 770 020 P-308*]*. •*CR* **Casa A Marchanta** €100 ✆ 629 809 198 Primera Trv. Seara, 50.
**▮ Combarro-Poio:** •*H* **Combarro** *x30* €49 ✆ 986 772 131 *www.hotelcombarro.es* (Apr-Sept) PO-308. •*H* **Hogar del Puerto** €35-50 ✆ 986 770 116 *www.hogardelpuerto.com.es* & •*H* **Stella Maris** €40+ ✆ 986 770 366. ☕/*H* **Xeito** €39 ✆ 986 770 039 Rúa da Cruz, 35 (PO-308). +100m ●*Alb.* **N.S. del Camino** *Priv. [12÷2]* €18 +5 €45+ ✆ 649 053 236 Trv. Casalvito, 16.

**■ ARMENTEIRA:** •**Pousada Armenteira** *x30* €90+ ✆ 986 716 372 *www.pousadadearmenteira.com* ●**Albergue de Peregrinos** *Muni [34÷2]* €6 ✆ Carmen 670 757 777. •*Hs* **Mosteiro de Santa María da Armenteira** €35-50 (dinner *cena* €10) ✆ 627 097 696 *www.monasteriodearmenteira.org* adj. 🍴/☕ *O Comercio*. adj. ☕/*bar O Comercio*.

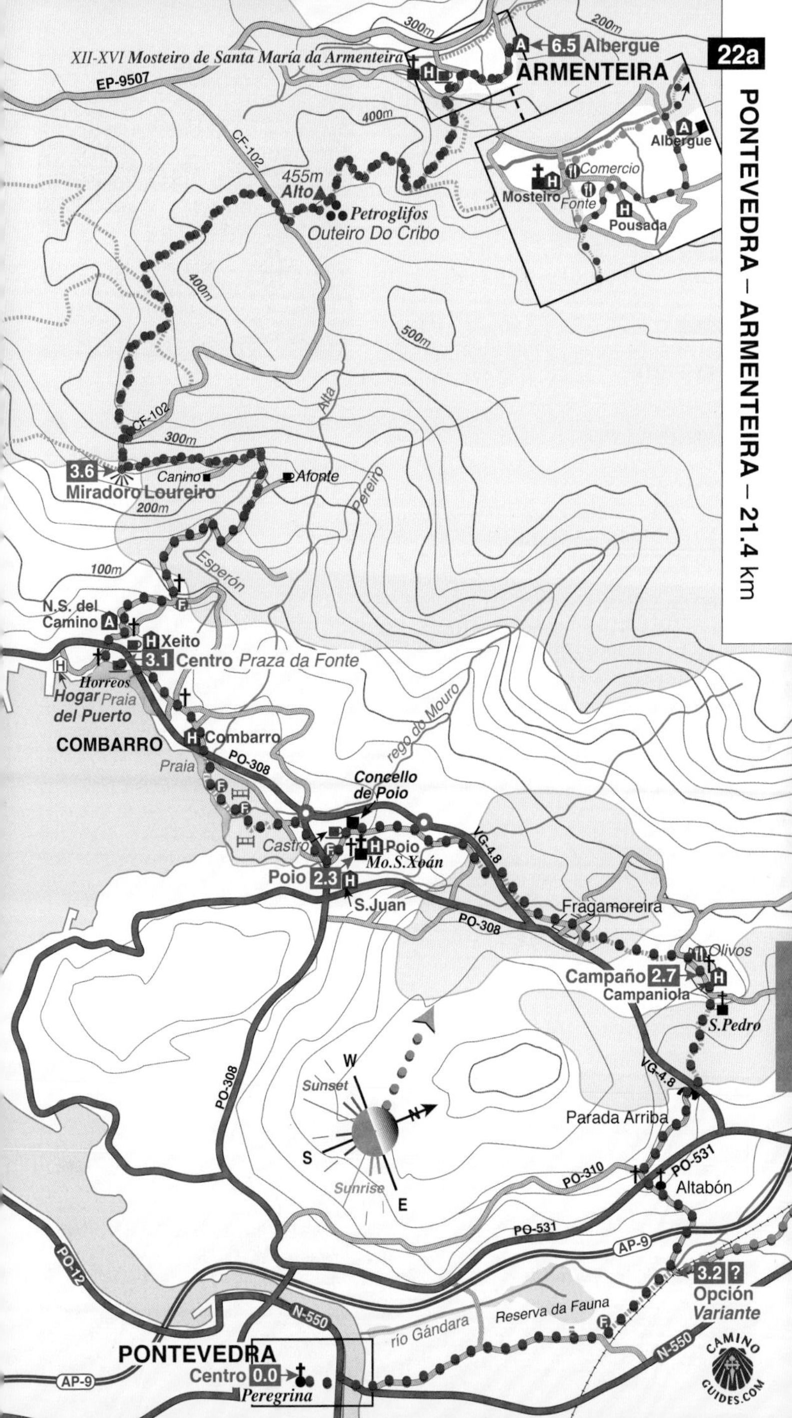
22a
PONTEVEDRA – ARMENTEIRA – 21.4 km
XII-XVI Mosteiro de Santa María da Armenteira
6.5 Albergue
ARMENTEIRA
EP-9507
Albergue
Comercio
Mosteiro
Fonte
Pousada
455m
Alto
Petroglifos
Outeiro Do Cribo
CF-102
400m
500m
300m
200m
100m
3.6
Miradoro Loureiro
Canino
Afonte
Alta
Pereiro
Esperón
N.S. del Camino
Xeito
3.1 Centro Praza da Fonte
Horreos
Hogar del Puerto
Praia
COMBARRO
Combarro
PO-308
rego do Mouro
Concello de Poio
Castro
Poio
Mo.S.Xoán
Poio 2.3
S.Juan
VG-4.8
Fragamoreira
Olivos
Campaño 2.7
Campaniola
S.Pedro
W
N
S
E
Sunset
Sunrise
Parada Arriba
PO-310
PO-531
Altabón
AP-9
3.2
Opción Variante
Reserva da Fauna
río Gándara
PO-12
N-550
PONTEVEDRA
Centro 0.0
Peregrina
CAMINO GUIDES.COM

# 23a ARMENTEIRA – V.N. de AROUSA

Santiago – 86.9 km *(54.0 ml)*

| | | |
|---|---|---|
| ----- | 17.2 | *70%* |
| ----- | 7.4 | *30%* |
| ----- | 0.0 | 0% |
| **Stage Total** | **24.6** km *(15.3 ml)* | |

Total ascent **1,190**m ±*2.0 hr*

Alto *m* Armenteira 275m *(900 ft)*

<A H> Barrantes **6.4**. Av.Cambados **19.7** km (+200m) Terrón **22.3** km.

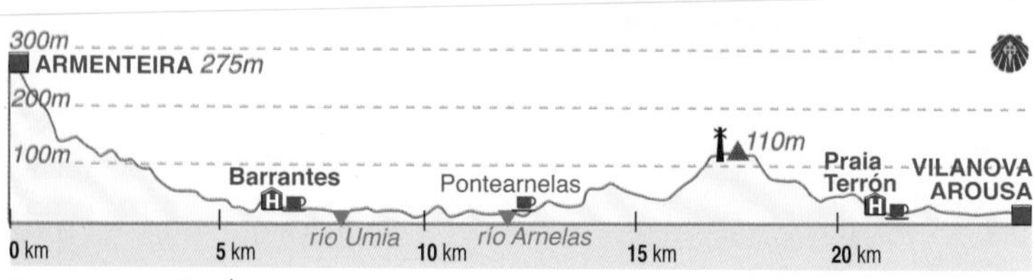

**Barrantes:** •*Hs* **Os Castaños** €25-35 © 986 710 236 rúa Torre, Ribadumia. **Cruce (PO-549): Monte San Roque:** *Chantada* & *Mississippi* + •*H* **Alte Frankfurt** €25-45 © 986 554 165 www.altefrankfurt.es (+200m Av. de Cambados). **Praia Terrón:** /*Hs* **Luz de Luna** *x8* €15-35 © 986 550 054 m: 618 195 967 Elena. •*H* **Arco Iris** *x40* €35-55 © 986 555 444 www.arcoirisweb.net •*H* **Dinajan** €40 © 986 561 534 c/ Terrón. •*H* **Torres** *x24* €35 © 986 561 010 **Vilanova de Arousa:** *Alb.*❶ **Vilanova de Arousa** *Mun. [20÷1]* €6 © Emilio 633 906 490 / 616 701 798 deportivo. •*H* **Bradomin** *x51* €25+ © 986 561 038 www.hotelbradomin.com Av. Juan Carlos I, 29. *Alb.*❷ **A Salazón** *[11÷2]* €18 +*2* €45 Fran © 606 365 561 Callejón do Boliche, 7. *Alb.*❸ **A Corticela** *[10÷2]* €18 Angeles © 655 884 136 Rua A Basella www.acorticela.com Meson *O Timon* Av. Galicia opp. ***Bahia-Sub*** ±€20 © 607 911 523. ***Turismo Casa-Museo De Valle Inclán*** (10-14 + 16.30-19.30) © 986 555 493 c/ Luces de Bohemia.

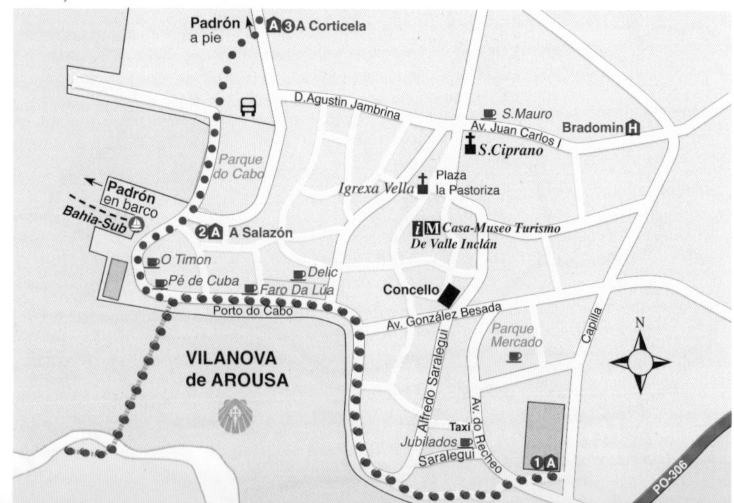

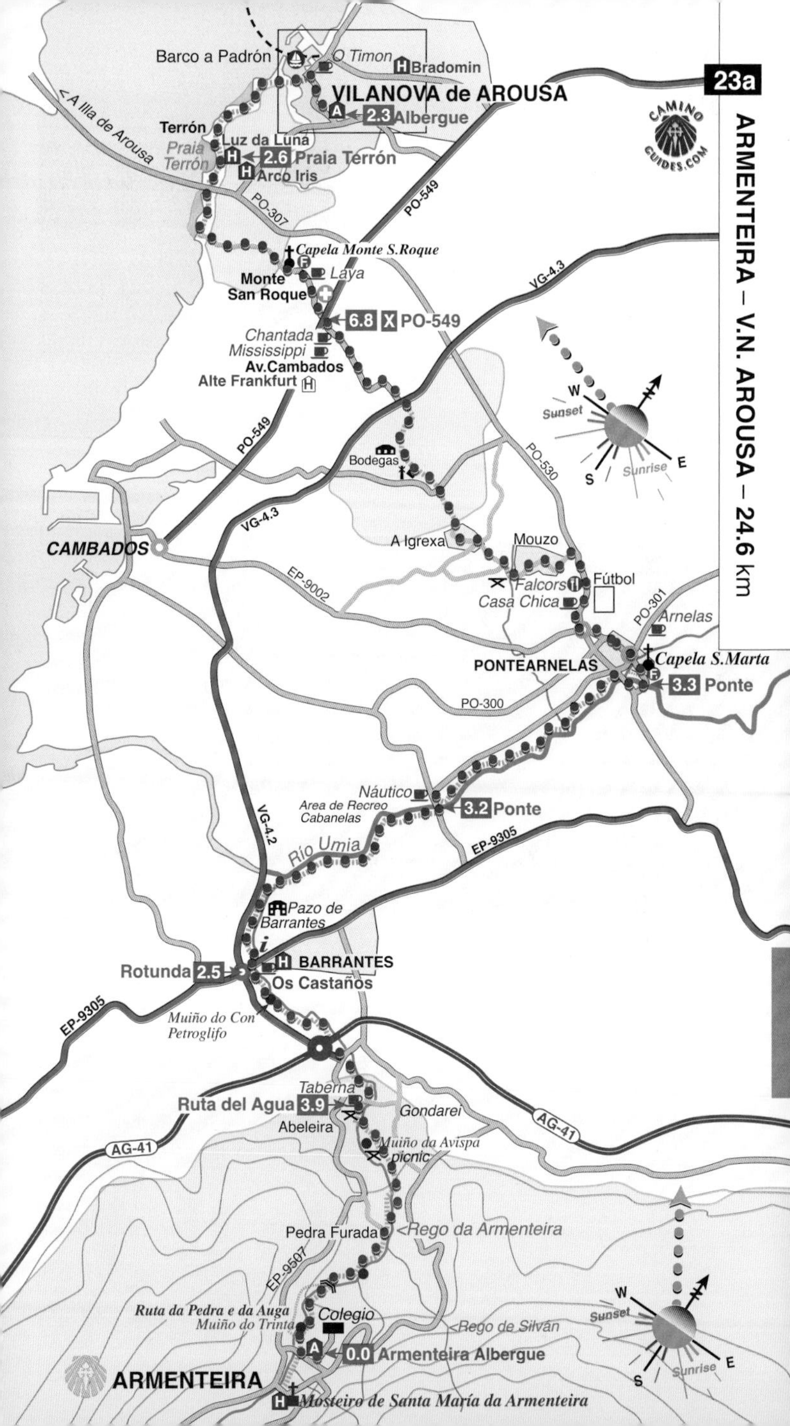

23a
ARMENTEIRA – V.N. AROUSA – 24.6 km
CAMINO GUIDES.COM
Barco a Padrón
O Timon
Bradomin
VILANOVA de AROUSA
2.3 Albergue
<A Illa de Arousa
Terrón
Luz da Luna
Praia Terrón
2.6 Praia Terrón
Arco Iris
PO-307
PO-549
Capela Monte S.Roque
Laya
Monte San Roque
6.8 PO-549
Chantada
Mississippi
Av.Cambados
Alte Frankfurt
VG-4.3
W
Sunset
E
S
Sunrise
Bodegas
PO-530
CAMBADOS
A Igrexa
Mouzo
EP-9002
Falcors
Fútbol
Casa Chica
PO-301
Arnelas
Capela S.Marta
PONTEARNELAS
3.3 Ponte
PO-300
Náutico
Area de Recreo Cabanelas
3.2 Ponte
VG-4.2
Río Umia
EP-9305
Pazo de Barrantes
BARRANTES
Rotunda 2.5
Os Castaños
Muiño do Con Petroglifo
Taberna
Ruta del Agua 3.9
Gondarei
Abeleira
AG-41
Muiño da Avispa
picnic
Pedra Furada
<Rego da Armenteira
EP-9507
Ruta da Pedra e da Auga
Muiño do Trinta
Colegio
<Rego de Silván
0.0 Armenteira Albergue
ARMENTEIRA
Mosteiro de Santa María da Armenteira

# 24a VILANOVA de AROUSA – PADRON

Santiago – 62.3 km *(38.7 ml)*

| | | | | |
|---|---|---|---|---|
| ▯▯▯ | --- --- | 8.5 | --- --- | *23%* |
| ▭ | --- --- | 22.9 | --- --- | *63%* |
| ▬ | --- --- | 5.3 | --- --- | *14%* |
| **Stage Total** | | **36.7** km | | *(22.8 ml)* |

Total ascent **640**m ±***1.0*** *hr*

▲ Alto *m* Bamio 80m *(262 ft)*

< A H > ➲Vilagarcia **9.5** km ➲Carril **12.6** ➲*Cores* **19.1** ➲*Catoira* **21.5** km

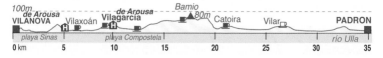

100m
VILANOVA de Arousa
Vilaxoán
Vilagarcía de Arousa
Bamio 80m
Catoira
Vilar
PADRON
playa Sinas
playa Compostela
río Ulla
0 km 5 10 15 20 25 30 35

▮ **Playa As Sinas:**. •*H** **Leal La Sirena** €21-33 ✆ 986 554 112. ●*Alb.* **Juvenil** *Xunta* ✆ 986 554 081. •*H** **Playa Las Sínas** €35 ✆ 986 555 173 San Pedro, 31. ▮ **Rial:** •*H**** **Pazo O Rial** €46+ ✆ 986 507 011 Av. de Vilanova. ☕ *Bar Carboa*. ▮ **Vilagarcia de Arousa**: •*H**** **Castelao** €50 ✆ 986 512 426 Rúa Arzobispo Lago, 5. •*Hs* **Nogal** *Cafetería* €30 ✆ 986 505 600 Rúa Alcalde Rey Daviña, 20. ▮ **Carril:** *Playa de la Concha* •*H*** **Playa Compostela** €35 ✆ 986 504 010 Av. Rosalía de Castro, 138 & •*H***** **Carril** €56 ✆ 86 511 507 r/ Lucena, 18.

▮ **Aldea Cores Catoira:** *Tanatoria de Catoira. [+250m •Motel*** ***Abalo*** *x5 €70 ✆ 986 546 900 Aldea Cores, Catoira].* ▮ **Catoira:** ☕ *Taberna Vikinga [+200m •CR* ***Os Migueliños*** *x5 €55+ ✆ 986 546 132 c/Barral, 12].* ***Torre do Este*** *paseo marítimo.* ▮ **Valga:** *[+ ½ km •H*** ***Corona De Galicia*** *x30 €40* ✆ 986 557 575 *Rúa da Devesa, 28].* ▮ **Pontecesures:** •*H*****A Casa Do Rio** €40 ✆ 986 557 575 Rúa Víctor García 1.

■ **Padrón** (Stage *Etapa 24) p.70*

**Capela da dos desa** *Pontecesures*

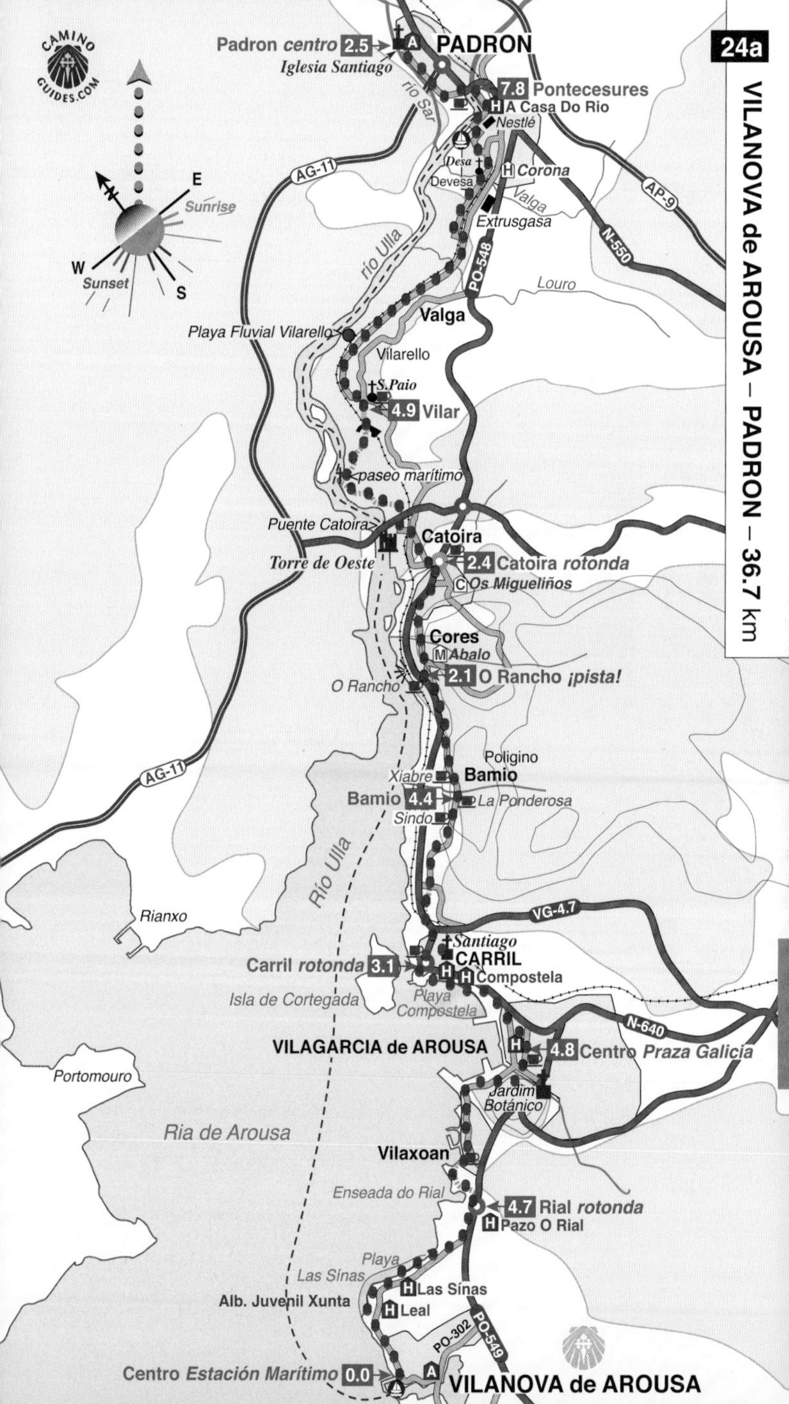
24a
VILANOVA de AROUSA – PADRON – 36.7 km
CAMINO GUIDES.COM
E
Sunrise
W
Sunset
S
Padron centro 2.5
PADRON
Iglesia Santiago
7.8 Pontecesures
A Casa Do Rio
río Sar
Nestlé
AG-11
Desa
Devesa
Corona
Valga
Extrusgasa
AP-9
N-550
río Ulla
PO-548
Louro
Valga
Playa Fluvial Vilarello
Vilarello
S.Paio
4.9 Vilar
paseo marítimo
Puente Catoira
Catoira
Torre de Oeste
2.4 Catoira rotonda
Os Migueliños
Cores
Abalo
2.1 O Rancho ¡pista!
O Rancho
AG-11
Poligino
Xiabre
Bamio
Bamio 4.4
La Ponderosa
Sindo
Río Ulla
Rianxo
VG-4.7
Santiago
CARRIL
Carril rotonda 3.1
Compostela
Isla de Cortegada
Playa Compostela
N-640
VILAGARCIA de AROUSA
4.8 Centro Praza Galicia
Portomouro
Jardim Botánico
Ria de Arousa
Vilaxoan
Enseada do Rial
4.7 Rial rotonda
Pazo O Rial
Playa Las Sínas
Las Sínas
Alb. Juvenil Xunta
Leal
PO-302
PO-549
Centro Estación Marítimo 0.0
VILANOVA de AROUSA

## Claves para las leyendas del mapa:

| | |
|---|---|
| **Total km** | Distancia total de la etapa indicada |
| | Adaptado para el desnivel (100 m verticales + 10 minutos) |
| (850m) Alto ▲ | Curva de desnivel / Punto más elevado de cada etapa |
| < A H > | Alojamiento intermedio |
| ◄ 3.5 | Distancia exacta entre puntos (3,5 km = ± 1 hora de camino) |
| ● 50m > / ^ / < | Distancias parciales: a150 m a la derecha>/seguir recto^/<izquierda<br>c. = aprox. / adj. = junto / incl. = incluido |
| | Camino o sendero (*verde*: caminos naturales / *gris*: hormigón) |
| | Carretera secundaria (*gris*: asfalto) / Rotonda |
| N-11 | Carretera principal [N-] (*rojo*: mayor tráfico y peligro) |
| A-1 | Autopista (*azul*: color habitual) |
| | Vía de tren / Estación |
| | El camino primordial de peregrinación: el camino interior del Alma. |
| | Ruta principal (*amarillo*: ± 80% peregrinos) |
| | Ruta escénica (*verde*: más alejada / menos servicios) |
| | Rodeo opcional a un punto de interés (*turquesa*) |
| | Ruta por carretera (*gris*: más asfalto) |
| | Cruce / Punto de Opción / Atención especial |
| | Molino de viento / Mirador / Antena de radio |
| | Frontera estatal / Límites de provinciales |
| | Río / Arroyo |
| | Lago o estuario / Bosque |
| | Iglesia / Capilla / Crucero |
| | Fuente de agua potable [ ] / Café bar / Mini-mercado |
| *menú* *V.* | Restaurante / Menú del peregrino / *V.* Vegetariano |
| | Turismo / Quinta o Pazo / Área de descanso |
| | Farmacia / Hospital / Correos |
| | Aeropuerto / Estación de autobuses / Gasolinera |
| XII | Monumento histórico / Siglo XII |
| A 1 J | Albergue(s) de peregrinos / Albergue(s) juveniles |
| H P C | Hotel *H*–H***** 30–90 / Pensión *P** €20+ / *Casa rural CR €35+* |
| Q B.V. | *Quinta Q €50–90* / Estación de bomberos *BV* € 5–10 |
| H A J | (*Alojamiento* fuera *de ruta*) |
| *[32 ]* | Número de plazas de cama (normalmente literas) |
| *[ ÷4]+* | ÷ número de dormitorios + *también habitaciones privadas* |
| ***Par.*** | Albergue parroquial *donación* €5+ |
| ***Conv.*** | Albergue en un convento o monasterio *donación* €5+ |
| ***Muni.*** | Albergue municipal €5+ |
| ***Xunta*** | Albergue de la Xunta de Galicia €6 |
| ***Asoc.*** | Albergue de una asociación |
| ***Priv. (*)*** | Albergue privado €10–15<br>**Los precios medios (temporada baja) para efectos comparativos*<br>*Hs.=Hostal / Hr.=Hotel Residencial* |
| | Plano de ciudad |
| *(Pop.–Alt. m)* | Población – Altitud en metro |
| | Periferia (gris) |
| | Centro Histórico (marrón) |

En las vidas de todos nosotros hay un exceso de parafernalia. Con la pretensión de aligerar la carga, hemos creado esta delgada edición de mapas. Ello ha sido posible gracias al trabajo desinteresado de las asociaciones de peregrinos que han señalizado el recorrido de tal forma que, hoy en día, tan solo necesitamos la información más básica para alcanzar nuestro destino. Resulta difícil perderse si en todo momento permanecemos concentrados y atentos a las flechas amarillas que apuntan en dirección a Santiago: en la concentración está la clave. Tómate un tiempo para familiarizarte con los símbolos del mapa que hallarás en la página de enfrente.

La sección entre Lisboa y Oporto está ahora completamente señalizada y abierta a peregrinos expertos con conocimientos básicos del portugués. Los servicios son adecuados y mejoran año a año, con una oferta de alojamiento a lo largo de cada etapa y líneas de atención 24 horas desde Lisboa: ***Via Lusitana S.O.S. Peregrinos (+351) 915 595 213.*** La sección de Oporto a Santiago tiene buenos servicios para todos los peregrinos. Comprueba las actualizaciones en *www.caminoguides.com* antes de viajar.

Esta edición incluye la principal ruta del ***Camino Central*** ● ● ● ● de Lisboa y las zonas costeras de Porto a Redondela ***Camino de la Costa*** ● ● ● ● y la ***Senda Litoral*** ● ● ● ● La ruta no está bien marcada y sólo se debe tratar con mapas detallados y guía de camino*. La Variante Espiritual ● ● ● ● a través de la Ría Arousa también se incluye para el primer equipo.

Estos mapas multilingües son un reconocimiento al compañerismo internacional del camino. Éste favorece el sentimiento de camaradería y comunión; una intención espiritual compartida que yace en el corazón de la peregrinación. Es esta focalización transcendente lo que distingue al peregrinaje del senderismo de larga distancia. Te recomendamos usar una guía con notas sobre cómo preparar bien un viaje largo de esta naturaleza, como el libro complementario ***A Pilgrim's Guide to the Camino Portugués**** un manual práctico y místico para el peregrino moderno.

Todos recorremos dos caminos simultáneamente: el camino exterior, por el que arrastramos nuestro cuerpo, y el camino interior del alma. Debemos ser conscientes de los dos y tomarnos el tiempo para prepararnos adecuadamente. El camino tradicional del peregrino es viajar solo, a pie, cargando con todas las posesiones materiales que podamos necesitar en el viaje que tenemos por delante. Esto brinda la primera lección al peregrino: dejar atrás todo lo supérfluo y viajar tan sólo con lo estrictamente necesario. La preparación para el camino interior es similar: comenzamos soltando la basura psíquica acumulada a lo largo de los años, como resentimientos, prejuicios y sistemas de creencias pasados de moda. Con una mente y un corazón abiertos asimilaremos con mayor facilidad las lecciones con las que nos encontraremos a lo largo de este Camino de las Averiguaciones.

Llevamos mucho tiempo dormidos. Pese al caótico mundo que nos rodea, o tal vez a causa de él, hay algo que nos sacude para que despertemos de nuestra amnesia colectiva. Una señal de este despertar es el número de personas que se sienten atraídas por hacer los caminos. El ritmo frenético de la vida moderna, que experimentamos no sólo en el trabajo sino también en nuestra vida familiar y en la social, hace que cada vez revoloteamos más lejos de nuestro centro. Hemos consentido en ser arrojados a la superficie de nuestras vidas, al confundir estar ocupados con estar vivos, pero esta existencia superficial resulta intrínsecamente insatisfactoria.

La peregrinación nos brinda la oportunidad de reducir el ritmo y de dotar a nuestras vidas de una cierta amplitud. En este espacio más tranquilo se puede reflexionar acerca del significado más profundo de nuestras vidas y las razones por las que hemos venido aquí. El camino nos anima a hacernos la pregunta perenne: ¿quién soy? Y, lo que resulta crucial, nos proporciona el tiempo para poder comprender y asimilar las respuestas. Así que no te apresures en recorrer el camino: tómate el tiempo que sea necesario, porque podría resultar ser el punto de inflexión de tu vida.

*Buen camino...*

**Explicação das legendas dos mapas:**

| | |
|---|---|
| **Total km** | Distância total da etapa |
| | Ajustado para subida (100 m na vertical + 10 minutos) |
| (850m) *Alto* ▲ | Linha de relevo / Ponto mais alto da etapa |
| < A H > | Alojamento intermédio |
| ◄ 3.5 | Distância exacta entre pontos (3.5 km = ± 1 hora andar) |
| –● 50m > / ^ / < | Distâncias intermédias 150 metros virar à direita> / seguir em frente^... c. = (cerca de) / adj. = adjacente / incl. = Incluindo |
| | Caminho ou carreiro (*verde*: caminho rural / *cinzento*: concreto) |
| | Estrada secundária (*cinzento*: asfalto) / Rotunda |
| N-11 | Estrada principal (*vermelho*: mais trânsito e perigo) |
| A-1 | Auto-estrada (*azul*: cor convencional das auto-estradas) |
| | Estação caminho-de-ferro |
| ● ● ● ● ● ● | O caminho primordial de peregrinação: o caminho interior da Alma |
| ● ● ● ● ● ● | Percurso principal (*amarelo*: ± 80% de todos os peregrinos) |
| ● ● ● ● ● ● | Percurso rural alternativo (*verde*: mais afastado/menos pontos de apoio) |
| ● ● ● ● ● ● | Desvio opcional para ponto de interesse (*turquesa*) |
| ● ● ● ● ● ● | Percurso alternativo (*cinzento*: mais estradas – asfalto) |
| X ? ! | Cruzamento / Opção / ¡Cuidado! |
| | Moinho / Miradouro / Antena de transmissão |
| | Fronteira nacional / Limite de província |
| | Rio / Ribeiro |
| | Estuário marítimo ou fluvial / Área florestal |
| | Igreja / Capela / Cruzeiro |
| F | Fonte [ ] / Café-bar / Mini-mercado |
| *menú* *V.* | Restaurante / menu peregrino / vegetariana |
| i | Posto de turismo / Solar / Picnic |
| | Farmácia / Hospital / Posto de correios |
| | Aeroporto / Estação autocarros / Bomba gasolina |
| XII | Monumento histórico / Século 12 |
| A 1 J | Albergue(s) de peregrinos *Alb.* / Pousada de juventude |
| H P C | Hotel *H**–*H***** €30–90 / Pensão *P* €20+ / Casa rural *CR* €35+ |
| Q B.V. | Quinta *Q* €50–90 / Quartel de Bombeiros *BV* € 5–10 |
| H A J | *(alojamento perto mas fora)* |
| *[32 ]* | Número de lugares (geralmente beliches) |
| *[ ÷4]+* | ÷ numero de dormitórios + *quartos particulares* |
| ***Par.*** | Alojamento paroquial (da igreja) *donativo* €5+ |
| ***Conv.*** | Alojamento em convento ou mosteiro *donativo* €5+ |
| ***Muni.*** | Alojamento municipal €5+ |
| ***Xunta*** | Alojamento oficial *Xunta Galego* €6 |
| ***Asoc.*** | Alojamento de uma associação €7+ |
| ***Priv. (*)*** | Alojamento privado €10–15 |

*Os preços são aproximados e apenas a título de comparação*
*Hs.=Hostal / Hr.=Hotel Residencial*

| | |
|---|---|
| | Planta da cidade |
| *(Pop.–Alt. m)* | População - altitude, em metros |
| | Subúrbios (*cinzento*) |
| | Centro histórico (*castanho*) |

Todos carregamos demasiados acessórios nas nossas vidas – num esforço para aliviar o peso produzimos este leve e fino volume de mapas básicos. Isto foi possível devido ao trabalho altruísta de organizações de apoio aos peregrinos que sinalizaram o Caminho de modo a que, hoje em dia, necessitemos de um mínimo de informações para nos levar ao destino. Será difícil perdermo-nos se nos mantivermos atentos às setas amarelas que indicam o caminho até Santiago.

A secção entre Lisboa e o Porto já está perfeitamente sinalizada, e é acessível a qualquer peregrino com um mínimo de treino. Os apoios são suficientes e melhoram todos os anos, havendo já hipótese de escolha em quase todas as etapas. Os peregrinos dispõem de duas linhas telefónicas de apoio: **Via Lusitana S.O.S. Peregrinos (+351) 915 595 213**. A secção do Porto a Santiago tem todos os apoios necessários, sendo acessível a qualquer peregrino. Antes de começar a peregrinação consulte as actualizações em *www.caminoguides.com*

Esta edição inclui a rota principal ***Camino Central*** ● ● ● ● de Lisboa e as rotas costeiras do Porto até Redondela ***Camino da Costa*** ● ● ● ● e ***Senda Litoral*** ● ● ● ●. A última rota não está bem marcada e só deve ser tentada com mapas detalhados e guia *. A ***Variante Espiritual*** ● ● ● ● através da Ría Arousa também está incluída pela primeira vez.

Estes mapas multilingues reconhecem a irmandade internacional do Caminho. Espera-se que ajudem a forjar um sentido de camaradagem e comunhão – a partilha de uma intenção comum que está na base da peregrinação. É este objectivo transcendente que distingue uma peregrinação de uma mera caminhada. Se não está habituado a percorrer a pé grandes distâncias recomenda-se que procure um guia com informações sobre a preparação de uma viagem desta natureza. O livro complementar ***A Pilgrim's Guide to the Camino Portugués*** * contém extensas notas práticas e históricas (ver no verso da contra-capa).

Todos percorremos dois caminhos simultaneamente – o caminho exterior ao longo do qual transportamos o nosso corpo e um caminho interior, da alma. Devemos estar conscientes de ambos e encontrar o tempo de preparação adequada. A maneira tradicional do peregrino é viajar sozinho, a pé, carregando todas as possessões materiais necessárias para a viagem que tem pela frente. Isto proporciona a primeira lição do peregrino – deixar para trás tudo o que é supérfluo e viajar com o que é realmente necessário. A preparação para o caminho interior é semelhante – devemos começar por abandonar o lixo psíquico acumulado ao longo dos anos, os ressentimentos, os preconceitos e as crenças antiquadas. Com uma mente aberta poderemos assimilar mais facilmente as lições a tirar ao longo deste Caminho de Busca.

Há muito tempo que andamos adormecidos. Apesar do mundo caótico à nossa volta ou talvez por isso, algo está a compelir-nos para o despertar da nossa amnésia colectiva. Um sinal deste despertar é o número de pessoas atraídas pelo Caminho. O ritmo agitado da vida moderna, que sentimos tanto no nosso trabalho como na nossa vida familiar e social, atira-nos para longe de nós próprios. Deixámo-nos afastar para a periferia da nossa vida confundindo estar ocupado com estar vivo, mas esta existência superficial acaba por ser inerentemente insatisfatória.

A peregrinação oferece uma oportunidade de abrandar e dar amplitude à nossa vida. É nesse espaço mais calmo que se torna possível reflectir no significado mais profundo das nossas vidas e nas razões porque estamos aqui. O Caminho encoraja-nos a fazer a pergunta essencial – quem sou eu? E fundamentalmente dá-nos tempo para que as respostas sejam compreendidas e absorvidas. Portanto não apresse o Caminho – leve o tempo que precisar, ele pode-se tornar um ponto essencial de mudança na sua vida.

*Bom caminho...*

## Zeichenerklärung:

| | |
|---|---|
| **Total km** | Gesamtentfernung für angezeigte Etappe |
| | An Höhenunterschied angepasst (100 m Höhe + 10 minuten) |
| (850m) *Alto* ▲ | Etappenprofil / Höchster Punkt jeder Etappe |
| < A H > | Unterkunft unterwegs |
| 3.5 | Genaue Entfernung zwischen Punkten (3,5 km = ± 1 Stunde Wandern) |
| 50m > / ^ / < | Zwischenentfernungen – in 150 m nach rechts>/geradeaus^/<links |
| | c. = (Ungefähr) / adj. = Angrenzend / incl. = Inklusive <nach links |
| | Weg oder Pfad (*grün*: natürliche Wege / *grau*: beton) |
| | Nebenstraße (*grau*: Asphalt) / Kreisverkehr |
| N-11 | Hauptstraße [N-] (*rot*: mehr Verkehr und größere Gefahr) |
| A-1 | Autobahn (*blau*: herkömmliche Farbe) |
| | Bahn / Bahnhof |
| | Der ursprüngliche pfad ist der innere Pfad der Seele |
| | Hauptroute (*gelb*: ± 80% pilger / vorwiegend Wege) |
| | Route mit Ausblick (*grün*: abgelegener / weniger Versorgung) |
| | Möglicher Abstecher desvío zu Sehenswürdigkeit (*türkis*) |
| | Landstraßen-Route (*grau*: mehr Asphalt) |
| X ? ! | Kreuzung *cruce* / Optionspunkt / Besondere Vorsicht |
| | Windrad / Aussichtspunkt / Antennenmast |
| | Landesgrenze / Provinzgrenze |
| | Fluss *río* / Bach |
| | See oder Flussmündung / Wald |
| | Kirche / Kapelle / Kreuz am Wegesrand |
| | Trinkwasser-Quelle *fuente* [ ] / Café Bar / Mini-Markt |
| *menú* *V.* | Restaurant / Pilgermenü *menú* / Vegetarier |
| | Tourismus / Herrenhaus / Rastplatz *Área de descanso* |
| | Apotheke *farmacia* / Krankenhaus / Post *correos* |
| | Flughafen / Busbahnhof / Tankstelle |
| XII | Altes Denkmal / 12. Jahrhundert |
| A 1 J | Pilgerherberge(n) *Albergue(s)* / Jugendherberge *Albergue juvenil* |
| H P C | Hotel *H*–H***** 30–90 / Pension *P** €20+ / *Casa rural CR* €35+ |
| Q B.V. | Herrenhaus *Quinta Q €50–90* / Feuerwehrhaus *Bombeiros BV € 5–10* |
| H A J | *(Unterkunft abseits der Route)* |
| *[32 ]* | Anzahl der Bettplätze (gewöhnlich Etagenbetten *literas*) |
| *[ ÷4]+* | ÷ Anzahl der Schlafsäle + *auch Privatzimmer* |
| *Par.* | Gemeinde-Herberge (Kirchengemeinde) Spende *donación (€5+)* |
| *Conv.* | Klosterherberge Spende *donación (€5+)* |
| *Muni.* | Städtische Herberge €5+ |
| *Xunta* | Herberge der Landesregierung Galiziens (Xunta) €6 |
| *Asoc.* | Herberge einer Vereinigung €5–8 |
| *Priv. (*)* | Private Herberge €10–15 |

**Alle Preise sind annähernd und nur zum Vergleich angegeben*
*Hs.=Hostal / Hr.=Hotel Residencial*

| | |
|---|---|
| | Stadtplan |
| *(Pop.–Alt. m)* | Stadtbevölkerung – Höhe in Metern |
| | Außenbezirke (*grau*) |
| | Altstadt centro histórico (*braun*) |

Wir alle haben zu viel Trödel in unserem Leben – um die Last zu erleichtern, haben wir diese schlanke Karten-Edition hergestellt. Ermöglicht wurde dies durch die selbstlose Arbeit von Pilgerorganisationen, die die Route dergestalt markiert haben, dass wir heute nur die grundlegendste Information brauchen, um an unser Ziel zu gelangen. Es ist schwer, sich zu verlaufen; wir müssen nur in jedem Moment gegenwärtig sein und auf die gelben Pfeile achten, die den Weg nach Santiago weisen – Achtsamkeit ist der Schlüssel. Nimm dir Zeit, dich mit den Karten-Symbolen auf der gegenüberliegenden Seite vertraut zu machen.

Der Abschnitt von Lissabon nach Porto ist jetzt vollständig mit Wegweisern markiert und offen für reife Wallfahrer mit grundlegendem Verständnis des Portu¬giesischen. Die Versorgungs¬mög¬lichkeiten sind angemessen und werden jedes Jahr besser, mit einer Auswahl an Unterkünften entlang jeder Etappe und 24-Stunden-Hotlines für Pilger aus Lissabon: **Via Lusitana S.O.S. Peregrinos (+351) 915 595 213**. Der Abschnitt von Porto nach Santiago hat gute Versorgungsmöglichkeiten für alle Pilger. Überprüfe Aktualisierungen in *www.caminoguides.com* vor der Reise.

Diese Ausgabe beinhaltet die Hauptroute ***Camino Central*** ● ● ● ● von Lissabon und die camino von Porto nach Redondela ***Camino da Costa*** ● ● ● ● und ***Senda Litoral*** ● ● ● ● Die letztere camino ist nicht gut markiert und sollte nur mit detaillierten Karten und Reiseführer *versucht werden. Die ***Variante Espiritual:*** ● ● ● ● über die Ría Arousa ist auch zum ersten Mal eingeschlossen.Die mehrsprachigen Karten würdigen die internationale Gemeinschaft des Camino. Dieser för¬dert das Gefühl von Freundschaft und Vereinigung; ein ge¬meinsames geistiges Ansinnen, das im Herzen der Wallfahrt liegt. Es ist dieser Fokus auf das Transzendente, was eine Wallfahrt vom Fernwandern unter¬scheidet. Wir empfehlen, einen Führer zur Hand zu nehmen mit Anmerkun¬gen, wie man sich am besten für eine weite Reise dieser Natur vorzubereiten hat; zum Beispiel das Begleitbuch ***A Pilgrim's Guide to the Camino Portugués****, ein praktisches und mystisches Handbuch für den zeitgenössischen Pilger.

Wir alle reisen gleichzeitig auf zwei Wegen; der äußere, entlang dessen wir unseren Körper schleppen, und der innere Weg der Seele. Wir müssen uns beider bewusst sein und uns die Zeit nehmen für eine entsprechende Vorbereitung. Traditionsgemäß ist der Weg des Wallfahrers eine Reise zu Fuß, alleine; wir tragen allen materiellen Besitz, den wir für die bevorstehende Fahrt benötigen mögen, mit uns. Dies bringt auch die erste Lektion für den Pilger – alles Überflüssige hinter sich zu lassen und nur mit dem wahrhaft Notwendigen zu reisen. Die Vorbereitung für den inneren Weg ist ähnlich – sie beginnt mit dem Ablegen vom psychischen Müll, der sich über die Jahre angehäuft hat, wie Groll, Vorurteile und überholte Glaubenssysteme. Mit offenem Verstand und offenem Herzen werden wir umso leichter die Lehren aufnehmen, die entlang dieses uralten Weges der Suche gefunden werden können.

Wir haben lange geschlafen. Trotz der chaotischen Welt um uns herum, oder vielleicht gerade ihretwegen, schüttelt uns etwas, auf dass wir aus unserer kollektiven Amnesie erwachen. Ein Zeichen dieses Erwachens ist die Anzahl der Menschen, die sich angezogen fühlen, die Caminos zu erwandern. Das hektische Tempo des modernen Lebens, das wir nicht nur in unserer Arbeit, sondern auch in unserem familiären und gesellschaftlichen Leben erfahren, wirbelt uns immer weiter nach außen, weg von unserem Zentrum. Wir haben es zugelassen, an die Oberfläche unseres Lebens geworfen zu werden – wir verwechseln Geschäftigkeit mit Lebendigkeit, doch dieses oberflächliche Dasein ist in sich unbefriedigend.Eine Wallfahrt bietet uns die Gelegenheit, langsamer zu werden und etwas Weite in unser Leben hineinzulassen. In diesem stilleren Umfeld können wir über die tiefere Bedeutung unseres Lebens nachdenken und über den Grund, wozu wir hierher kamen. Der Camino ermutigt uns, die immerwährende Frage zu stellen – wer bin ich? Und entscheidend ist: er bietet uns Zeit dafür, die Antworten zu verstehen und zu integrieren. Also hetzt nicht auf dem Camino – nimm dir die Zeit, die er erfordert, denn er könnte sich als ein entscheidender Wendepunkt in deinem Leben entpuppen.

**Legenda:**

| | |
|---|---|
| **Total km** | Distanza totale della tappa indicata |
| | Adatto al dislivello (100 m verticali + 10 minuto) |
| (850m) **Alto▲** | Curva di dislivello / Punto più elevato di ogni tappa |
| < A H > | Alloggio intermezzo *(di solito meno occupato)* |
| ◄ 3.5 | Distanza esatta tra punti (3,5 km = ± 1'ora di cammino) |
| 50m > / ^ / < | Distanze parziali: a 150 m a destra > / proseguire dritto ^ / < a sinistra<br>c.= circa / adj.= adiacente / incl.= incluso |
| | Cammino o sentiero (*verde*: cammini naturali / pista di ghiaia) |
| | Strada secondaria (*grigio:* asfalto) / Rotonda |
| N-11 | Strada principale [N-] (*rosso:* maggiore traffico e pericolo) |
| A-1 | Autostrada (*azzurra*: colore abituale) |
| | Via di treno / Stazione |

| | |
|---|---|
| | Percorso principale del pellegrinaggio; il percorso interno dell'Anima. |
| | Itinerario consigliato (*giallo*: ± 80% dei pellegrini /cammini naturali) |
| | Itinerario scenico (*verde*: più lontana / meno servizi) |
| | Giro opzionale a un punto di interesse (*azzurrino*) |
| | Itinerario per strada (*grigio*: più asfalto) |

| | |
|---|---|
| X ? ! | Croce / Punto di Opzione / Attenzione speciale |
| | Mulino di vento / Belvedere / Antenna di radio |
| | Frontiera statale / Limiti di provinciali |
| | Fiume / Fiumicello |
| | Lago oppure estuario / Bosco |
| | Chiesa / Cappella / Croce |

| | |
|---|---|
| F | Fontana di acqua potabile *Fuente* [ ] / Caffè bar / Mini-mercato |
| *menú V.* | Ristorante / menú de peregrino / vegetariano |
| | Turismo / casa signorile / Picnic |
| | Farmacia / Ospedale / Posta |
| | Aeroporto / Stazione degli autobus / Distributore di benzina |
| XII | Monumento storico / Secolo XII |

| | |
|---|---|
| A 1 J | Ostello (-i) di pellegrino *Alb.* / Ostello (-i) per la gioventù |
| H P C | Hotels *H-H**** €30-90 / Pensione *P** €20+ / Casa rurale *CR* €35+ |
| Q B.V. | Casa signorile *Quinta Q* €50-90 / Stazione di pompieri *B.V.* €5-10 |
| H A J | *Alloggio fuori itinerario* |
| *[32 ]* | Numero di posti letto (in genere letti a castello) |
| *[ ÷4]+* | ÷ numero di dormitori + anche stanze private €20+ |
| ***Par.*** | Ostello parrocchiale donazione (€5+) |
| ***Conv.*** | Ostello in un convento o monastero donazione (€5+) |
| ***Muni.*** | Ostello municipale €5+ |
| ***Xunta*** | Ostello della Xunta di Galizia €6 |
| ***Asoc.*** | Ostello di un'associazione |
| ***Priv. (*)*** | Ostello privato (della Red di Albergues* Rete di Ostelli) €10–15<br>*I prezzi sono indicativi; ai soli fini comparativi*<br>*Hs.=Hostal / Hr.=Hostal Residenziali* |
| | Cartina della città |
| *(Pop.–Alt. m)* | Popolazione – Altitudine in metri |
| | Periferia (*grigio*) |
| | Centro Storico (*marrone*) |

Nelle vite di tutti noi c'è un eccesso parafernale. Con la pretensione di alleggerire il carico, abbiamo creato questa sottile edizione di mappe. Tutto ciò è stato possibile grazie al lavoro disinteressato delle Associazioni di Pellegrini che hanno segnato il percorso in modo tale che, oggi giorno, soltanto ne abbiamo bisogno della informazione più di base per raggiungere la nostra destinazione. Risulta difficile perdersi se in tutti i momenti rimaniamo concentrati e attenti alle frecce gialle che spuntano verso Santiago: nel raccoglimento c'è la chiave. Prendi un tempo per familiarizzarti con i simboli della mappa che troverai sulla pagina di fronte.

Il percorso tra Lisbona e Oporto è adesso completamente segnato e aperto a pellegrini esperti con conoscenza di base di portoghese. I servizi sono adeguati e migliorano ogni anno, con un'offerta di alloggio lungo ogni tappa e linee di attenzione 24 ore da Lisbona: **Via Lusitana S.O.S. Peregrinos (+351) 915 595 213**. La sezione da Oporto a Santiago ha bei servizi per tutti i pellegrini. Verifica gli aggiornamenti in *www.caminoguides.com* prima di viaggiare.

Questa edizione comprende il percorso principale di ***Camino Central*** ● ● ● ● di Lisbona e le rotte costiere da Porto a Redondela ***Camino da Costa*** ● ● ● ● e ***Senda Litoral*** ● ● ● ● Quest'ultimo percorso non è ben marcato e dovrebbe essere solo tentato con mappe dettagliate e guida *. ***Variante Espiritual*** ● ● ● ● per la Ría Arousa è inclusa per la prima volta.

Queste cartine multilingue sono una riconoscimento alla fratellanza internazionale del Cammino. Esso favorisce il sentimento di cameratismo e comunione; un'intenzione spirituale condivisa che giace nel cuore del pellegrinaggio. È questa focalizzazione trascendente quello che distingue il pellegrinaggio dal trekking di lunga distanza. Vi consigliamo di usare una guida con delle note su come preparare bene un viaggio lungo di questa natura, come il libro complementare ***A Pilgrim's Guide to the Camino Portugués****, un manuale pratico e mistico per il pellegrino moderno.

Tutti percorriamo due cammini simultaneamente: il cammino esteriore, per cui trasciniamo il nostro corpo, e il cammino interiore del anima. Dobbiamo essere consapevoli di tutti e due e prenderci il tempo per preparaci adeguatamente. Il cammino tradizionale dl pellegrino è viaggiare s olo, a piedi, portando in carico tutti i possessi materiali di cui ne abbiamo bisogno nel viaggio che abbiamo davanti. Questo offre la prima lezione al pellegrino: lasciare indietro tutto quello superfluo e viaggiare soltanto con quello strettamente necessario. La preparazione per il cammino interiore è simile: incominciamo buttando via la spazzatura psichica accumulata lungo gli anni, come risentimenti, pregiudizi e sistemi di credenze fuori moda. Con una mente e un cuore aperti assimileremo con maggior facilità le lezioni con cui ci troveremo lungo questo Cammino delle verifiche.

È da tanto tempo che siamo addormentati. Pur il caotico mondo che ci gira attorno, o forse a causa di esso, c'è qualcosa che ci scuote affinché svegliamo della nostra amnesia collettiva. Un segnale di questo risveglio è il numero di persone che si sentono attratte per fare i cammini. Il ritmo frenetico della vita moderna, che esperimentiamo non soltanto al lavoro ma anche nella nostra vita famigliare e nella sociale, fa si che ogni volta sfarfalliamo più lontano del nostro centro. Abbiamo consenso di essere lanciati alla superficie delle nostre vite, al confondere essere occupati con essere vivi, ma questa esistenza superficiale risulta intrinsecamente insoddisfacente.

Il pellegrinaggio ci offre l'opportunità di ridurre il ritmo e di dotare le nostre vite di una certa ampiezza. In questo spazio più tranquillo si può riflettere riguardo al significato più profondo delle nostre vite e le ragioni per cui siamo venuti qui. Il Cammino ci anima a farci la domanda perenne: chi sono?. E, quello che risulta cruciale, ci fornisce il tempo per poter capire e assimilare le risposte. Quindi non ti affrettare a percorrere il Cammino: prendi il tempo di cui ne abbia bisogno, perché potrebbe diventare il punto di inflessione della tua vita.

*Bom caminho...*

## 12 Caminos de Santiago

❶ Camino Francés* **778** km
St. Jean – Santiago
Camino Invierno*
Ponferrada – Santiago **275** km

❷ Chemin de Paris **1000** km
Paris – St. Jean via Tours

❸ **Chemin** de **Vézelay 900** km
Vezélay – St. Jean via Bazas

❹ Chemin du Puy **740** km
Le Puy-en-Velay – St. Jean
Ext. to Geneva, Budapest

❺ Chemin d'Arles **750** km
Arles – Somport Pass
*Camino Aragonés* **160** km
Somport Pass – Óbanos
*Camí San Jaume* **600** km
Port de Selva – Jaca
*Camino del Piamonte* **515** km
Narbonne - Lourdes - St. Jean

❻ **Camino de Madrid 320** km
Madrid – Sahagún
**Camino** de **Levante 900** km
Valencia – Zamora
Alt. via Cuenca – Burgos

❼ Camino Mozárabe **390** km
Granada – Mérida
*(Málaga alt. via Baena)*

❽ Via de la Plata **1,000** km
Seville – Santiago
Camino Sanabrés Ourense **110** km

❾ Camino Portugués *Central** **640** km
Lisboa – Porto 389 km
Porto – Santiago 251 km
Camino Portugués *Costa** **320** km
Porto – Santiago
*via Caminha &* **Variante Espiritual***

❿ Camino Finisterre* **86** km
Santiago – Finisterre
via – Muxía – Santiago **114** km

⓫ Camino Inglés* **120** km
Ferrol & Coruna – Santiago

⓬ Camino del Norte **830** km
Irún – Santiago via Gijón
Camino Primitivo **320** km
Oviedo – Lugo – Melide